You will never need to worry
about a steady income.

You are person of strong
sense of duty. ☺

Other Resources from Kaplan and John Douglas

John Douglas's Guide to Careers in the FBI

John Douglas's Guide to the Police Exams

John Douglas's Guide to the California Police Officer Exam

by John Douglas

Simon & Schuster
Sydney • London • Singapore • New York • Toronto

Kaplan Books
Published by Simon & Schuster
1230 Avenue of the Americas
New York, NY 10020

Contributing Editor: Trent Anderson
Project Editor: Donna Ratajczak
Cover Design: Cheung Tai
Interior Page Design: Jude Bond
Interior Page Production: Joseph Budenholzer and Jobim Rose
Production Editor: Maude Spekes
Desktop Publishing Manager: Michael Shevlin
Managing Editor: Dave Chipps
Executive Editor: Del Franz

Special thanks to: Sara Pearl and Larissa Shmailo.

The names and events appearing in test examples in this book are fictitious. Any resemblance to actual people and events is unintentional.

Manufactured in the United States of America
Published simultaneously in Canada

April 2000

10 9 8 7 6 5 4 3 2 1

Library of Congress Cataloging-in-Publication Data is available.

ISBN: 0-684-85508-9

TABLE OF CONTENTS

Part One: How to Apply for a California Police Job

Part Two: Preparing for the Written Test

Part Three: Practice POST Exams

Appendix 1: California Law Enforcement Agencies 293

Appendix 2: Sample Personal History Statement 325

About the Author

During 25 years with the FBI, John Douglas became a leading expert on criminal personality profiling. Early in his career, he served as a recruiter for the Bureau; later, he conducted the first organized study into the methods and motivations of serial criminals, and became known as the pioneer of modern criminal investigative analysis. As a consultant, he continues assisting in criminal investigations and prosecutions throughout the world. An Air Force veteran, Douglas holds a doctorate in adult education, and is the author of numerous articles and presentations on criminology. He coauthored two landmark criminology texts: *Sexual Homicide: Patterns and Motives* and the *Crime Classification Manual*. With Mark Olshaker, he's coauthored several best-selling nonfiction books: *Mindhunter: Inside the FBI's Elite Serial Crime Unit; Unabomber: On the Trail of America's Most-Wanted Serial Killer; Journey into Darkness: The FBI's Premier Investigator Penetrates the Minds and Motives of the Most Terrifying Serial Killers;* and *Obsession: The FBI's Legendary Profiler Probes the Psyches of Killers, Rapists, and Stalkers, and Their Victims, and Tells How to Fight Back.* He lives in the Washington, D.C., area.

Part One

How to Apply for a California Police Job

CHAPTER ONE

Introduction

Let me ask you a question: Why do you want to be a cop? I'm assuming you know it's a tough job: extended periods of tedium interrupted by moments of butt-puckering panic. High rates of divorce, alcoholism, hypertension, and every other stress indicator you can think of. The pay and benefits can be pretty good, but they can also be pretty lousy.

So why do you want to be a cop? The best reason, of course, is that you have a kind of vocation for it. You want a career that lets you do something meaningful, something more important than pushing papers or answering e-mail. And that's good. When everybody's running away from the danger, someone's got to run toward it.

PREPARATION TIP NO. 1: PRACTICE SAYING, "YES, SIR!"

You'll be saying it a lot as soon as you get into the Academy. Law enforcement agencies are organized like the military, with strict hierarchies of rank and well-defined areas of responsibility. Within each rank, there are usually two or more levels, such as Detective I, II, and III. Higher levels mean higher pay and increased responsibility, often supervising those at the levels just below.

The description that follows is a fairly general one; the details for the department you're interested in could vary. But one thing all police departments have in common is bureaucracy, and lots of it. If you have trouble working "within the system," you might want to reconsider your career choice.

Police Officer

These are the foot soldiers—the largest and most visible part of any department. Most often, a police recruit fresh from the academy is assigned to a specific patrol under the supervision of a training officer. After a probationary period, he or she then advances to the next level, and can go on to specialized patrols, such as the K-9 division, motorcycle patrol, or narcotics.

Right from the beginning, police officers handle the day-to-day work of law enforcement: responding to the scene of a crime or an accident; interviewing suspects and witnesses; writ-

MONTHLY WAGES

Nobody goes into police work to get rich—but that doesn't mean you don't care what you're making. The good news is that California pays its law enforcement officers well. The Labor Relations Information System compiles information on pay and other personnel issues for "public safety professionals," which includes police officers and firefighters. These are the LRIS's best-paying—and worst-paying—police forces:

Top Ten		**Bottom Ten**	
Milpitas, CA	$6,002	McAllen, TX	$2,371
Santa Clara, CA	5,778	Baton Rouge, LA	2,367
Santa Ana, CA	5,569	Greenville, SC	2,349
Middletown, NJ	5,297	St. Joseph, MO	2,315
Huntington Park, CA	5,287	Louisville, KY	2,309
Vallejo, CA	5,096	Odessa, TX	2,285
Fremont, CA	5,087	Great Falls, MT	2,283
Hayward, CA	5,071	Huntington, WV	2,260
Anchorage, AK	5,006	Monroe, LA	1,642
Alameda, CA	4,997	Lake Charles, LA	1,517

(These figures cover top step monthly wages, in 305 municipal police forces surveyed.)

For more information on benefits and other related information, go to the Labor Relations Information System Web site, http://www.lris.com.

ing crime reports; responding to radio calls; coordinating vehicular traffic; booking suspects and evidence and transporting them to the appropriate Police Department facility; responding to citizens' and visitors' questions; and attending and coordinating neighborhood watch meetings.

A Police Officer assigned to a specialized division handles all these duties, plus whatever's required by the division's mission. For instance, an officer assigned to Juvenile Narcotics Division might conduct undercover narcotics investigations or patrol the school area to monitor criminal activity and to maintain contact with the school officials. Desk officers take care of administrative and coordination duties at station houses and department headquarters.

As an officer gains experience, he or she becomes eligible for more specialized duties and assignments, such as recruiting, teaching at the academy, or providing security for the chief or the mayor.

Years ago, a good patrol officer could stay on patrol his entire career. These days, officers often feel pressure to move up or move out. I think this is unfortunate, because it means that rookie officers are working patrols with officers who really don't have that much more experience. There's a kind of competence and confidence that comes only with experience; it's a shame that experience often isn't available to the cops who are the most visible, who deal with the public just about every working minute.

Police Detective

These are the guys (and gals) you see in the TV cop shows. While uniformed officers handle the initial, ground-level work on a case, the detectives are responsible for follow-through—actually solving the crime. Their duties include conducting preliminary and follow-up investigations; preparing the required investigative reports; identifying and apprehending the suspect; preparing the case for a successful prosecution; and testifying in court. Depending on their specific assignments, detectives also might conduct narcotics investigations; establish and maintain contacts with informants; and investigate gang-related crimes. Often, detectives develop an area of expertise, such as electronic surveillance, and will be asked to use that expertise to assist in cases other than those they're assigned to. As with officers, detectives who move up within the detective rank generally end up supervising other detectives.

Police Sergeant

Sergeants supervise geographic patrol divisions, specialized divisions and administrative units of these divisions. On patrol, the Sergeant may be a Watch Commander or Assistant Watch Commander. This means the sergeant handles administrative duties such as preparing daily car plan assignments; preparing and presenting roll call training; supervising the desk and patrol officers; handling radio calls and dispatching personnel; keeping the supervisors informed of important developments or issues; and training and supervising probationary officers.

Police Lieutenant

Just as a sergeant is in charge of a patrol, a lieutenant oversees an area made up of several patrols, supervising the sergeants, police officers, and detectives who carry out the day-to-day law enforcement. The lieutenant acts as an assistant to a captain, and is the commander in the captain's absence; his or her job is to take care of the details, so the captain can concentrate on the big picture. This means deploying officers to meet crime trends or emergencies; responding to scenes of serious crimes such as officer-involved shootings, homicide, major robbery, and theft; keeping an eye on follow-up investigations to make sure they're complete and accurate; and—this is often the hardest part—deciding what the captain needs to be told, and when. In keeping with the rank's operational focus, the lieutenant often is the chief administrative officer in an area. That means a lot of paperwork and meeting-and-greeting: reviewing and responding to correspondence; overseeing training; and attending community functions as a department representative.

Police Captain

The captain is the lieutenant's boss, the person in charge of overall, long-term operations for an area or a division. A captain will keep an eye on his or her area to ensure compliance with department policies; inspect the area's personnel, facilities, and tactics for safety or training needs; oversee budgeting and planning; and maintain contact with other civic departments, community groups, and private citizens.

Past the rank of captain, things get a little more complicated. Small departments may have only a rank or two between captain and chief; larger ones may include more layers. Also, the way a police chief or commissioner is selected varies from department to department. In some cities, selecting the chief is handled pretty much as another civil service appointment; in others, the chief is picked by the mayor or city council or some other governmental body. Again depending on the agency, the chief or commissioner may bring in his or her own assistants, or may be bound to keep the personnel already in place.

Police Commander or Supervisor

In large agencies, the police department will be broken down into four or five bureaus or departments, according to geography or function or both. These bureaus are overseen by deputy chiefs or assistant commissioners; the day-to-day operations of the bureaus are handled by commanders, or supervisors. (The names for these ranks change from department to department.) For instance, in Los Angeles, a deputy chief is in charge of the Operations-Headquarters Bureau; he or she will be assisted by a fleet of Police Commanders, each of whom runs a department within the bureau: Community Affairs, Uniformed Services, Detective Services, Juvenile Services, Criminal Intelligence, Personnel, Training, Internal Affairs, Administrative, and Transit Groups. Each of these Groups are subdivided into more specialized divisions such as Narcotics, Organized Crime and Vice, Antiterrorist, Burglary/Auto Theft, Air Support, Crime Suppression, Labor Relations, and Robbery/Homicide; each of these divisions are overseen by a police captain.

In general terms, the commander–deputy chief relationship is like the lieutenant-captain relationship; the former handles the details, while the latter does the long-term thinking and planning.

Police Deputy Chief or Deputy Commissioner

The deputy chief or deputy commissioner reports directly to the chief or commissioner and oversees a departmental bureau. Large agencies will have several deputy chiefs or commissioners. These men and women are the eyes and ears of the commissioner; their job is to keep on top of the department and make sure the chief's mission is communicated and enacted through the agency.

Chief of Police, or Police Commissioner

This is the big cheese, the highest-ranking officer in a police department. If the uniformed cops are the most visible as a group, the chief is the most visible individual. The chief gets to take the heat when things go wrong (as with a controversial police shooting) and take the credit when things go right (as when the crime rate drops). While his deputies oversee current operations, the chief or commissioner plans for the department's needs in the future. The chief has the large-scale jobs: developing and maintaining good relationships with the mayor, the governor, the police commission, or whatever other governmental body oversees the department; anticipating social and economic changes that could affect local law enforcement; and building and strengthening community-police relations. The job pays well, but talk about stress!

COPS OFFER INMATES REWARDS WITH LUNCH

Some detectives in South Florida are tapping a new source for leads on crimes—the county lockup. Broward County Sheriff's Office investigators are handing "investigative flyers" to inmates, sticking them in lunch bags with a crime description and a number for inmates to call if they know anything, said Veda Coleman-Wright, a Sheriff's Office spokeswoman. They also offer rewards for information that leads to an arrest.

The flyers are 5-by-7-inch sheets that include a photo or sketch of a suspect and provide aliases and a description, Coleman-Wright said. Since the program started a little more than a year ago, officers have placed more than two dozen different flyers in the inmates' lunch bags, and they've netted at least 45 tips—though they have not handed out any rewards yet, said homicide investigator Sgt. Bob O'Neil.

"[The flyers] generate a lot of tips, but usually they're not pertinent to the flier," O'Neil said. "However, [the inmates] are using the flyer as a means of contacting the detectives in a range of other cases."

Sheriff's officials say unconventional programs like these have helped improve their homicide clearance rate so it's better than that of the FBI or the Florida Department of Law Enforcement. Sheriff's officials also say they have also noticed a significant increase in calls to their Crimestoppers tip line, which is also listed on the flyers, since the inception of the program, Coleman-Wright said.

The flyers have profiled crimes ranging from homicides to a dry cleaners bandit to sexual abusers, and offer rewards as high as $15,000. "It's really opening up communications from the inmates to the detectives," O'Neil said. "After all, they're a captive audience."

—Adapted from an APBNews.com article by Scott A. Pignone, July 2, 1999

WHERE SHOULD YOU APPLY?

One of the biggest decisions you need to make now is where to apply. There's nothing wrong with applying to several agencies at the same time, but you don't want to overdo it and lose track. Before you apply anywhere, you need to do some serious thinking about what you want out of a career in law enforcement. When you imagine yourself as a cop, do you see Sipowicz, or Andy Griffith? (Actually, if the first thing you see is a TV cop, you should cancel your cable service and get out more.) There's a big difference between working in a three-man force or in one with thousands of officers.

Small Departments

People are people anywhere, so even in a small agency, you'll run into all kinds of crime. The only exceptions are the most extreme, brutal crimes, such as homicide; small departments may handle one, or none, per year, year after year. In a small department, there's no rigid division of duties, no specialization, so you'll get a range of experience you might not ever get in a large force. Friends who've worked in small departments have told me that in a small town, you get to know the people you deal with pretty well; they feel like they had a chance to really make a difference, instead of just operating a revolving door in and out of the jail. The pay tends to be lower, but so does the cost of living.

Large Departments

If you're an adrenaline junkie, large urban departments definitely offer more action. (Keep in mind, though, that police work anywhere is at least 95 percent tedium.) Big departments contain highly specialized divisions, such as SWAT teams, hostage rescue teams, and bomb squads. If you have a strong interest in a particular area, a large agency is the way to go. On the other hand, big agencies, and big cities, can feel chaotic and brutal; it's easy to get burned out and bitter.

Just to illustrate the differences, let's take a look at two municipal police departments.

Cloverdale Police Department

Cloverdale is a pretty little town about 80 miles north of San Francisco, on the Russian River. The Cloverdale Police Department has 11 sworn officers, five full-time dispatchers, and a Records/Communications Supervisor. The department covers the town, with its 6,000 citizens, plus a service area with another 4,000 people. Cloverdale's programs include a bicycle team on electric bikes; Adopt-a-Cop, which sends officers into elementary schools to develop long-term relationships with the kids; and a community-oriented policing program. Total crimes reported for 1998: 446. Here's the breakdown by type of case: 8 arsons, 15 auto thefts, 243 thefts, 81 burglaries, 93 assaults, 6 robberies, no rapes, no homicides.

Los Angeles Police Department

The LAPD patrols 467 square miles, with a population of 3.4 million residents. The department employs over 12,500 sworn and civilian employees, organized into eight bureaus and over 50 divisions, groups, units or sections. Specialized divisions include Organized Crime and Vice, Narcotics, Antiterrorist, Robbery/Homicide, Burglary/Auto Theft, Bomb Squad, Scientific Support, and Air Support. In addition, they've developed more than a dozen programs, including community policing, a Safe House Community Program for juveniles, and neighborhood watches. LAPD compiles crime statistics using the FBI's classification system; for 1998, they reported 183,707 Part I crimes. These include: 28,441 vehicle thefts; 79,997 larcenies; 26,067 burglaries; 31,545 aggravated assaults; 15,835 robberies; 1,395 forcible rapes; 427 homicides.

Don't misunderstand me—I'm not making any sort of comparison between these two departments as far as the value of their work. Small town or big city, cops lay their lives on the line to protect others. That's always worthy of respect. But if your big dream is to fly a police helicopter, or become a hot-shot homicide detective, Cloverdale is not the place for you.

PREPARE YOURSELF

You've already taken a big step toward becoming a cop: You've been proactive, seeking out assistance to make yourself a better candidate. Keep that attitude, and you'll do fine.

The best thing you can do to prepare yourself is to inform yourself. Talk to cops. Read about cops. Get on the Internet and research the agencies that interest you. Throughout this book, you'll read some pithy comments from active-duty cops; these quotes come from one of the best law-enforcement Web sites I know of—ABPNews, at http://www.apbnews.com. (Of course, the fact that I have a page on the site doesn't make me biased.) This is just one of literally hundreds of Web sites that will let you walk in the shoes of a cop, before you even get into the Academy.

PARKING TICKET LEADS TO SERIAL RAPE SUSPECT

A parking ticket led police to identify and apprehend a serial rape suspect wanted for a seven-month string of attacks involving mostly teenage girls in Orange County, the district attorney said today.

Steven Morales, 32, of Chino was arrested after police discovered it was his late-model pick-up truck victims described in two of the assaults in Seal Beach and Irvine. He was charged today with 23 counts of sexual assault, five kidnappings and two burglaries, and he faces multiple life sentences if convicted.

Officials said that because the suspect had no criminal record, DNA evidence wasn't leading anywhere. Instead, a Seal Beach detective decided to check randomly for any parking tickets issued around the time a rape occurred in his town. He turned up a citation on a late-model Chevrolet pickup truck two blocks from a rape scene. He then obtained a driver's license photo and discovered the descriptions matched. When police went to Morales' home, they found the pickup in his driveway.

At that point, police obtained a search and arrest warrant along with an order that the suspect provide DNA samples. When the samples matched four incidents committed in Seal Beach, Irvine, Huntington Beach, and Tustin, he was arrested and ordered held without bail at Huntington Beach City Jail.

"This was great police work," District Attorney Tony Rackauckas said. "If this puzzle had not been pieced together, there would be more innocent victims suffering."

Morales is charged in the following rapes, burglaries and kidnappings:

- The June 16, 1998, abduction and rape of a 17-year-old walking down Carbon Canyon Road in Brea.

- The Aug. 27, 1998, abduction and rape of a 16-year-old walking near Utt Middle School in Tustin.

- The Oct. 19, 1998, abduction and rape of 13- and 16-year-old sisters from a Huntington Beach shopping center, in which the suspect posed as a police officer and said he was stopping the victims for skipping school.

- A Dec. 22, 1998, incident in which the suspect broke into the Tustin home of a woman in her mid-40s and raped her upon her return.

- A Jan. 8, 1998, incident in which the suspect broke into the Irvine home of an 18-year-old and raped her when she got home.

Because rape is a generally underreported crime, police and prosecutors suspect there may be more victims, authorities said.

—Adapted from an APBNews.com article by Pete Brush, July 7, 1999

CHAPTER TWO
Managing the Application Process

GIVE YOURSELF A COMPETITIVE EDGE

The sections that follow will give you specific information about the process of applying to a police force. These are more general ideas about how to make yourself a standout candidate. If you have some time before you actually apply, use it wisely. The more of the following suggestions you can put into practice, the better.

Add to Your Education. The basic requirement for most police jobs is a high school diploma or a G.E.D. But you'll be a much more attractive candidate if you've taken some college-level courses, especially in the criminal-justice area. Continuing your education will take a serious commitment of time, but it doesn't have to cost a fortune. Get a course catalog from your local community college; see if there's anything there that looks interesting. Take a look at the distance learning that's available online. At the very least, use your local library to look up professional articles in an area that interests you.

Develop Your Language Skills. If you have any familiarity with a foreign language, work on it. Of course, some languages will be more useful than others. A basic working knowledge of Spanish will come in handy just about anywhere; depending on the ethnic mix of the area you're interested in working, you might want to familiarize yourself with Vietnamese, Croatian, Farsi, or some other language. You'll have to make this a priority in terms of your time, but you can accomplish a lot without spending much money. Check out self-taught courses, either in a book or a computer program. Distance learning opens up real opportunities here, too.

Get Involved. Cops have to work with all kinds of people—not just their high school buddies. Show your adaptability, and your community-minded dedication, by volunteering for a local organization. Pick a group you really believe in, one whose mission you whole-heartedly support. If it's also got a law-enforcement alliance, so much the better. If you're a jock, call the local Police Athletic League. If you're more of a one-on-one person, think about a victims'-rights organization or a crisis hotline. But whatever you pick, make sure you're genuinely interested in it. That's the key to doing well, and sticking with it.

Focus on Useful Skills. How's your marksmanship? Do you know C.P.R.? Any first-aid training? These skills that are immensely useful in a law-enforcement career; don't wait until you get into the academy to start thinking about them. Check the phone book for target ranges; they often have inexpensive courses that will let you get used to shooting handguns. Local community colleges and hospitals are a good source for first-aid certification courses.

Network. If you're interested in a law enforcement career, chances are you have friends or family already on the force. Take one of them, or all of them, out to lunch and pick their brains. Ask them what they wish they'd known at the beginning of their career. And keep going from there. Most police departments have community outreach programs; call your local precinct or department. Get to know as many people as you can—not for greater opportunities to brownnose, but to give you as many sources of information as possible.

Get up off the Couch. You're going to have to pass a physical test. Stuffing your face with chips and beer isn't going to make it any easier. And regular physical activity will give you a healthy way to deal with the stress you're going to face.

ON THE BEAT

"The patrolman should walk with purpose, energetically and on the alert, avoiding the appearance of one who has nothing to do but put in time. His movement should be unhurried, even while apprehending a criminal unless there is something definite to be gained by speed; a running policeman will attract a crowd quickly. The patrolman should ordinarily patrol to the left, that is, with his shield to the curb. This is done for the reason that superior officers patrol to the right and, therefore, can more readily find the patrolman. Patrolling should never under any circumstances be reduced to a habit so that the patrolman is ordinarily at a given spot at a given time; the patrol should be irregular. The competent beat patrolman stops occasionally and casually looks back to observe what is going on. He cuts through alleys, yards, and private passageways; he retraces his steps. At night he occasionally stands in dark spots in order to scrutinize closely all passersby. Patrolling after dark is ordinarily done along the property line in order to try more readily doors and windows. The patrolman keeps on the outside in patrolling a crowded thoroughfare so that he may be seen. That is the reason the patrolman wears a uniform; its presence distinctly acts as a deterrent to crime….

"Patrolling a beat properly is both a science and an art. Improper and incompetent patrolling is a nuisance to the public and a cause of unhappiness and dissatisfaction to the beat patrolman.

"The outstanding patrolman knows almost every person on his beat and has their unqualified confidence. They know him, they respect him, and they bring their troubles to him. Consequently, they admire him and look up to him; in a sense, his relationship with the people on his beat is like that of a father of a large family. No reward is as rich in the esteem of one's fellowmen. The work of the beat patrolman can bring that and, therefore, be full of happiness. The beat patrolman has the opportunity to reap rewards far beyond his monetary salary."

—From *Basic Police Procedure,* published by the Pennsylvania Chiefs of Police Association, 1940

WHAT'S POST?

POST stands for Peace Officer Standards and Training; the POST Commission oversees selection and training for just about every law enforcement agency in California. It's a state agency, originally established in 1959, headed up by 14 commissioners—the State Attorney General and 13 commissioners nominated by the governor and approved by the state legislature.

POST has a three-part goal:

- Meet the statewide need for consistent selection standards by refining and updating job-related selection standards
- Assure access to useful training so California peace officers can acquire and develop the skills, knowledge, attitude, and behaviors needed for their work
- Encourage productive professional structures by offering leadership development programs and management counseling services

Obviously, once you become a law enforcement professional, you'll deal with POST on a regular basis. If you're interested in finding out more about POST, or the law enforcement training they offer, visit their Web site at http://www.post.ca.gov. For right now, what means the most to you is the selection process they've set up. And that's what we're going to go over now.

WHAT ARE THEY LOOKING FOR?

The POST Commission has spent a lot of time tweaking and tuning the application process—devising ways to see how well you're likely to perform as a police officer. They've identified fifteen "job dimensions" required for entry-level law enforcement personnel; the screening process as a whole measures you in these areas:

Communications Skills—Ability to express oneself clearly in writing and speech. Ability to read with good comprehension. Ability to write a report that accurately describes what happened. Ability to speak clearly and make oneself understood.

Problem-Solving Ability—Knowing how to size up a situation, identify the problem, and make a logical decision. Knowing when to take action and what kind of action is appropriate. Using good judgment in making decisions. Ability to see the similarities and differences between many situations confronted on a daily basis.

Learning Ability—Ability to comprehend and retain a good deal of factual information. Ability to recall factual information pertaining to laws, statutes, codes, etcetera. Ability to learn and to apply what is learned. Capability of learning the factual material that is required of a law enforcement officer.

Judgment Under Pressure—Applying good common sense in dealing with pressure situations. Capability of making sound decisions on the spot. Using good judgment in dealing with a potentially explosive situation. Ability to make effective, logical decisions under pressure.

Observational Skills—Mental alertness, good observational skills, memory for details. Alertness to signals that indicate that something is wrong. Inquisitive; senses when something is wrong. Suspicious and inquisitive; able to sense when things are not satisfactory.

Willingness to Confront Problems—Ability to be asserting in a potentially explosive situation. Won't back away. Willingness to stop people who are behaving in a suspicious manner and to challenge them. Having the courage to confront a potentially dangerous situation.

Interest in People—Desire to understand people and to work with them. An active interest in working with people. Fairness in dealing with the public regardless of ethnic race, economic level, etcetera. Having a public service orientation. Wanting to help people.

Interpersonal Sensitivity—Resolving problems in a way that shows some sensitivity to the feelings of others. Showing empathy in working with people. Does not enforce the law blindly. Effective in dealing with people without needlessly arousing antagonism. Understanding the motives of people and how they are likely to react.

Desire for Self-Improvement—Desire to seek out the knowledge needed to be a competent law enforcement officer. Seeing oneself as responsible for learning the job. Displaying a willingness to put in the time needed to stay up-to-date. Having a high degree of self-motivation in wanting to improve skills and knowledge.

Appearance—Demeanor as determined by physical appearance, grooming, and personal care. Having personal and professional pride in one's demeanor and appearance. Showing pride in self. Professional bearing as determined by neatness and overall grooming.

Dependability—Well-motivated; habitually and consistently submitting reports on time, responding quickly and actively to all calls. Follows through on assignments without extensive supervision. Will take the extra effort required to be accurate in all details. Willingness to put in the hours needed to complete the job.

Physical Ability—Showing the endurance required to do the job. Having good physical coordination, stamina, and agility.

Integrity—Refusing to yield to the temptation of bribes, gratuities, payoffs, etcetera. Refusing to tolerate unethical or illegal conduct on the part of other law enforcement personnel. Showing strong moral character in dealing with the public. Being honest in dealing with the public.

Operation of a Motor Vehicle—Ability to possess a valid California driver's license. Ability to drive safely. Ability to control a motor vehicle at high speeds. Ability to operate motor vehicles in all types of weather conditions.

Credibility as a Witness in a Court of Law—Ability to give testimony in a court of law without being subject to impeachment due to his or her character for honesty or veracity (or their opposites) or due to a prior felony conviction.

As you move through the screening process, these are the qualities you need to be able to demonstrate. If you're lacking in one of these areas, start working on it. And if you've got real strengths in others, make sure that gets across.

INITIAL APPLICATION STRATEGIES

I'm going to walk you through the Idiot's Guide to Applying for a Police Job here. Some of this might seem painfully obvious to you, but it's better to overprepare than skip something important.

Up to the Written Test

Assuming you meet all the requirements, the written test is the first yes/no point. You need to pass it before moving on to any of the other steps.

What's on the test? What are they looking for?

Basically, they want to check out your communication skills—if you can read accurately and write clearly. The POST test is a standardized, two-part test; most of the questions are multiple choice, with a few fill-in-the-blanks.

Some agencies stop right there. Others add their own tests to the basic POST version. For instance, San Diego includes questions on observation and memory (Do you notice and remember details?) and directional ability (Can you get from Point A to Point B?), plus an essay question. Later in the book, I'll spend some time on these kinds of questions, but you'll be getting a real workout on the POST questions.

1. *Speak to the recruiting officer in the department (or departments) you're interested in; ask about the specifics of their application process.* This is critical. I'm going to say it over and over and over: Speak to your recruitment officer. With over 600 law enforcement agencies in the state, there's no way that one book can provide the details of every single application process. Your recruitment officer will give you the info you need to make sure you're well prepared for the process.

    If you've got online access, go to the Police Officers Internet Directory at http://www.officer.com. It's a great source for information about law enforcement, with links to Web sites for agencies all over the United States and the world. Chances are, the department you want has a Web site, with all the info you need just a click or two away.

2. *Identify the requirements and make sure you're eligible.* These are the basic, minimum requirements for an entry-level law enforcement job in the state of California:

    *   A high school diploma or G.E.D. certificate.
    *   Proof that you meet the age requirement. This is either 18 or 21, depending on the department.
    *   Proof of United States citizenship.
    *   A valid driver's license and a clean driving record.
    *   A clean military and police record. That means no felony convictions in any jurisdiction. Depending on the agency and the specifics of your situation, misdemeanor convictions may or may not knock you out of the running. If you served in the military, you can't have a dishonorable discharge.

- Vision that's better than 20/100, correctable to 20/20, and normal color vision.
- Minimum physical requirements specified by the relevant agency.
- No history of excessive drug or alcohol abuse.

However, your agency might have additional requirements, such as a maximum age or a college credit requirement. Check with your recruiting officer.

3. *Check the test schedule.* Again, you'll need to find out the specifics for the agency you want. Smaller departments may offer the test locally, or send you to the nearest POST facility; your recruiting officer will tell you the time and place for the next test.

   Larger departments, such as Los Angeles and San Francisco, have set up their own schedules and offer tests more frequently than POST does. So check the agency's Web site, or call the recruitment officer.

4. *Find out what you need to do to register for the test.* Check with your recruiting officer. Some agencies ask you fill out an application in advance; others let you walk into the test and fill out an application on the spot.

5. *Will you need any documentation up front?* Again, policies vary. Sometimes all you need is a photo ID, such as your driver's license; for other departments, you'll need proof of age, proof of residency, or some other piece of paper. Ask early; if you need any documentation that's not handy, you want time to get a copy.

6. *Do your best to prepare.* That's why you're here, right? We'll go into more detail about this later. The most important thing to do is study the test packet from the department. Just about every agency includes information about the test format they use; most even provide sample questions. You'll be able to use your prep time efficiently once you know exactly what to expect.

7. *Once it's over, let it go.* Some people are good test takers and breeze through; others struggle and barely finish in time. The style doesn't make much difference in the score. So don't second-guess yourself, don't beat yourself up over specific questions. You probably didn't do as badly as you think you did. And if you did—well, what you learned will help you do better next time.

8. *Wait for your score.* At the test itself, or in the application packet, you'll be told when to expect to find out whether you passed. Some agencies post an answer key and let you leave the test with a "cheat sheet" to check your answers; others don't. If you pass the test, your notification letter will give you all the details about the next step in the process.

As always, if you have any questions, ask your recruiting officer. But do not call every day to ask if the scores are in; you won't find out faster, and you'll just make yourself a pain in the butt.

If I fail, can I take the test again?

Most agencies require you to wait six months before signing up for another session. Take advantage of the time to prepare yourself. What, specifically, gave you the most trouble? Focus on that area.

What if I pass the test, but decide not to apply for a couple of years—will I have to take the test again?

Probably not. As far as most departments see it, once you pass the written test, you've passed for good. However, if you bow out later in the process, you may have to retake the physical or psychological tests.

After the Written Test

Now that you've passed the first written test, you'll embark on the really fun stuff: the background check, the psychological tests, the interview. If you have a good recruitment officer, he or she will guide you through the whole process. Here's some general advice on reducing stress and staying organized.

1. *Make photocopies of all blank forms.* You are going to be filling out a lot of paperwork. As soon as someone gives you a form to take home and fill out, hustle down to a copy shop and make three or four copies. And do it right away, before the papers get coffee spilled on them. You'll want to have a couple of copies to make your mistakes on before you write out the finished version.

2. *Using one of the photocopies, fill out everything accurately and truthfully.* Don't try to hide anything on your application. Tell the truth. Let's say you're filling out your Personal History, and you have a small problem. There's a gap in your work record because you took three months off to hike the Appalachian Trail. Just say so. You'll only cause trouble for yourself if you try to fudge the answer to make yourself look better. Or, what if you dropped out of high school and did a little of this and a little of that before you got back on track and got your G.E.D.? Well, it's certainly not going to help you much, but by itself, it might not knock you out of the running either. Your history doesn't mean as much as how you're doing now, what strides you've made to straighten up your life. Recruiters know they're dealing with human beings here. One problem is not necessarily going to torpedo your application.

    On the other hand, maybe the blemish is significant—"I have a six-month gap in my work record because I was in jail on a D.W.I." In that case, my question to you is, "Why do you think law enforcement is the place for you?"

3. *Proofread and revise the whole application.* Check your spelling and grammar. If you're not sure about anything, look it up. Have someone else read what you've written to make sure it makes sense. Write in any corrections. Then let it sit for a day or so before you read it again. You might see problems—or good points you missed earlier. Make any last corrections.

4. *Recopy the application, in ink, on the original form, as carefully and legibly as you can.* Okay, this might seem obvious. But you wouldn't believe the sloppy mess some people send in.

Believe me, people notice when a document arrives looking like it's spent a week curled up at the bottom of someone's laundry basket. And they're not impressed.

5. *Do not attach a résumé.* It's just a waste of effort—and money, if you have to pay someone to write it up for you. The standard, private-sector résumé won't tell a law enforcement agency what they need to know; that's why agencies have such detailed application forms.

6. *Make a photocopy of your final application.* If you're applying to several different agencies, you'll definitely want a copy of at least the first application you fill out. Most forms cover a lot of the same ground, and there's no sense starting from scratch every time. And, every once in a while, an application does get lost. It simplifies things if you can just pull out a copy and use it to fill out the resubmission.

THE BACKGROUND CHECK

Congratulations; you've aced the written test. Now you'll be asked to come in and fill out a Personal History statement. You'll document, in detail, your education, your job history, where you've lived. You'll also be asked to supply names and addresses for personal and professional references. We've included a sample copy of the POST Personal History statement at the back of the book, so you can get a jump on gathering the information.

Once you've submitted your completed statement, an officer will go through it with you, asking you to explain any blank spots or discrepancies. Again, be honest. You're not facing an enemy here; no one wants to knock you out of the running. Assuming you don't have a felony conviction, the worst thing you can do is lie about your past.

The first thing the investigators will do is establish your paper trail, requesting copies of your transcripts, military records, credit report, and any other relevant information. All of this becomes part of your file.

Then he or she starts verifying what you've told them, step-by-step.

What if I've got shaky credit?

I can't say your financial history doesn't matter at all. You want to demonstrate that you're responsible and reliable, and good credit definitely helps do that. Obviously, that's the best position to be in.

At the other extreme, let's say the investigators find out that right now you've got liens and judgments and foreclosures on everything from your house to your socks. Well, that doesn't show a lot of responsibility. You need to, at the minimum, clear up debts that have gone into collection.

However, if you had trouble managing your money a while back and can show that you've gotten things under control, the black marks probably won't sink your application. The important thing to remember is that they're going to be looking at your application as a whole; one flaw isn't going to cancel out a bunch of strengths.

Whom do they talk to?

The investigators will contact the people you've listed as references in your personal history statement; they'll also develop their own sources by asking those folks to recommend other people who know something about you.

This isn't an undercover operation. The investigator will always identify himself and explain that he's conducting a background investigation on you because you've applied for a job with the Blankety-Blank Police Department.

Whom should I list as references?

The first rule is *always tell the truth.* Don't try to get a coworker to play like he's boss for the interview. It just gets too complicated, and if the scheme doesn't work, your application is finished right there. Who needs the stress?

When they ask for a former boss, give your former boss's name. When they ask for your brother's name, give your brother's name. Of course, you may have a choice of people to list—several coworkers, for example. In that case, definitely list the guy you got along with well, not the one you argued with all the time. That's just common sense.

But never, ever, lie or try to manipulate the process. I can guarantee you it won't work, and it will completely eliminate you from the applicant pool.

Should I tell people I've listed them?

Absolutely. In fact, before you list anyone as a reference, check with them. Make sure they're comfortable talking to an investigator, and that what they have to say is both truthful and helpful. Of course, you can't speak to the secondary contacts; that's okay. I've done a few background investigations, and I've found that people almost always bend over backwards to be fair and accurate.

What if they talk to my ex-wife and she tells them about all the problems we had?

The POST guidelines state that any information obtained from a "prior spouse . . . should be impartially evaluated and carefully corroborated." As I've said, the investigator is putting together a complete picture of you and your life up to this point. The info from any one person is just a detail of that picture. By itself, it can't make or break you. What you have to worry about is if the problems with your ex are representative of bigger problems in your background.

Is there anything the investigators can't ask about?

Definitely. According to POST guidelines, the investigators must strictly limit the areas of inquiry to *job-related* aspects of your history and current status. Your medical history is off-limits, except to determine your current physical ability. The citizenship status of your family members can't be investigated or asked about. The gender of your roommate, the quality of your housekeeping, your lack of previous employment—unless the investigator strongly suspects an illegal activity or other issues that would affect your fitness for the job, none of these things matter.

THE INTERVIEW

For most people, this is the real sweaty-palm time. Don't worry. Just prepare yourself ahead of time, and you'll do fine.

Two Weeks Before the Interview

Do Your Homework. How many cops are on the force you're applying to? What's the major crime problem in your community? Have there been any big changes in policy or focus recently? Any cases or investigations that have been widely covered in the news? Who's the police chief? How long has he been there? Did he come in from outside or was he promoted from within? How does he get along with the mayor? You can get information like this from local newspapers or from the department itself; work it into your answers *where appropriate,* and you'll impress your interviewers.

For example, if a question refers to gang graffiti, you can say something like, "Well, the gang problem is the main target of the new Street Shield unit, and they've been having some success—gang activity is down 12 percent since last year. In light of that, I'd coordinate my efforts with the unit to build on their success."

Of course, you won't impress anyone if your information is wrong, or doesn't really connect with what you're saying. So think about the information you're going to use. Don't just blurt it out. The key is preparation.

Anticipate the Questions. I can't tell you exactly what the interviewers are going to ask you, but I can tell you what they're looking for. They want to know if you can deal with conflict, get along with other people, and learn from mistakes. To get at that information, they'll ask you for details about your previous experience and education. To further probe for these qualities, they'll give you a hypothetical situation and ask for your response. This also tests your ability to make good decisions and think on your feet.

Here are some ways you can prepare yourself:

- Look at your own application and put yourself in the interviewers' shoes. They're going to push to find out if you've got what it takes to be a good, responsible cop. Come up with your own questions, and *the best honest answers.*

  Here's an example: "I see you left your job at Kasper Dry Cleaning after only three months. Why is that?"

  Do not say: "I had to quit because the manager was a pushy jerk and he kept trying to make me do stuff that wasn't in my job description." That makes you sound like someone who A) has no initiative and B) is always looking for a scapegoat. If that's accurate, I'm assuming you've worked on that; you need to demonstrate how you've improved your work skills.

  Instead, put it like this: "I had a personality conflict with the manager that we just weren't able to resolve. That was one of my first jobs out of school, and since then I've really worked on my people skills. In fact, at my current job, I was able to negotiate with the boss to get a better scheduling system set up for all the employees."

This shows that you're able to learn from your mistakes, and that you've developed the ability to work with others—both important aspects of being a good cop.

This is an important step in your preparation, so take your time. Ask for a friend to help you, if you're having trouble coming up with hard questions. You really can't overprepare; even if the interviewers don't ask exactly the same questions you come up with, they'll probably be in the ballpark. And there's less chance you'll be caught off guard.

- Imagine some difficult situations a cop might face, and come up with your responses. You'll need to have some practice at making good decisions quickly. These are the kinds of things you'll be asked:

  "You're on patrol and you see a car being driven erratically. You pull it over, and the driver is the police chief's 16-year-old daughter. There are empty beer bottles in the front seat and her eyes are red. She says they were left by her boyfriend, who she just dropped off, and her eyes are red because they had a fight and she was crying. What do you do?"

  "You're working on a narcotics case, and you make a big bust. Another cop, your partner's brother-in-law, pockets some of the cash before it's booked into evidence. You tell your partner, and he just shrugs, says that the guy's a bum but his sister loves him. What do you do?"

  "The station gets an anonymous call about child abuse at a certain address. You're sent to check it out. When you get there, the man who answers the door says there's no problem. You hear a kid screaming in the background. When you ask to come in and take a look, the man tells you to come back with a warrant. What do you do?"

When you're in the interview, the officers will keep upping the ante on you, adding complications to the original situation. Don't rush into an answer, and don't change your answer once you've given it. Most of the time, there's not a black-and-white answer they're looking for; they just want to see how you react to stress and whether you're able to make reasonable decisions under pressure. The *only* time you should take back your answer is if you realize that there really is a better solution than the one you first gave. Whatever you do, don't change any answer more than once. You don't want to seem like someone who's always second guessing herself, or letting her decision be swayed by whoever she's spoken to last.

Practice with a Friend. Get someone you trust to do some role playing with you. Ideally, this will be a friend who's a cop and who's been through the interview process. But whoever it is, make sure it's someone who can give you honest feedback.

Give that person the questions and situations you've come up with, along with your application. Ask him or her to write out some more questions and then put you through an interview. This'll seem weird at first, and neither one of you will want to take it seriously, but keep at it. This is the best way to prepare yourself, so you can walk into that interview room feeling confident.

Take notes while you're practicing, and ask your friend to do the same. What do you need to work on? What are your strengths? Keep thinking about how to improve your performance, and incorporate those ideas into your notes.

Prepare a Closer. At the end of the interview, you'll almost always be asked, "Do you have any questions?" Have your answer prepared. If you have a couple of good questions, ask them. *Don't* ask about retirement benefits or how soon you can be promoted to detective. That really sends the wrong signal—that you're assuming you're going to be hired, and that you're focused a bit too much on your own personal goals. If you can't think of any questions, just say something like, "I don't have any questions, but I would like to say that becoming a police officer has been a lifelong goal, and I believe my skills would make me an asset to this department."

Make Sure You Know How to Get to the Interview Site. Don't assume it's at the police station. Check your notification form. Even if you've been to the station, or the courthouse, or wherever it is you're supposed to go, make another trip. If you can, go at the same time of day you'll be heading in for your interview. Time the trip, then add a safety margin for traffic jams, sick subway passengers, flat tires, or any other transportation disaster.

The Night Before the Interview

Check Your Transportation. If you're driving, do you have enough gas in the tank? Been having problems with your car? If so, arrange a backup—get a friend to stand by in case you need a ride, or make sure you have enough money for cab fare and the number of a good company. If you're using mass transit, make sure you've got tokens or change.

Check Your Clothes. For most women, this is second nature, but we guys may need a little prompting here. Men, wear a suit, or a sport coat and tie. Women, wear a dress, or skirt and blouse. You're not heading for a fashion show or a velvet-rope nightclub, so don't pick anything flashy. Lay out every single thing you're going to wear to the interview, including your underwear. Make sure it's all clean, matching, no buttons missing or seams ripped. If you haven't worn those pants for a while, try them on now—while there's still time to find an alternative, in case they don't fit. You want to minimize any nasty surprises in the morning.

Go Over Your Notes. Read through your application, so it's fresh in your mind. The interviewers will have read it, will probably have it in front of them, and you won't want to just repeat what you've already told them. Read the notes from your mock interview. Think about the positive aspects about yourself that you want to get across.

Get a Good Night's Sleep. This is not the time to go out barhopping with your buds. And it's a good idea not to even go down that path. Have a good dinner, watch some TV, but don't make any wild plans.

The Day of the Interview

Make Sure You Get up Early. You don't want to be rushed, so give yourself plenty of time to get ready. If you're a sound sleeper, set two alarms, and have a friend call you.

Eat Breakfast, but Don't Overdo the Coffee. You want to give yourself some fuel, but you don't want to be jangling all over the place, hyped up on caffeine. And this is not a good morning to chow down on the huevos rancheros with the incinerator salsa.

INTERVIEW TIPS

If the very idea of going into an interview starts your knees shaking, you're not alone. Some people are natural performers, and some people panic at asking directions from a stranger. Most of us are somewhere in the middle, maybe closer to one end or the other. If you're more of a panicker, take some tips from professional speakers—people who make their living talking to strangers. Here are some ways to handle the common symptoms of performance anxiety:

If You Get Dry Mouth

- Drink room-temperature water. There'll probably be a glass and pitcher in the interview room; don't be afraid to use it.

- Don't drink milk, soda, coffee, alcohol, or anything sugary for an hour before the interview. All these things will only dehydrate you more.

- Bite the tip of your tongue. This will help your mouth produce more saliva.

If You Get Sweaty

- Use talcum powder when you get dressed.

- Carry a handkerchief. Wipe off your hands just before you go into the interview room.

If Your Hands Get Shaky

- Move them around some. Before the interview, practice gesturing. Watch yourself in a mirror to make sure you don't look like a windmill.

- Press your palms gently against your thighs.

If Your Heart Starts Pounding

- Take a few deep breaths. If you practice a bit before the interview, you'll be able to do this without sounding like an overheated buffalo.

—This was adapted from *Speaking Is an Audience-Centered Sport* by Marjorie Brody, and originally appeared in the September 1998 issue of *Presentations* magazine.

Leave Early. You want to be in the waiting room fifteen minutes before your appointment—regardless of traffic on the freeway or a slooooow bus. Believe me, people notice promptness, and it makes a good impression. Bring your notes and you can use the waiting time for a little last-minute reviewing. If you're starting to get stressed out, take a few really deep breaths. Don't start worrying about all the things that could go wrong; instead, focus on doing well, making a good impression. That should be the image you carry into the room.

In the Interview

Acknowledge Everyone. Someone will take the lead and introduce him- or herself, and the other interviewers. This person may or may not be the chief decision maker in this situation, so you need to acknowledge and address all the interviewers—now and throughout the interview. When you're introduced, smile, shake hands, and greet *each* of the interviewers. When you answer questions, make eye contact with everyone. I'm not saying you should sit there with your eyes bouncing around like Ping-Pong balls, but you do need to acknowledge that you're addressing more than one person.

Listen to the Questions. One of the biggest mistakes people make is answering the question they *think* they've heard, instead of the question that's been asked. Pay attention and *focus*. If you're in any doubt, ask for a clarification.

Don't Blurt out Your Answer Right Away. You don't get extra points for speed. Give yourself a second or two to gather your thoughts and focus on the best answer to the question. You don't want to have to retract your answer later.

Identify the "Bad Cop." In just about every interview situation, one of the interviewers will play the heavy, the one who challenges your answers and tries to get you to back down. Don't be aggressive with this person, but don't let him bully you either. Address the Bad Cop directly; don't get thrown by his questions or his tone. And *don't* take it personally. He's not out to get you—the point is to see how you react to stress and confrontation.

Thank the Interviewers. When you get up to leave, again shake hands with each of the interviewers and thank them for the opportunity to speak with them.

THE POLYGRAPH

Polygraphs are not part of the POST requirements, but more and more police departments are requiring them. If you've never taken one before, the idea can be intimidating. How does it work? What are they going to ask about? What if I'm nervous during the test? Can you beat the polygraph? Well, here are the answers:

How Does It Work?

The polygraph measures several involuntary physiological responses to stress—specifically, the stress involved in lying. When you're actually "hooked up," you'll be seated in a chair near the polygraph. Three sensors will be attached:

- Blood pressure cuff, to measure heart rate
- Convoluted rubber tubes, attached around the abdomen and chest, to measure respiratory activity
- Two small metal plates, attached to the fingers, to measure sweat gland activity.

The questioning phase also has three parts:

Pretest: Before you're hooked up to the polygraph, the examiner asks you several questions. There are the baseline questions—"Is your name Jane Doe? Were you born in Peoria, Illinois?" Then there are the real questions—questions such as "Have you ever manufactured, transported, or sold illegal drugs?" You're not going to lie about your name or where you were born; even if your heart is beating faster than it normally would because you're nervous, that elevated heart rate is going to register as the baseline for the test.

Chart Collection Phase: You're then hooked up to the polygraph, and the examiner goes through the questions again. Then, there's the follow-up—"Did you lie when you told me you haven't manufactured, transported or sold illegal drugs?" This is the key to the use of the polygraph—the specific questioning and the immediate response.

COPS IN THE NEIGHBORHOOD

Law enforcement, like anything else, has its fads and fashions. But sometimes a fad actually turns out to be a classic—a pair of jeans, instead of plaid polyester bell-bottom hip-huggers. Community oriented policing is becoming a classic.

The Department of Justice defines community oriented policing as "a policing philosophy that promotes and supports organizational strategies to address the causes and reduce the fear of crime and social disorder through problem-solving tactics and community-police partnerships. A fundamental shift from traditional, reactive policing, community policing stresses the prevention of crime before it occurs." This doesn't mean that cops are expected to become social workers, or that station houses should be turned over to the local P.T.A. But it does require more flexibility from law enforcement officers—and it's not an idea that's going to go away anytime soon. The increase in community oriented policing, among other things, is credited with the recent drop in crime rates across the country.

To get more details, check out the DOJ's Community Oriented Policing Services (COPS) site: http://www.usdoj.gov/cops/. You'll find useful information about basic practices and tools, success stories from police departments throughout the country, a bibliography of relevant research, and much more. This site alone should help you prepare for an interview.

Test Data Analysis Phase: The examiner reviews the charts and notes areas where deception is indicated. When appropriate, the examiner will ask the subject to explain or clarify any unusual physiological responses—something along the lines of, "You seemed to react strongly to the questions about theft. Is there a specific reason for that?"

What Are They Going to Ask About?

Law enforcement agencies maintain very high ethical standards among its employees. Even so, they're not looking for saints, or robots. Drug use isn't defined as being in the same room as a marijuana cigarette; theft isn't defined as making a few personal phone calls on company time.

The questions on a polygraph are very carefully designed to be limited and specific, and thus useful. They won't ask you if you've stolen sticky-notes from work. They'll ask questions like, "Have you ever significantly defrauded an employer?" or "Have you ever manufactured or sold illicit drugs?"

What If the Polygraph Shows I'm Lying When I'm Not?

During the pretest, the examiner will assess the subject's emotional state and physical condition and allow for any effect these might have. The control questions help identify subjects who are extremely responsive or extremely nervous; there are specialized tests for use in these circumstances. The examiners make every effort to get an accurate reading from the polygraph.

If you know a deceptive response on your polygraph is inaccurate, you can request a second polygraph with a second examiner, or you can ask to have the first polygraph reviewed by another examiner.

As far as trying to beat the polygraph—forget it. It's not the machine you're trying to fool, it's the examiner—and a skilled, experienced polygraph examiner is almost impossible to fool.

THE PSYCHOLOGICAL TEST

I know people tend to get nervous at the mention of "psychological" anything, but there's really no point in getting wound up about this. Actually, I think this the easiest part of the whole process. You can't study for this test, you can't outguess it, so there's really nothing to do to prepare.

The Written Test

Almost all departments give applicants a standardized, multiple-choice test, either one they've designed themselves or one that's commonly used in psychological settings. The most common test is the Minnesota Multiphasic Psychological Inventory, or MMPI—500 true-false statements, which you read and respond to. Just to give you some idea of what it's like, the statements range from things like, "I prefer romance novels to mysteries," to "My father is a good man," to "My thoughts are insects." Your mark your answers, depending on whether the statement never applies to you, sometimes applies to you, often applies to you, or always applies to you. And that's it.

Other tests may ask you to complete sentences, or react to specific phrases: "When I'm at home _____" or "My mother's favorite _____." Don't obsess over your answers, and answer honestly, but think about what you're writing. "My mother's favorite color is purple" will probably send a better message than "My mother's favorite was always my worthless brother." But *do not* waste a lot of time trying to come up the "right" or the "best" answers. You're better off just answering honestly. The MMPI and all psychological tests are specifically designed to pick up inconsistencies that indicate someone's manipulating the answers. You don't gain anything by not being honest and up-front in your responses.

The Psychological Interview

In some departments, you'll have an interview with a psychologist, usually a few days after you complete the written test. The psychologist will probably ask you some follow-up questions about the results of your written test, and he or she may also ask other questions to find out a little more about what makes you tick.

Don't worry too much about this. Anything you say is private, and you're not going to leave the testing room in a straitjacket. You *will* be asked questions no one's ever asked you before—things like "Have you ever had any homosexual impulses?" or "What's the worst thing you've ever done?" or "Do you have a happy marriage?" Don't say, "None of your damn business"—although that'll probably be your first impulse. Just answer the question as honestly as you can.

THE PHYSICAL TEST

POST doesn't require one, but some agencies do. Doughnut jokes aside, you have to be reasonably fit to do a good job as a cop. If you don't already have some sort of physical fitness routine, start one. It can be as simple as walking up the stairs at work instead of taking the elevator. If you want to go all out, check with your physician first. But I firmly believe that physical health enhances all areas of your life. It helps you handle stress (always a big part of any law enforcement job), it increases your stamina, and it really does help you think more clearly. So that's my little physical fitness sermon.

Once you get into the academy, you'll be tested on:

- Agility Run: Run at least 99 yards (almost the length of a football field), while going around, over, or between obstacles. None of the obstacles will be very tall, and you won't have to crawl under anything.
- Body Drag: Drag a nonresisting person at least 32 feet (about ten yards) as rapidly as you can, without assistance. (You've got to feel sorry for the poor guy who's the dragee.)
- Chain Link Fence Climb: Climb a 6-foot chain-link fence, with footholds and handholds, as rapidly as you can.
- Solid Fence Climb: Climb a 6-foot solid fence with no handholds or footholds, as rapidly as you can.
- 500-yard Run: Run 500 yards (about one-and-a-half laps around a standard running track).

Check with the department you're applying to. They'll give you specifics as far as their application procedures. Some of the larger forces, such as Los Angeles, have a scheduled training program to get applicants up to the required fitness level. And even if you don't have to pass a physical at this point, it's not a bad idea to get a head start.

How The LAPD Polices the World

Foreign criminals who flee to their homelands are learning that they can't hide from the long arm of the Los Angeles Police Department. The city, which boasts a huge immigrant population and is near a long, porous international border, maintains a unique LAPD unit charged with pursuing criminals who flee the country. Suspects are apprehended by authorities in their homeland, then tried in that nation's courts. If convicted, they do time in their own prisons. Convincing authorities abroad to arrest and try someone is an often laborious process requiring sophisticated linguistic skills, cultural awareness, sensitivity—and patience.

Detective Arturo A. Zorrilla, 52, a 29-year LAPD veteran, has been with the Foreign Prosecutions Unit since it was organized in 1985 and is now its boss. "Our officers must understand the other country's system and how it works, and know how to treat people with respect, courtesy, and understanding. We must be as much diplomats as police," says Zorrilla.

In addition to pursuing criminals, the unit also has helped find witnesses. Zorrilla once escorted a deputy district attorney to war-torn Guatemala, where they tracked a murder witness to a remote village near the Honduran border. After days on rebel-controlled roads, they walked miles on jungle footpaths. Zorrilla convinced the witness to return, and a murderer went to death row.

Few crimes qualify for the squad's efforts. "Most of our cases are murders," explains Zorrilla. "We don't have the manpower to address every type of case, so each is carefully reviewed before we accept it."

One memorable case involved Rene Cruz Reynoso, a 29-year-old American who in 1991 hired two hit men to murder his landlord. To make the hit look like road rage, the gunmen followed the victim on a motorcycle and shot him as his car left the freeway. When police arrested the motorcycle driver, Reynoso vanished. Then his photo aired on America's Most Wanted, and somebody in Guadalajara spotted him.

"We tried to have him arrested," recalls Zorrilla. "But the Guadalajara federales were reluctant to touch this guy. We asked the director of Interpol in Mexico City for help. He sent two guys with two of ours to Guadalajara, and they grabbed him." Despite this unusual arrest by Interpol operatives, the only Mexican charge against Reynoso was for being an undocumented worker. "He claimed to be a Mexican citizen, but his Spanish was horrendous," chuckles Zorrilla. "He presented a phony birth certificate that belonged to a cousin."

While in custody, Reynoso hired a battery of lawyers to press for his release on the relatively minor charge. "By the time we could have produced an airtight case on the murder, translated it and presented it, he would have been free," recalls Zorrilla. Racing against the clock, Zorrilla's squad rounded up fingerprints, a voter registration document and a birth certificate to prove that Reynoso was a U.S. citizen. After months of high-level negotiations, Reynoso was deported. He pleaded guilty to murder and is serving 20 years.

Cases presented by the LAPD that convince foreign judges to issue an arrest warrant almost always result in convictions. Similar cases tried in the United States bring fewer convictions. The difference is that Americans enjoy more expansive civil liberties, including the right to an attorney to cross-examine witnesses and reveal contradictions in their testimony.

"The suspect gives up his right to a trial under our system when he flees the country," says Zorrilla. "He or she gets the kind of justice that's practiced in their homeland."

—Adapted from an APBNews.com article by Marvin J. Wolf, Oct. 31, 1999

Part Two

Preparing for the Written Test

I'll say it again—the most important thing you can do to prepare for the written police test is get all the information you can from the department you're applying to. Tests vary from agency to agency, and I can't give you the specific info you'll need to do well.

However, I *can* give you some general guidelines to help you get ready for the test. First, I'll give you some tips on test-taking in general. Then, I'll cover the spelling, grammar, and reading comprehension skills you'll be be tested on. Finally, you'll practice answering questions in the same format you'll see on the POST test.

CHAPTER THREE
Test-Taking Basics

In this chapter, we'll look at some things you can do to be a better test taker. We'll start with some general advice for improving your performance on a standardized test. The rest of this chapter will help you with memory and observation questions.

- *Pace yourself.* Wear a watch, and keep track of the time. You don't want to focus so intensely on one section that you never even get to the others.

- *Don't stall out.* If you get stuck on a particular question, just put a big check mark next to it and move on. If you have time when you finish the test, go back and work on the checked questions.

- *Limit your choices.* Most of the time, at least one of the multiple-choice answers is obviously wrong. Look for that one first, and cross it out. That narrows down your choices and saves you time.

- *No wild guesses.* If you've narrowed things down to two answers, go ahead and choose the one that makes the most sense. But if you have absolutely no idea how to answer the question, leave it blank. Not answering questions won't hurt you as much as giving the wrong answers.

- *Go with your first answer.* It's almost always the best one. Unless you realize that you've read the question wrong or made some other mistake, stick with your first choice. If you start second-guessing yourself, you'll never get past the first five questions.

- *Once it's over, it's over.* Once you walk out of the room, don't torture yourself thinking about "what ifs" or "shouldas." You probably didn't do as badly as you think you did. And even if you fail the test, you can take it again. And the next time, you'll be better prepared.

MEMORY AND OBSERVATION

You know that one of the requirements for being a police officer is vision correctable to 20/20. Well, that perfect vision won't do you any good if you can't use it intelligently. And that's where memory and observation come in.

As a police officer, you need to be able to take in a scene and sort through all the thousands of details to come up with the relevant information. And you've got to do it quickly—almost unconsciously.

You might or might not encounter memory and observation questions on your written test; it's not required by POST, but some departments test you on it anyway. As always, check with your recruiting officer and take a look at the prep packet from the department.

The "Inspector Clouseau" Questions

One category might test your ability to detect disguises. I call it the "Inspector Clouseau" category, because the questions usually involve looking at a set of goofy drawings showing even goofier disguises. One drawing shows the "subject"; four or five other drawings represent possible disguises adopted by the subject. You're asked to determine which of the possibilities is most likely to be the actual subject. These tests are slowly being phased out, so they're not as common as they once were. But if you do come across this category, here's how you handle it:

- Focus on facial characteristics that can't easily be changed: nose breadth and length, the shape of the chin, the size of the eyes, the way the ears are set on the head.

- Don't be distracted by differences (or similarities) in qualities that are easier to manipulate: hair length, color, and texture; facial hair; size and shape of eyebrows; general shape of the face, which can be affected by weight gain or loss. These days, even eye color can be disguised with contacts.

And that's about it. Don't rush your decision; take your time and evaulate all your choices. Stick to the underlying facial structure, and the right choice will become obvious.

The Scene

You'll be given a certain length of time (usually 15 minutes) to look at a photograph of a street scene or a simulated street scene. Then you'll be asked to answer several questions about the action and details shown.

If you're lucky, you already have a good memory. But you can sharpen it. And even if your memory isn't so great, you can learn better memory skills.

Street Scene

Think of the drawing you're given as a movie scene, and focus on the three basics of any movie:

Characters

- How many people are there?

- Ages? Gender?

- Use two words to describe the physical appearance of each person. For instance, "tall, hairy man" or "plump, elderly woman."

- If one of the characters has an especially distinctive physical characteristic, note it: "Tall hairy man with eye patch."

- What about their facial expressions?

- What, if anything, is each character carrying?

Action

- What is each person doing?

- Group them, using your two-word descriptions: "Tall, hairy man escorting plump, elderly woman across the intersection."

- What can you tell about the relationships among the members of the group? Are they boss/coworkers, friends, spouses, strangers?

- Are any of the groups interacting? For instance: "Tall hairy man escorting plump, elderly woman across intersection. Young slender man with blond ponytail is running behind them, reaching toward her shopping bag."

Setting

- Take note of any numbers, such as street addresses and license plate numbers.

- Look for other useful identifiers—business signs, names on buildings, statues, or other landmarks.

- Does the area seem prosperous or struggling? Crowded or deserted? Can you tell whether it's a weekday or weekend, daytime or evening or night?

The Crime Scene

These don't contain as many details as the street scenes, but each detail is more important.

Think of the photograph as a clock. What's at 12 o'clock? Then work your way around the dial, assigning each element in the photograph its appropriate number. Just keep going over the objects in the same order, and you'll be able to recall them more accurately.

Of course, you'll want to take particular notice of:

- Anything that indicates time or date

- Anything personalized

- Documents or letters of any kind
- Physical appearance and peculiarities of any people present

The best way to prepare for this kind of test is to practice noticing. For the next few days, make a point of going through this exercise with as many things as you can—news photographs, advertisements, even the crowd in a movie theater or sports arena. Do this often enough, and it'll become second nature.

MAP READING

You may be given a map of few blocks in a fictional city, and asked to select the best route from Point A to Point B from four choices. The key to answering these questions is remaining focused. It's easy to get confused and lose track of where you are.

- *Look out for one-way streets.* These will be indicated on the map with an arrow.
- *Check your directions.* Make sure you're clear on which way is north.
- *Draw your path.* Unless you're hopeless at map reading, it's almost always faster to come up with the best route and look for the answer that matches, rather than test all of the answers.

CRIME JUSTICE SAFETY

MURDER INVESTIGATIONS CHANGE DRAMATICALLY

Over the last two and a half decades, the process of investigating homicides has changed radically. Twenty years ago, for example, if a homicide detective recovered a fingerprint that didn't match any of the suspects', he was stymied. There was no practical method for comparing a recovered print with the millions of individual prints that a police department might have on file. Instead, the recovered fingerprint would be filed away and, as time permitted, manually compared to the fingerprints of certain newly arrested people.

That was before the advent of the Automated Fingerprint Identification System (AFIS), the computer system that uses "recognition points" to electronically code fingerprints stored in its memory. Today, the recognition points of a fingerprint recovered at a crime scene can be compared at lightning speed with the millions of fingerprints stored in a computer's memory. Within minutes, if there is a match, the computer will display it.

Another daily tool that has been dramatically altered by computer technology is the old mug shot book, a collection of photographs of known criminals. Today, digitized mug shots are stored on mug shot computers. This advance in technology has also largely done away with another tradition of homicide investigators: the live lineup of suspects. Now, detectives can enter the suspect's information into the mug shot computer, which generates a digital photographic lineup of the suspect and any number of others who resemble to him. The witnesses can then pick the suspect out of a photo array. This computer system can also pull up pictures of suspects based on physical characteristics such as scars, tattoos, deformities, etcetera.

The single biggest change we've seen over the decades in homicide involves the nature of the crime itself. Twenty years ago, we had half as many homicides as today, and a large number of the murders investigated were either "smoking gun domestics," in which one spouse killed another and was still holding the proverbial smoking gun when the police arrived, or murders committed during disturbances such as tavern fights, where tempers flared and a murder resulted.

The widespread use of crack cocaine and other drugs has dramatically altered homicide trends. Life in today's drug culture is cheap and violent—individuals in that drug world carry guns and tend to use them almost indiscriminately.

Few people outside of law enforcement fully appreciate how many of the murders committed today have some sort of drug connection. But homicide detectives do. "The drug man can't go to small claims court," said Sgt. Richard Combs, a homicide investigator for nearly 25 years. "When you owe the drug man, he's going to get his money, or he's going to kill you." These new types of murders are, of course, much more difficult to solve than domestics or tavern fights because often little or no connection exists between the murderer and the victim.

Fortunately, the advances in science and technology can give homicide detectives the extra edge they often need to solve these more difficult cases.

—Adapted from an APBNews.com article by Robert L. Snow, June 1, 1999

CHAPTER FOUR
Grammar and Spelling

The POST test measures your ability to spot incorrect or awkward sentences. If you're a good reader and enjoy reading for pleasure, you'll probably do fine with just a little review. If language is not your strong point, work a little harder here.

This chapter covers the basics that are likely to trip you up, and gives you a bunch of practice questions. In each section, the first set of questions will improve your skills in a particular area. Then, you'll apply those skills on questions in the same format you'll see on the POST test.

GRAMMAR BASICS

This is the structure of language—how words fit together to form meaningful sentences. I'm going to give you a little refresher course in grammar here, plus a rundown on the most common mistakes people make. I'm going to assume you know nothing, and start from the very beginning. This is not to insult you, but just to make sure you understand the basics before we build on them.

What's a Sentence?

I told you we were going to start from the very beginning.

A sentence needs, at the minimum, a **subject** and a **verb**. The subject is most often a noun (a person, place or thing); it's the actor in the sentence. The verb is the action; it tells you what the subject is doing.

For now, we'll just make a very simple sentence.

The dog barked.

"The dog" is the subject, "barked" is the verb.

Okay, you've got that. Now let's complicate the sentence a little:

The dog barked at the man.

So what does "man" do in this sentence? It's not the subject; the dog is still doing the barking. Because the man is on the receiving end of the barking, he's the **object** in this sentence.

The subject's action is directed at the object.

That's easy to figure out, but if a sentence gets more complicated and you're having trouble identifying the subject and verb, ask yourself these questions:

- To find the verb, ask: "What's happening?"
- To find the subject, ask: "Who, or what, is making it happen?"
- To find the object, ask: "Who, or what, is it happening to?"

Why should you care about finding the subject, verb, and object? Because words often change, depending on their place in the sentence. The subject and verb are most important because they're always there, and they always have to match in person and number.

Person indicates who the speaker or writer is talking about or talking to. First person means the speaker is referring to or describing him- or herself—"I am." Second person means the sentence is addressed to or describing the audience—"you are." Third person, or "he is," describes or refers to someone or something ("it") that's neither the speaker nor the audience.

Then there's *number*—singular or plural. The examples above are all singular in number. "We are, you are, they are"—that's first person plural, second person plural, and third person plural.

All the examples above match in person and number, which is grammatically correct. You wouldn't say, "I are a good student"—not if you wanted anyone to believe you. In our dog/man sentence, the subject and verb match. Here are some examples of mismatched subjects and verbs:

The dog bark at the man.

"Bark" is third person plural ("the dogs bark") while the subject is still third person singular.

The dog barking at the man.

Okay. I'll explain exactly why this is wrong in a minute, but first we have to talk about *verb tense*—when the action is taking place. Don't worry about the names of these tenses; that's not important. Focus on learning how the words fit together, so you'll be able to spot and correct a mistake.

Base form	*to bark*	This is the basic verb, your starting point.
Past	*barked*	The action happened at some earlier time.
Present	*bark*	The action is taking place now.
Future	*will bark*	The action will take place later.

That covers the simplest, most basic tenses. Of course, real events can't be as easily divided into just three time categories. Which brings up the following tenses:

Present participle	*is barking*	Emphasizes the ongoing act.
The dog is barking too much.		
Past participle	*was barking*	Again, emphasizes the activity in the past.
Before the break-in, the dog was barking very loudly.		
Present perfect	*has barked*	The action began in the past and it (or the effects of it) are continuing now.
The dog has barked so much that his throat is sore.		
Past perfect	*had barked*	The action started and ended in the past.
The dog had barked so much that the entire neighborhood was awake.		

Believe it or not, there are other tenses, all with increasingly complex and confusing names, like future pluperfect. We're just going to skip those, because they're not used very often in the kind of writing you'll be dealing with.

Remember the second example of incorrect grammar? I said I was going to get into why it was wrong later. Well, later is now.

The dog barking at the man.

"Barking" is the **infinitive** form of the verb; it's used with the helping verbs (such as "is," "was," and "has") to form the more complicated tenses. The infinitive form can't stand alone as a verb.

Beyond Subjects and Verbs

Okay, back to our sentence.

The dog barked at the man.

What about "at"? This is a **preposition**, a word that describes the relationship between two ideas, in this case, the barking and the man. Prepositions almost always relate to time and place, and the same prepositions can be used for either time or place; you have to sort it out by context. Here are the most common prepositions and some examples of usage.

Time

*I'll take care of it **in** the morning.*

*The plane is due here **at** 3:05.*

*My brother is arriving for a visit **on** May 5th.*

*The baby screamed **for** an entire hour.*

*She hasn't worked **since** her car accident.*

Place

*There's hardly any peanut butter **in** this jar.*

*I left a memo **on** your desk.*

*She kept her money **under** her mattress.*

*He's waiting **at** the theater.*

*The hurricane swept **over** the island.*

In all these examples, the preposition is at the end of the sentence. It doesn't *have* to be there:

***Since** her car accident, she hasn't worked.*

Now let's add some more to our dog/man sentence.

The tiny dog barked at the laughing man.

"Tiny" and "laughing" are **adjectives**. They add descriptive detail to a noun.

The vicious dog barked at the trembling man.

The tiny white dog barked at the laughing fat man.

What if you want to modify the verb? You can do that. A word that adds descriptive detail to a verb is called an adverb. You turn an adjective into an adverb by adding the ending "-ly." (There are some exceptions to this rule, but not many.)

The tiny dog barked fiercely at the laughing man.

There are two words in this sentence we still haven't talked about (actually, one word used twice): "the." This is an article, one of two in English; the other is "a" or "an." "The" is the definite article; it's used when referring to a specific, particular thing. "A" or "an" is the indefinite article; it's used when referring to one of a number of similar things. "A" is used in front of words that start with a consonant ("a cat"), while "an" is used in front of words that begin with a vowel ("an icicle").

The dog barked at the man.

There's a specific man and a specific dog the writer has in mind.

A dog barked at a man.

The writer is talking about some dog, somewhere, barking at some man, somewhere.

Now, let's build a more complicated sentence:

The tiny dog barked fiercely at the laughing man, and then ran to its doghouse.

(Notice that as long as it's clear who "its" refers to, you don't have to repeat the subject.)

Look at "and," the word that's linking these two sentences. "And" is one example of a **conjunction**. If sentences are bricks, conjunctions are the mortar that holds them together. Different conjunctions imply different relationships between the ideas they connect. Here are the most common conjunctions, the ones you're most likely to see on the test, plus what they mean in the sentence.

***And*—Connection:** There's a clear, logical connection between the two ideas:

- One idea follows the other in time:

Bradley sent in his applications and waited for a response.

- One idea causes the other:

Natasha worked hard at her job and was rewarded with a raise.

***But*—Contrast:** The second idea is a little bit of a surprise; in some way, it's contrary to the first idea.

He doesn't seem to have a job but he always has plenty of money to spend.

I'd like to go to the beach but I have to study for my test.

***Or*—Choice:** Only one idea of the two presented is true or will happen.

We can see a movie or we can go bowling.

You must eat less and exercise more, or you're going to keep gaining weight.

There's another group of conjunctions that contain two or more words. You need to know which two words match—like matching your socks.

Two-Part Conjunctions

Both . . . and—includes two separate ideas

Both the plumbing and the wiring in the old house had to be replaced.

Either . . . or—a choice between two ideas

The two of you can either stop arguing or walk home.

Neither . . . nor—rejects both ideas

Look for a diet and exercise program that's neither too restrictive nor too complicated.

Not only . . . but also—contrast between the first idea and the second.

He motivated his students not only with verbal encouragement but also with tangible rewards.

That covers the basic rules and structures of grammar. As I said earlier, don't make yourself nuts trying to memorize the names for verb forms or modifiers. This is the important thing: *Think about how grammar works.* Make yourself familiar with the function of each part of the sentence. You don't have to explain it to anyone, or teach a course on it. Just be able to use it.

The next section covers some of the most common grammatical mistakes people make. See if you're prone to any of them, and focus on that area.

COMMON MISTAKES

Double Negatives

In English, two wrongs don't make a right. If a sentence contains two negatives—words such as "not" or "without"—the words cancel each other out. Sometimes people intentionally use double negatives, especially when they're trying to sound classy. Saying, "The little bistro was not without charm," means it was a cute place. But it takes a second to figure that out. It's better to avoid double negatives altogether.

Watch out for the low-key negatives—"hardly," "barely," "scarcely," "cannot." They do count as negatives.

Here are a couple of examples of double negatives and ways to fix them.

The suspect said that he didn't commit no burglaries.

People do talk this way, but you shouldn't write this way. "Didn't" is a contraction for "did not"—that's one negative. Combined with "no," you've got a double negative. Here's how to fix it:

The suspect said he didn't commit any burglaries.

The suspect said he committed no burglaries.

***

Recruit Smith hasn't hardly any worries about how he'll do on the running portion of the test.

"Hasn't" is a contraction for "has not," and "hardly" is one of those tricky negatives. You've got one too many. You've got two ways to fix it:

Recruit Smith has hardly any worries about how he'll do on the running portion of the test.

Recruit Smith hasn't any worries about how he'll do on the running portion of the test.

***

With the new computerized databases, it doesn't take scarcely any time to run a license check.

Nope, that's not right—unless the computer's down. Try these:

With the new computerized databases, it doesn't take any time to run a license check.

With the new computerized databases, it takes scarcely any time to run a license check.

Misplaced Modifiers

Modifying phrases can help describe something more precisely, or explain something more fully. But if they're not clearly linked to the noun they're modifying, these phrases also can make a sentence confusing. For example:

Noxious gases pouring out the rear, Lieutenant Stanley ran toward the overturned tanker truck.

Well, whose rear are we talking about here? It's probably the tanker truck's, but for Lieutenant Stanley's sake, the writer really should have made it clear.

Lieutenant Stanley ran toward the overturned tanker truck, which had noxious gases pouring out the rear.

Vague Pronoun Reference

Pronouns stand in for other nouns in a sentence. (Check out the table listing the different kinds of pronouns.) They're used most often to eliminate repetitiveness—"The health club offers a wide range of classes for the health club's members" becomes "The health club offers a wide range of classes for its members." The original noun is called the antecedent. You should always make sure that there's no confusion about which noun is the antecendent of a pronoun. This grammatical error is called ambiguous pronoun reference.

Here are a couple of examples:

I've always been interested in forensic psychology, so I've decided to be one.

One what? No one can *be* a psychology, forensic or not. Here's one way to make the sentence clearer:

I've always been interested in forensic psychology, so I've decided to make that my specialty.

Or, you could also write:

I've always been interested in forensic psychology, so I've decided to study it in college.

***

Officers Smith and Jones jumped into their cruiser and, hitting the siren, raced to the scene. It was brand new.

What's new—scene, siren, or cruiser? No telling. Here's a possible fix:

Officers Smith and Jones jumped into their brand-new cruiser and, hitting the siren, raced to the scene.

Personal Pronouns: Stand in for People or Things

I, me, you, he, she, him, her, it, we, us, they, them, one

- "John and Latisha have been friends for years; they went to kindergarten together."

Relative Pronouns: Used in Clauses Relating to Someone or Something

Who, whom, which, that, where, whose

- "The suspect, who had been arrested many times before, seemed quite comfortable with the processing routine."

Possessive Pronouns: Refer to Things Belonging to Some Individual or Group

Mine, yours, his, hers, theirs, ours

- "Enriqué did well on the screening test, but Sally did even better; in fact, her score was the highest in the state."

Sentence Fragments

Sentence fragments are usually pretty easy to spot. When you read one, your reaction is usually, "Huh?" There's something crucial missing. In more technical terms, a sentence fragment is a group of words that looks like a sentence, but is either grammatically or logically incomplete. Here's the grammatical test: to be a sentence, the group of words has to contain both a subject and a verb related to one another.

Take a look at this example:

The man in the lineup wearing the plaid shirt.

Well, you've got a subject—"The man." And you seem to have a verb—"wearing." But "wearing the plaid shirt" really just modifies the subject, giving us more details about the man. There *is* no verb. What *about* the man in the lineup? Did he do something? Or did someone do something to him? What was going on? Who knows?

You can complete the sentence by adding a verb:

The man in the lineup wearing the plaid shirt mumbled so much the witness couldn't understand him.

The man in the lineup wearing the plaid shirt was the witness' first choice.

But some sentence fragments do have a subject and verb; these are the sentences that are logically incomplete. Look at this:

When the sergeant has to fill out a lot of paperwork.

Yep, you've got the subject, the sergeant. And he has a verb attached—he has to fill out paperwork. But what about that "when"? That leads us to expect information that just isn't there. Here's how that fragment can be turned into a full sentence:

When the sergeant has to fill out a lot of paperwork, he gets very cranky.

Believe me, you're going to run into that sergeant at some point.

Subject/Verb Agreement Problems

We've already talked about subject-verb disagreement in sentences like "I are a good student." That's a pretty easy mistake to spot, but it can get trickier. Here are some of the easy-to-miss situations.

Compound Subjects

One tricky situation occurs when you have a sentence in which the subject is a list of some kind:

The applicant told the interviewers that his drive, determination, and intelligence makes/make him an ideal recruit.

The correct answer is "make"—that list of three singular nouns adds up to one compound subject, which requires a plural verb.

Compound Impostors

As if compound subjects weren't tricky enough, there are some sentences that seem to have compound subjects, when they really don't. Watch out for phrases containing or beginning with "neither/nor," "either/or," "along with," "as well as," "in addition to." These are the compound impostors.

> *Neither the rookie nor the old-timer* knows/know *how to handle the situation.*

Here, the right answer is the singular verb—"knows"—even though this looks like a list of two nouns. To make it clearer, rewrite the sentence as, "Neither **one** knows how to handle the situation." And that's the implied meaning of "either/or" and "neither/nor."

However, what if you had "rookies" and "old-timers"? Then you're dealing with plural subjects in both situations, so you'd need the plural verb— "Neither the rookies nor the old-timers *knew* how to handle the situation."

> *Neither the rookie nor the old-timers* knows/know *how to handle the situation.*

Here the sentence takes a plural verb, "know." That's because the verb is closer to the plural noun "old-timers."

> *Officer Tremblay, along with half of the 9th Precinct,* was/were *a rabid softball player.*

The sentence takes a singular verb—"was." Officer Tremblay is the real subject of the sentence. The phrase "along with half of the 9th Precinct" is just a kind of detour; grammatically, it doesn't become part of the subject.

Subject Separated from the Verb

Don't get distracted by phrases that come between the subject and verb. Take a look at this sentence and see if you can tell which verb is correct.

> *Officer Prince, who spends many days off jumping with an elite group of skydivers,* remain/remains *calm under the most stressful circumstances.*

The right answer is the singular form, "remains." The subject of the sentence is Officer Prince, a singular noun, even though there's a plural noun right in front of the verb. Everything between the commas just gives you more information about the singular subject; it doesn't *replace* the subject.

Tricky Subject

Sometimes, some loony rule just pop up out of nowhere and trips you up. For instance:

> *The rain is pouring down the window.*

> *The raindrops are pouring down the window.*

You're talking about the same thing, but one subject is considered singular, the other plural.

Here's how to figure out which verb to use:

If the noun isn't divided into parts, it's considered singular:

*The **water is** so clear in this bay.*

*I can't believe how quickly my **money is** disappearing.*

*The **time is** slipping away from us.*

*I know **exercise is** healthy, but I still hate it.*

However, if the noun is divided into parts, it's plural:

*The **droplets are** slapping down faster now.*

*My **dollars aren't** going far enough.*

*The **minutes are** creeping by.*

*Abdominal **crunches are** torture.*

Punctuation

I'm sorry to say there are no shortcuts here. You've just got to learn what the different punctuation marks are, and the rules for using them. And there is a good chance this will show up on your test.

Period

The period (.) simply indicates the end of a complete sentence.

Comma

A comma is a separator. Use commas between elements of a list:

When Officer Jubaya ran the driver's license, he discovered that the driver was wanted for arson, burglary, and vehicular assault.

Take a look at the first comma in that sentence. This demonstrates the second use of the comma: to separate a modifying phrase from the rest of the sentence.

Sergeant Finn rarely loses his temper, unless someone insults his wife.

And what's a modifying phrase? It's a word or a group of words that adds to the information in the sentence itself. Look for words like this:

after

along with

although

before

between

generally

sometimes

throughout

unless

until

when

within

The Apostrophe

This bit of punctuation is, as far as I know, the only one that can indicate two totally separate ideas: *possession*, or a *contraction*.

Possession indicates ownership. For instance, when you write, "That locker is Tammy's," the apostrophe tells readers you're talking about a locker that belongs to Tammy, not a locker built out of several people named Tammy. ("That locker is Tammys.")

If the subject is plural, you want the plural possessive. In that case, you add the apostrophe after the "s" indicates the plural—"The flowers' scent was almost too sweet."

Then there's the second use of the apostrophe. If you write, "That locker can't be Tammy's," the apostrophe in "can't" signals a *contraction*—a shortened combination of two words, with the apostrophe marking the place of the missing letter or letters.

We use contractions all the time when we're talking or writing something like a personal letter.

Because contractions are considered casual or informal, they're rarely used in professional documents. Here are some other common contractions:

should not	shouldn't
cannot	can't
will not	won't
she will	she'll
had not	hadn't
he has	he's
should have	should've

You get the idea, right?

In everyday life, we don't always stick to the rules of grammar, and we don't always speak slowly and enunciate properly. In fact, some of us *rarely* do. That's fine, for conversation between friends. But when you're writing a report, it's definitely not fine.

Don't write what you hear. *Avoid these mistakes.* They show that you're not paying attention to what you're writing.

What You Hear	What It Is
should of	should've
buncha	bunch of
kinda	kind of
hadda	had to
wanna	want to
gone	going
axe	ask

Semicolon

The semicolon (;) joins two complete sentences when the ideas in the sentences are closely connected.

This was Officer Frankel's first murder case; he hoped that his nervousness wasn't completely obvious.

It takes at least 15 minutes to drive around Hollinghurst Park; most people take the shortcut across the park.

Instead of a semicolon, you can use a comma and a connecting word or phrase:

This was Officer Frankel's first murder case, and he hoped that his nervousness wasn't completely obvious.

It takes at least 15 minutes to drive around Hollinghurst Park, which is why most people take the shortcut across the park.

But it's one or the other. Don't use a semicolon and the connecting phrase.

Colon

The colon (:) introduces something: a new idea, a list, an broader explanation. It's an indication that the sentence is about to change direction.

You know what old cons say: two people can keep a secret, if one of them is dead.

There are three things you need on a stakeout: patience, determination, and a strong bladder.

Grammar and Spelling

Quotation Marks

Quotation marks ("") most often indicate speech.

After Mrs. Helden identified her daughter's body, she said, "I know her husband did this."

Notice the punctuation in that sentence. Use a comma just before the beginning of the quotation mark, and include the period within the marks.

Quotation marks also signal that the writer is using words originally used by someone else, or somewhere else. Notice that when I repeat a word from an example in the explanation, I put it in quotes. That sets the example word apart, so it's not confused with the rest of the sentence.

You also use quotation marks the first time you introduce an unfamiliar term, usually a professional term your readers probably wouldn't know.

The psychological term for extreme and sudden mood changes is "lability."

Finally, you can use quotation marks to cast doubt on something, or let the reader know you don't believe it.

The man said that the flashily dressed woman next to him was his "wife."

SPELLING

In some languages, words are spelled pretty much the way they sound. Not English. Take a look at *through* and *rough*. Or *through* and *threw*. Well, I'm afraid there aren't many shortcuts here. There are a few rules, but each one has dozens of exceptions. The best tactic here is to become aware of fairly common words that trip you up, then simply memorize the correct spelling.

Here's a list of some of that are misspelled often.

Incorrect	Correct
alot	a lot
athelete	athlete
calender	calendar
docter	doctor
eleminate	eliminate
excelerate	accelerate
oppertunity	opportunity
persued	pursued
seperate	separate

Do any of these words pose problems for you? Make a list of the words that consistently trip you up. Then write them on index cards and carry the cards around with you. Anytime you have a few minutes, take a look. Make yourself as familiar as possible with them, so you'll be more likely to spot the correct spelling right away.

Some of the most common spelling mistakes occur when people confuse words that sound similar, but mean totally different things. This confusion often arises when it comes to words with an apostrophe.

their/there/they're
- "Their" indicates possession by more than one person, not including the speaker—"That's their car."
- "There" indicates distance from the speaker—"That's their car over there."
- "They're" is a contraction for "they are"—"That's their car over there, and they're sitting inside it."

your/you're
- "Your" indicates possession by someone the speaker is talking to—"Your golf game has improved."
- "You're" is another contraction, meaning "you are"—"Your golf game has improved. You're just about to break par." (Note that "a lot" is *two* words, not one.)

its/it's
- "Its" is the possessive form of "it"—as in "The department has really lowered its standards."
- "It's" is a contraction of "it is"—"The department has really lowered its standards, and it's a shame."

Of course, the apostrophe isn't responsible for every source of confusion. Certain words are close to others in sound and meaning, but different in spelling; it's important to know the difference so you can express yourself accurately.

lay/lie
- "Lay" is a transitive verb, one that indicates an action done *to*. Transitive verbs are incomplete without an object: "I'm going to lay tile in the new family room."
- "Lie" is a regular verb, one that indicates an action done *by*: "I'm going to lay tile in the new family room, and then I'm going to lie down for a nap."

raise/rise

This difference is similar to that between "lay" and "lie."
- "Raise" is done *to* someone or something: "The candidate is going to have to raise a lot of money."
- "Rise" is done *by* someone or something: "The candidate is going to have to raise a lot of money before he can rise in the political structure."

accept/except
- "Accept" means taking possession or acknowledging ownership of something: "The professor said he wouldn't accept late papers."
- "Except" indicates a special case: "The professor said he wouldn't accept late papers, except in situations involving medical emergencies or large sums of cash."

effect/affect

- "Effect" is noun, a result of some action: "The effect of the earthquake is devastating."
- "Affect" is a verb, resulting in an effect: "The effect of the earthquake is devastating; nothing this disastrous has ever affected the region before."

site/sight

- "Site" indicates a location: "The site of the outdoor music festival was a pasture south of town."
- "Sight" is related to vision, either the sense itself or something that's seen: "The site of the outdoor music festival was a pasture south of town. After three days of crowds and rain, the area was quite a sight."

persecute/prosecute

- "Persecute" means inflicting some kind of torment on someone: "I don't know why he keeps persecuting his assistant with lewd remarks and sexual comments."
- "Prosecute" involves bringing legal action: "I don't know why he keeps persecuting his secretary with lewd remarks and sexual comments. If he doesn't watch it, she might try to have him prosecuted for harassment."

precede/proceed

- "Precede" means to come before: "A Secret Service team always precedes the president as he travels."
- "Proceed" means to continue: "A Secret Service team always precedes the president as he travels. If the security team doesn't feel a site is secure, the event will not proceed."

marital/martial

- "Marital" means having to do with marriage: "He suggested they go to marital counseling."
- "Martial" means having to do with war: "He suggested they go to marital counseling, before the atmosphere in the house grew more martial."

(Feel free to add your own cheap joke here.)

principal/principle

- "Principal" can be used as a noun or an adjective. As a noun, it's the title for the chief administrator at a school: "The principal gave a speech to our entire school."
  As an adjective, it means "essential" or "most important": "The principal gave a speech to our entire school, outlining his principal goals for the upcoming year."
- "Principle" is a moral belief or a code of conduct: "The principal gave a speech to the entire school, outlining his principal goals for the upcoming year and the principles that would guide us."

SO WHY IS ENGLISH SPELLING SO CONFUSING?

For the answer to that, you have to know a little bit about etymology—the study of where words come from.

English contains a mishmash of words from all over the globe. There was the original Anglo-Saxon language, which had similarities to German. This language was adulterated by the Latin brought over by the Roman conquerors. Then the Normans (from what's now France) took over, and a lot of their words became part of English. Because the Romans and the Normans made up the ruling class, their languages were considered more elegant. That bias continues today. All of the four-letter words for basic bodily functions, the words we can't print in this book, George Carlin's famous seven words—those words come straight from the original Anglo-Saxon. The more "proper" terms are descended from either Latin or French.

As English explorers traveled the globe, they picked up bits and pieces of other languages. Often, the spelling was either based on the original language, or was a vague approximation of sounds and letters that don't exist in English. And that's why there's no logic to spelling in English.

Here are three English words we've borrowed from other languages:

- *assassin*—Off and on, during the eleventh, twelfth, and thirteenth centuries, Christian soldiers marched off to the Middle East on a mission to retake the Holy Land. These campaigns, known collectively as the Crusades, didn't accomplish much, except to waste a lot of money and kill a lot of people. During the Crusades, the Christians encountered a Muslim sect that, like the Christians, took on murder as a religious duty. Unlike the Christians, this particular sect fueled themselves with hashish; their zeal apparently impressed the English Crusaders. The sect is commemorated in the English word "assassin," which originated in the Arabic word "hashshashin," meaning "eaters or smokers of hashish."

- *gorgeous*—Around the same time as the Crusades, in the late Middle Ages, the hot fashion for women was a *gorgias*, a cloth headdress wrapped over the hair and under the chin, so only the face showed. (Some of the more traditional orders of Roman Catholic nuns still wear these headdresses, called wimples.) Fashion being what it is, anyone who had the resources decorated her gorgias with embroidery or jewels. Over time, the decorations became more and more elaborate and eye-catching. As an adjective, *gorgayse*, the word became a synonym for "beautiful" or "highly decorative."

- *cigar*—This word was lifted from the Spanish word *cigarro*, which means exactly the same thing. According to some sources, *cigarro* came from the Mayan verb *sicar*, "to smoke rolled tobacco leaves."

I don't know what any of this has to do with police tests, but it gives you a new, more interesting excuse for being a crummy speller.

SECTION 1—GRAMMAR AND SPELLING REVIEW

The following two tests will help you review the topics covered in this chapter.

Review Exercise 1

For the following twenty questions, choose the right word from the italicized words in the sentence. Answers appear at the end of the chapter.

1. Coffee grown in Latin American countries *taste/tastes* better than coffee grown anywhere else in the world.

2. Pancakes, eggs, biscuits, and sausage *is/are* Officer Stone's favorite breakfast.

3. The one positive *affect/effect* of the accident was the subsequent installation of the stop sign at the dangerous intersection.

4. Both my mom and dad *supports/support* my decision to become a police officer.

5. Of all the injuries Officer Ruiz sustained in the fender bender, the bruising of her ribs *bothers/bother* her the most.

6. Officer Gill, along with the rest of the squad, *is/are* determined to apprehend the rapist before he strikes again.

7. Officer Washington tries to *rise/raise* early enough to run five miles every day.

8. Although Josh never thought of himself as an outdoorsy person, the physicality, risk taking, and strategizing involved in rock climbing *appeal/appeals* to him.

9. Neither the approaching storm nor the warnings on all radio frequencies *persuades/persuade* Officer Norton to give up searching for survivors.

10. Polls show that the number of people who don't care about the latest government scandal *has/have* increased.

11. Basketball, with its flashy stars and their spectacular plays, *have/has* become America's favorite sport.

12. Many residents, especially those from the converted hotel, *were/was* extremely upset by the string of robberies.

13. The detective refused to *accept/except* the suspect's evasive answers and kept pressing him for the truth.

14. The courtroom had to be cleared of spectators before the trial could *precede/proceed*.

15. Greed, along with gullibility, *cause/causes* many people to fall for Ponzi schemes and other financial scams.

16. Neither the attorneys nor the courthouse observers *expect/expects* the trial to last more than two weeks.

17. Some people believe it's difficult to *prosecute/persecute* Internet offenses because the statutes haven't been written to reflect the new technology.

18. There *is/are* a lot of evidence pointing to the suspect, but so far nothing strong enough to issue an arrest warrant.

19. Of the many recent advances in science, DNA analysis *has/have* the biggest impact on law enforcement.

20. Unfamiliarity with the material, in addition to nervousness, *explains/explain* why many people don't do well on standardized tests.

Review Exercise 2

To answer the following twenty questions, rewrite the sentence to eliminate confusion or correct grammatical errors. Use the lines following the sentences for your rewrites. Suggested answers appear at the end of the chapter.

1. The number of people who call tech support to ask questions about computers demonstrates that they are confusing.

   _____

   _____

2. Staggering and weaving, the officer approached the old man who had just left the bar.

   _____

   _____

3. Officer Ryan hadn't been on duty but five minutes when the call came in about a burglary in progress.

   _____

   _____

4. The desk sergeant, after weighing the pros and cons, deciding not to change the duty roster.

   _____

   _____

5. Staring blankly, the computer screen flickered while Joanna sat at her desk.

   _____

   _____

6. Upon discovering the theft in the office, the employees, suspecting one another.

   _____

   _____

7. Officer Jasek drove the cruiser into the garage, running on only one cylinder.

   _____

   _____

8. The actors on that TV cop show are great, but they don't get the details of real-life
   police work right.

   _____

   _____

9. Officer Chang searched the available files to see what kind of rap sheets they had.

   _____

   _____

10. The driver, traveling at a high rate of speed, losing control on the slick road.

    _____

    _____

11. Don't believe everything you read in the papers because you don't know if they are
    telling the truth.

    _____

    _____

12. Developed in secrecy, the scientist patented his vaccine for the deadly virus.

    _____

    _____

13. Some people prefer women's professional basketball because they don't talk as much trash.

    _____

    _____

14. Officer Melton couldn't hardly see out the windshield because of the heavy rain.

_____

_____

15. The point of going to school is not just getting an education but also socializing.

_____

_____

16. Reflecting the glare of the cruiser's lights, the tall weeds in front of the factory almost hid the shards of broken glass.

_____

_____

17. Because Officer Wilson genuinely liked talking to people, he sometimes missing his days on the street.

_____

_____

18. Officer Kwame told Officer O'Neil she wanted to trade shifts over the weekend.

_____

_____

19. The woman started crying, until her husband told her he didn't want none of her hysterics.

_____

_____

20. Street festivals being targets for pickpockets, because of the crowded conditions and many distractions.

_____

_____

SECTION 2—POST FORMAT

The following two tests are very close to what you'll actually see when you take the test. The first tests your use of grammar; the second checks spelling.

Exercise 1—Clarity

For each of the following pairs of sentences, select the sentence that is most clearly written.

1. A. The patrolman ate two bananas and a bowl of cereal for breakfast.

   B. The patrolman ates two bananas and a bowl of cereal for breakfast.

2. A. After work, the secretary, picked up a pizza for supper.

   B. After work, the secretary picked up a pizza for supper.

3. A. The best way to stay in shape is to eat well and exercise regularly.

   B. The best way to stay in shape is to eat well and exercise regular.

4. A. Guns should be kept wheres children can't reach them.

   B. Guns should be kept where children can't reach them.

5. A. The prowler left fingerprints, all over the windowsill, and these fingerprints provided the police department with an essential set of clues.

   B. The prowler left fingerprints all over the windowsill, and these fingerprints provided the police department with an essential set of clues.

6. A. After years of good service the deserving officer, was promoted.

   B. After years of good service, the deserving officer was promoted.

7. A. The witness said that the gunman fleed from the scene when he was hearing the sirens.

   B. The witness said that the gunman fled from the scene when he heard the sirens.

8. A. When investigating officers heard the back door slam, they knew the suspect was attempting to escape.

   B. When investigator officers heard the back door slam, they knew, the suspect was attempting to escape.

9. A. The assistance of neighborhood watch programs makes the police department's job more easy.

   B. The assistance of neighborhood watch programs makes the police department's job easier.

10. A. Business owners who hires formerly incarcerated individuals are performing an important civic function.

    B. Business owners who hire formerly incarcerated individuals are performing an important civic function.

11. A. It has been said that the best thing about working for the police department is helping people.

    B. It has been said that the most best thing about working for the police department is helping people.

12. A. The rate of murders committed every year in certain California cities has declined.

    B. The rate of murders committed every year in certain California cities was declined.

13. A. Judges are endowed with the ability to interpret laws and to judge each case on its own merit.

    B. Judges are endowed with the ability to interpret laws and to judge each case on their own merit.

14. A. The weapon was throwed into the river after the assault.

    B. The weapon was thrown into the river after the assault.

15. A. Buying stolen property, if the property is aware of the fact that it is stolen, is a crime.

    B. Buying stolen property is a crime if the buyer is aware of the fact that the property was stolen.

16. A. The woman's blood alcohol content was found to be three times the legal limit.

    B. The womans blood alcohol content was found out to be three times the legal limit.

17. A. The two drivers who was involved in the accident blamed each other.

    B. The two drivers who were involved in the accident blamed each other.

18. A. Following a tip from an anonymous source, the investigating officer drove to a warehouse and waited for something to happen.

    B. Following a tip from a anonymous source, the investigating officer drove to a warehouse and waited for something to happen.

19. A. The victim, said she did not get a good look at her assailant.

    B. The victim said she did not get a good look at her assailant.

20. A. The murderer was found guilty and sentenced, to twenty-five years in prison.

    B. The murderer was found guilty and sentenced to twenty-five years in prison.

21. A. He ran all the way home after the bully pushed him down.

    B. He run all the way home after the bully pushed him down.

22. A. They, chose the prettiest china, and ordered four place settings.

    B. They chose the prettiest china, and ordered four place settings.

23. A. He swore he could of eaten four entire pies.

    B. He swore he could've eaten four entire pies.

24. A. Her boss never offer her a raise.

    B. Her boss never offered her a raise.

25. A. He bought a pony instead of a horse.

    B. He bought a pony instead from a horse.

26. A. His flowers were large red and lovely.

    B. His flowers were large, red, and lovely.

27. A. High in the sky. There is a thin, gray cloud.

    B. High in the sky, there is a thin, gray cloud.

28. A. They forgotted where they had parked their car.

    B. They forgot where they had parked their car.

29. A. She ate her food and left in a hurry.

    B. She eat her food and left in a hurry.

30. A. Fried chicken is not the healthiest of all foods.

    B. Fried chicken is not the healthier of all foods.

31. A. Wishful thinking will get you nowhere.

    B. Wishful thinking will, get you nowhere.

32. A. She growed quickly.

    B. She grew quickly.

33. A. The bright lights were colorful and pretty.

    B. The bright lights was colorful and pretty.

34. A. Its a shame that we missed the concert.

    B. It's a shame that we missed the concert.

35. A. He and his girlfriend have a great idea for a fireworks display.

    B. He and his girlfriend has a great idea for a fireworks display.

36. A. Bullets that are designed to penetrate armor are intended for one thing: killing people.

    B. Bullets that are designed to penetrate armor are intended for one thing. Killing people.

37. A. After years, of being pursued, the arsonist was finally brought to justice.

    B. After years of being pursued, the arsonist was finally brought to justice.

38. A. Someone would probably receive a higher fine for exceeding the speed limit by twenty miles per hour than they would for exceeding it by ten miles per hour.

    B. Someone would probably receive the highest fine for exceeding the speed limit by twenty miles per hour than they would for if they exceeded it by ten.

39. A. Anyone who are facing a trial but cannot afford to hire an attorney will be provided an attorney by the court.

    B. Anyone who is facing a trial but cannot afford to hire an attorney will be provided an attorney by the court.

40. A. The violence escalated. On the South side of town after the victim died during surgery.

    B. The violence on the South side of town escalated after the victim died during surgery.

41. A. An officer on patrol should always be willingly helping of citizens who ask for assistance.

    B. An officer on patrol should always be willing to help citizens who ask for assistance.

42. A. The newly elected mayor established a commission to improve the quality of life in the inner cities.

    B. The mayor, who was new-elected, established a commission to improve the quality of life in the inner cities.

43. A. New cars were bought by the police department, and the old vehicles were sold at auction.

    B. New cars was bought by the police department, and the old vehicles were sold at auction.

44. A. Funding for city parks were increased, by a unanimous vote of the board.

    B. Funding for city parks was increased by a unanimous vote of the board.

45. A. The number of people arrested for shoplifting in the capital last year was lower than the year before.

    B. The number of people arrested for shoplifting in the capital last year was lower as the year before.

46. A. Due to his prior convictions and the brutal nature of the crime, the young man was tried as an adult.

    B. The young man, due to his prior convictions, was tried as an adult, as well as the brutal nature of the crime.

47. A. The officers believed that the fire was started by the serial arsonist for who they were looking for weeks.

    B. The officers believed that the fire was started by the serial arsonist for whom they had been looking for weeks.

48. A. Joggers are advised to wear reflected clothing when jogging at night.

    B. Joggers are advised to wear reflective clothing when jogging at night.

49. A. The public schools in one county began offering a daily vegetarian option for students who prefers not to eat meat.

    B. The public schools in one county began offering a daily vegetarian option for students who preferred not to eat meat.

50. A. The playground was been rusting for years, and the swing set finally collapsed.

    B. The playground had been rusting for years, and the swing set finally collapsed.

51. A. Residents of the waterfront homes were evacuated due to the approaching storm.

    B. Residents of the waterfront homes was evacuated due to the approaching storm.

52. A. The city council was convened for a special meeting about school violence.

    B. The city council was special convened for a school violence meeting.

53. A. There are streetlights at every corner of the seaside resort, this is to minimize the opportunity for criminals to take advantage of unsuspecting tourists.

    B. There are streetlights at every corner of the seaside resort; this is to minimize the opportunity for criminals to take advantage of unsuspecting tourists.

54. A. Due to strictly enforced emissions standards, air quality has improved greatly since 1980.

    B. Since 1980, the quality of air has improved greatly due to emissions standards that are enforced, strictly.

55. A. It is a crime to kill an animal whose species is endangered.

    B. It is a crime to kill an animal who's species is endangered.

56. A. The dogs were put to sleep after it was discovered that they had been poisoned.

    B. The dogs were put to sleep after it was discovered that they had been poison.

57. A. A person must have a valid driver's license in order to legally operate a motor vehicle.

    B. A person must have a valid drivers license in order to legally operate a motor vehicle.

58. A. The voting power of the senior citizens in this country is amazing.

    B. The voting power of the senior citizens' in the country is amazing.

59. A. Insurance fraud is not a victimless crime; we all pay in the form of increased costs.

    B. Insurance fraud is not a victimless crime; we all pay in the form of increase costs.

60. A. Their are laws against employing young children.

    B. There are laws against employing young children.

61. A. Excessive consumption of alcohol causes many deaths each year.

    B. Excessive consumption of alcohol, causes many deaths each year.

62. A. Knowing where the nearest located fire department is, is important.

    B. It is important to know where the nearest fire department is located.

63. A. Public transportation conserves energy.

    B. Public transportation conserves' energy.

64. A. Learning how to administer first aid and CPR could enable you to save someone's life.

    B. Learning how to administer first aid and CPR could enable you to save someone's lives.

65. A. The medical examiner, estimated that the victim had been dead for about three days.

    B. The medical examiner estimated that the victim had been dead for about three days.

Exercise 2—Spelling

For each of the following sentences, select the correct spelling of the missing word.

1. It was difficult to _____ which of the solutions was best.

   A. deterrmine

   B. determine

   C. dettermine

   D. determen

2. For years, _____ had been increasing on the southern shore.

   A. tourism

   B. tourrism

   C. tourisim

   D. turism

3. _____ devices may someday accomplish tasks that require very complicated reasoning.

   A. Robottic

   B. Robbotic

   C. Robotec

   D. Robotic

4. She was _____ to leave the courtroom as soon as the verdict was announced.

   A. anxuous

   B. ankshus

   C. anxious

   D. anxiuos

5. The officer's father was _____ by his son's bravery.

    A. empressed

    B. impresed

    C. emmpressed

    D. impressed

6. The second set of instructions was _____ and, therefore, unnecessary.

    A. redundant

    B. redondant

    C. reddundant

    D. redondent

7. An emergency room physician stated that the woman's injuries were _____ .

    A. superfisial

    B. superrficial

    C. superficial

    D. supperficial

8. _____ engineers designed a better suspension system for the new model.

    A. Autamotive

    B. Atomotive

    C. Automotove

    D. Automotive

9. The rate of unemployment increased as the country entered a _____ .

    A. resession

    B. recession

    C. recesion

    D. ressecion

10. Voters elected the candidate by a _____ .

    A. landslide

    B. landsslide

    C. lanndslide

    D. landslid

11. Many people _____ healthier living through a whole-foods diet.

    A. advoccate

    B. addvocate

    C.advokate

    D. advocate

12. The _____ kept in shape by running, swimming, and lifting weights.

    A. athleet

    B. athlete

    C. atlhete

    D. athlette

13. Neighbors complained that the _____ partygoers had become too loud.

    A. boisterous

    B. boisterious

    C. boastrous

    D. boasterous

14. Once, sailors depended upon the _____ to guide them to their destinations.

    A. constellations

    B. constelations

    C. constellashuns

    D. connstelations

15. The United States never fully adopted the _____ system of weights and measures.

    A. mettric

    B. meteric

    C. metric

    D. meetric

16. Attorneys often utilize legal _____ to persuade judges.

    A. presidents

    B. precedents

    C. presedents

    D. precidents

17. The infant's parents wanted to find a _____ baby-sitter.

    A. dependable

    B. dependible

    C. depindable

    D. dipendible

18. Senior citizens sometimes have special _____ needs.

    A. dietery

    B. diettary

    C. dieterry

    D. dietary

19. Students in _____ learn social skills by interacting with other children.

    A. kintergarten

    B. kindigarten

    C. kindergarten

    D. kindagarten

20. The lowest voice in the choir is the _____ .

    A. baritone

    B. barritone

    C. barytone

    D. baritonn

21. Long _____ is difficult for many people.

    A. divission

    B. divizion

    C. division

    D. devision

22. The infant _____ rate is higher in certain areas than in others.

    A. mortallity

    B. moretality

    C. mortalty

    D. mortality

23. The jet reached its _____ altitude of 10,000 feet.

    A. cruising

    B. cruiseing

    C. croosing

    D. cruizing

24. Military _____ tend to stay in touch with other former military personnel.

    A. retireys

    B. retirees

    C. retires

    D. reetirees

25. Driving at _____ speeds can be dangerous.

    A. excessive

    B. exessive

    C. excesive

    D. exesive

26. The house's _____ was sinking, and had to be repaired.

    A. foundashun

    B. fundation

    C. founddation

    D. foundation

27. After dating for four years, the individuals were joined in _____ .

    A. marrimony

    B. matrimony

    C. matriomony

    D. marimony

28. There is a great risk of _____ if proper presurgical precautions are not taken.

    A. infecttion

    B. innfection

    C. infectiun

    D. infection

29. The _____ was supported by most voters, and passed easily.

    A. referrendum

    B. refferendum

    C. referendum

    D. referendem

30. The contents of the box were _____ .

    A. frajile

    B. fraggile

    C. fragile

    D. frajule

31. Due to the _____ , hospitals were filled with patients.

    A. epidemic

    B. eppidemic

    C. epidemmic

    D. epedemic

32. Tennessee was once considered part of the American _____ .

    A. fronter

    B. frontier

    C. fronteer

    D. fronnter

33. The losing pitcher was _____ after the disappointing game.

    A. dejected

    B. dejeected

    C. degected

    D. dejacted

34. Workers stood on the street corner and offered _____ to people walking by.

    A. pamplets

    B. pamphlettes

    C. pamplettes

    D. pamphlets

35. The _____ mourned for his wife for years after she died.

    A. widower

    B. widoweer

    C. weddower

    D. wedower

36. The man _____ the neighborhood restaurant.

    A. frequnted

    B. frequented

    C. frequinted

    D. freequented

37. The students were eager to meet their new _____ .

    A. princaple

    B. prinnciple

    C. principple

    D. principal

38. Coupons provide _____ discounts on various items.

    A. siggnificant

    B. significent

    C. significant

    D. signeficant

39. People walking alone at night should be _____ of approaching strangers.

    A. werry

    B. wairy

    C. wery

    D. wary

40. It is said that there is _____ room for information on the Internet.

    A. infinate

    B. infinite

    C. infinnate

    D. infenate

41. It was amazing to learn how the shipwrecked people had _____ for so long.

    A. servived

    B. surfived

    C. survived

    D. surrvived

42. The large company was accused of being a _____ .

    A. monopoly

    B. monopely

    C. monnopoloy

    D. monnopoly

43. The officers instructed everyone not to _____ .

    A. panac

    B. panick

    C. paneck

    D. panic

44. Thousands of people watched the event from the _____ .

    A. bleechers

    B. bleachers

    C. bleackers

    D. blechers

45. _____ training sessions were offered to all of the company's supervisors.

    A. Manigement

    B. Manajement

    C. Management

    D. Mannagement

46. Participation in the educational program was _____ .

    A. voluntery

    B. volunteery

    C. volluntary

    D. voluntary

47. There must be _____ by which one lives one's life.

    A. standdards

    B. standards

    C. standerds

    D. stannderds

48. The food in the refrigerator _____ during the power outage.

    A. spolled

    B. spoilled

    C. spoiled

    D. spollied

49. He did not _____ his brother.

    A. reckonize

    B. recconize

    C. recognnize

    D. recognize

50. The criminal _____ after he was caught.

    A. confesed

    B. confessed

    C. connfessed

    D. confesed

Explanations for Section 1—Grammar and Spelling Review

Review Exercise 1

1. *Coffee grown in Latin American countries* tastes *better than coffee grown anywhere else in the world.* The subject is "coffee," a singular noun.

2. *Pancakes, eggs, biscuits, and sausage* are *Officer Stone's favorite breakfast.* This is a compound subject; don't be thrown off by that singular word, "sausage," just before the verb.

3. *The one positive* effect *of the accident was the subsequent installation of the stop sign at the dangerous intersection.* Remember, "effect" is the noun, "affect" is the verb.

4. *Both my mom and dad* support *my decision to become a police officer.* The two parents make up a compound, or plural, subject.

5. *Of all the injuries Officer Ruiz sustained in the fender bender, the bruising of her ribs* bothers *her the most.* The subject is "bruising," which is singular. Again, don't be thrown by the word just before the verb.

6. *Officer Gill, along with the rest of the squad,* is *determined to apprehend the rapist before he strikes again.* Phrases beginning with "along with" don't go into making up a compound subject, so Officer Gill is the singular subject.

7. *Officer Washington tries to* rise *early enough to run five miles every day.* If the subject is doing the getting up himself, he's rising. "Raising" is something done to a person or thing—you raise money, or raise a ruckus.

8. *Although Josh never thought of himself as an outdoorsy person, the physicality, risk taking, and strategizing involved in rock climbing* appeal *to him.* This is a compound subject, so you need a plural verb.

9. *Neither the approaching storm nor the warnings on all radio frequencies* persuade *Officer Norton to give up searching for survivors.* Remember that when "neither/nor" links a singular noun and a plural noun, the verb agrees with the subject that's closest to the verb.

10. *Polls show that the number of people who don't care about the latest government scandal* has *increased.* The subject is "number," which is singular.

11. *Basketball, with its flashy stars and their spectacular plays,* has *become America's favorite sport.* The subject is "basketball," which is singular. The phrase in commas just tells us more about the subject.

12. *Many residents, especially those from the converted hotel,* were *extremely upset by the string of robberies.* The subject is plural, "residents." Again, don't be thrown by the noun just before the verb. "Hotel" isn't the real subject of the sentence.

13. *The detective refused to* accept *the suspect's evasive answers and kept pressing him for the truth.*

14. *The courtroom had to be cleared of spectators before the trial could* proceed.

15. *Greed, along with gullibility,* causes *many people to fall for Ponzi schemes and other financial scams.* Phrases beginning with "along with" don't contribute to a compound subject.

16. *Neither the attorneys nor the courthouse observers* expect *the trial to last more than two weeks.* Unlike the situation in question 9, here you're dealing with a "neither/nor" linking two plural nouns. That means you'll have a plural subject, and a plural verb.

17. *Some people believe it's difficult to* prosecute *Internet offenses because the statutes haven't been written to reflect the new technology.*

18. *There* is *a lot of evidence pointing to the suspect, but so far nothing strong enough to issue an arrest warrant.* "A lot" of anything is considered one unit, so it's singular. However, "many pieces" of evidence would be plural.

19. *Of the many recent advances in science, DNA analysis* has *the biggest impact on law enforcement.* This is a singular subject, DNA analysis.

20. *Unfamiliarity with the material, in addition to nervousness,* explains *why many people don't do well on standardized tests.* Phrases beginning with "in addition to" don't go to make up a compound subject.

Review Exercise 2
There are a few ways you could have fixed these sentences. Here are some rewrites.

1. *The number of people who call tech support numbers to ask questions about computers demonstrates that people find computers confusing.* In the original sentence, it's not clear whether "they" refers to computers, numbers, or people.

2. *The officer approached the old man who, staggering and weaving, had just left the bar.* I *hope* it wasn't the officer staggering and weaving.

3. *Officer Ryan hadn't been on duty five minutes when the call came in about a burglary in progress.* Or, as an alternative: *Officer Ryan had been on duty but five minutes when the call came in about a burglary in progress.*

4. *The desk sergeant, after weighing the pros and cons, decided not to change the duty roster.*

5. *The computer screen flickered while Joanna, staring blankly, sat at her desk.* Who's doing the staring?

6. *Upon discovering the theft in the office, the employees began suspecting one another.* Or, equally correct: *Upon discovering the theft in the office, the employees suspected one another.*

7. *Officer Jasek drove the cruiser, which was running on only one cylinder, into the garage.*

8. *The actors on that TV cop show are great, but the writers don't get the details of real-life police work right.* It's really not the actors' fault the details aren't right. In the original sentence, "they" seems to refer to the writers, who aren't mentioned.

9. *Officer Chang searched the available files to see what kind of rap sheets the suspects had.* Again, "they" in the original sentence refers to a noun not included in the sentence.

10. *The driver, traveling at a high rate of speed, lost control on the slick road.* Or you could also write: *The driver, traveling at a high rate of speed, began losing control on the slick road.*

11. *Don't believe everything you read in the papers because you don't know if the writers are telling the truth.* Again, "they" in the original sentence refers to a noun not included in the sentence.

12. *The scientist patented his vaccine for the deadly virus, which had been developed in secrecy.* "For the deadly virus" modifies "vaccine," so it's fine to put another modifying phrase behind it.

13. *Some people prefer women's professional basketball because the players don't talk as much trash.*

14. *Officer Melton could hardly see out the windshield because of the heavy rain.* Or, *Officer Melton couldn't see out the windshield because of the heavy rain.*

15. *The point of going to school is not just to get an education but also to acquire social skills.*

16. *The tall weeds in front of the factory almost hid the shards of broken glass, which reflected the glare of the cruiser's lights.*

17. *Because Officer Wilson genuinely liked talking to people, he sometimes missed his days on the street.*

18. *Officer Kwame asked Officer O'Neil if he would be willing to trade shifts with her over the weekend.*

19. *The woman started crying, until her husband told her he didn't want any of her hysterics.* Or, *The woman started crying, until her husband told her he wanted none of her hysterics.*

20. *Street festivals are targets for pickpockets, because of the crowded conditions and many distractions.*

Explanations for Section 2—POST Format

Exercise 1—Clarity

1. **A**—The correct verb form is "ate." "Ates" is not a word.

2. **B**—In A, the comma between "secretary" and "picked" is unnecessary and incorrect.

3. **A**—"Regular" is incorrectly used as an adjective in B.

4. **A**—"Wheres" is not a word.

5. **B**—The comma between "fingerprints" and "all" in A is unnecessary and incorrect.

6. **B**—The correct placement of the comma is between "service" and "the."

7. **B**—"Fleed" is not a word, and "when he was hearing the sirens" is not in the past tense.

8. **A**—In B, the comma between "knew" and "the" is unnecessary and incorrect.

9. **B**—The correct comparative form of the adjective is "easier."

10. **B**—The appropriate verb form is "hire" because the subject, "business owners," is plural.

11. **A**—The correct comparative form of the adjective is "best."

12. **A**—The correct verb form is "has declined." In B, the phrase "was declined" gives the sentence a nonsensical meaning.

13. **A**—"Each case" corresponds with the possessive pronoun "its." In B, "their" is incorrect because "each case" is singular.

14. **B**—"Throwed" is not a word.

15. **B**—The sentence in A is illogical. How could "property" be "aware of the fact that it is stolen?"

16. **A**—In B, the word "out" is unnecessary and incorrect.

17. **B**—In A, the verb "was" is incorrect because the subject, "the two drivers," is plural.

18. **A**—Because "anonymous" begins with a vowel, the correct article is "an."

19. **B**—In A, the comma between "victim" and "said" is unnecessary and incorrect.

20. **B**—In A, the comma between "sentenced" and "to" is unnecessary and incorrect.

21. **A**—Since the sentence is in the past tense, the correct verb form is "ran."

22. **B**—In A, the comma between "they" and "chose' is unnecessary and incorrect.

23. **B**—The correct present perfect phrase is "could have eaten." "Of" is a preposition that is often used to indicate origin or connection, and is never used in a present perfect conjugation.

24. **B**—Since the sentence is in the past tense, the correct verb form is "offered."

25. **A**—The correct phrase is "instead of." The preposition "from," which is often used to indicate direction, is used incorrectly in B.

26. **B**—There should be commas separating the adjectives in A. The commas in B are placed correctly.

27. **B**—There is a sentence fragment in A.

28. **B**—The correct form of the verb is "forgot." "Forgotted" is not a word.

29. **A**—Since the sentence is in the past tense, and since the subject, "she," is singular, the correct verb is "ate."

30. **A**—The correct form of the adjective is the superlative "healthiest." If there were only two items being compared, "healthier" would be correct, as in: She is the healthier of the two children.

31. **A**—In B, the comma is unnecessary and incorrect.

32. **B**—The correct past tense form of the verb "grow" is "grew." "Growed" is not a word.

33. **A**—Because the subject, "the bright lights," is plural, the correct past tense form of the verb "was" is "were."

34. **B**—The correct pronoun is "it's," which is a contraction of the words "it" and "is." In A, the possessive pronoun "its" is used incorrectly.

35. **A**—Since the subject, "he and his girlfriend," is plural, the correct verb form is "have."

36. **A**—There is a sentence fragment in B.

37. **B**—In A, the comma between "years" and "of" is unnecessary and incorrect.

38. **A**—The correct comparative form of the adjective is "higher."

39. **B**—The correct verb form is "is" because the subject, "anyone," is singular.

40. **B**—There is a sentence fragment in A.

41. **B.**—The correct phrase is "willing to help." In A, "willingly helping of" is incorrect.

42. **A**—In B, the phrase "new-elected" is incorrect. "Newly elected" is appropriate.

43. **A**—The correct verb form is "were" because the subject, "new cars," is plural.

44. **B**—In A, the comma between "increased" and "by" is unnecessary and incorrect.

45. **A**—The correct conjunction is "than."

46. **A**—The meaning of the sentence in B is obscured by the awkward wording. The clause "as well as the brutal nature of the crime" does not appear to modify anything, and so its meaning in the sentence is lost.

47. **B**—The correct form of the word "who" is the objective pronoun "whom." The preposition "for" indicates that the noun or pronoun that follows will be in the objective case.

48. **B**—The correct adjective is "reflective." The word "reflected" implies that light has been thrown back from a surface, while the correct word, "reflective," indicates a surface that will throw back light.

49. **B**—Because the sentence is in the past tense, the correct verb form is "preferred."

50. **B**—The correct past perfect phrase is "had been rusting." The construction "was been rusting" is incorrect and nonsensical; past perfect verb phrases never begin with "was."

51. **A**—Because the subject, "residents," is plural, use the corresponding plural verb "were."

52. **A**—If you're going to use the adjective "special" to describe the verb "convened," as in B, you have to turn the adjective into an adverb by adding the suffix "-ly." "Specially convened" would work.

53. **B**—When you're connecting two complete sentences, use a semicolon instead of a comma.

54. **A**—There aren't any glaring errors in B, but it is far more confusing than it needs to be.

55. **A**—The possessive form of the pronoun "who" is "whose." "Who's" is a contraction of "who is."

56. **A**—When we're talking, it's easy to drop the "ed" suffix from words. But in writing, you have to use it when it's needed. Here, that suffix makes it clear that "poison" is used as a verb, not a noun.

57. **A**—The correct possessive form of the word "driver" is "driver's." The word "drivers" is the plural form of "driver."

58. **A**—You've already indicated what the senior citizens have with "of" so you don't need an apostrophe. The correct way to use the possessive form would be: "In this country, the senior citizens' voting power is amazing." I moved "in this country" to keep it from separating "senior citizens'" from "voting power."

59. **A**—The correct adjective is "increased."

60. **B**—"Their" is the possessive form of the pronoun "they."

61. **A**—You don't need the comma in B.

62. **B**—The wording in A is unclear and confusing.

63. **A**—The apostrophe in B leads you to think that "conserves" somehow has hold of something, which makes no sense at all.

64. **A**—"Someone" is singular. Unless we're talking about cats, "someone" has only one life.

65. **B**—You don't need the comma in A.

Exercise 2—Spelling

1. **B**—determine	26. **D**—foundation
2. **A**—tourism	27. **B**—matrimony
3. **D**—Robotic	28. **D**—infection
4. **C**—anxious	29. **C**—referendum
5. **D**—impressed	30. **C**—fragile
6. **A**—redundant	31. **A**—epidemic
7. **C**—superficial	32. **B**—frontier
8. **D**—Automotive	33. **A**—dejected
9. **B**—recession	34. **D**—pamphlets
10. **A**—landslide	35. **A**—widower
11. **D**—advocate	36. **B**—frequented
12. **B**—athlete	37. **D**—principal
13. **A**—boisterous	38. **C**—significant
14. **A**—constellations	39. **D**—wary
15. **C**—metric	40. **B**—infinite
16. **B**—precedents	41. **C**—survived
17. **A**—dependable	42. **A**—monopoly
18. **D**—dietary	43. **D**—panic
19. **C**—kindergarten	44. **B**—bleachers
20. **A**—baritone	45. **C**—Management
21. **C**—division	46. **D**—voluntary
22. **D**—mortality	47. **B**—standards
23. **A**—cruising	48. **C**—spoiled
24. **B**—retirees	49. **D**—recognize
25. **A**—excessive	50. **B**—confessed

CRIME JUSTICE SAFETY

SWAT TEAMS, SNIPERS SWARM INTO FLORIDA

During the last two decades, Florida, with its balmy climate and many entertainment options, has emerged as one of the most popular law enforcement training venues in the world. Overall, the range of topics and training offered by the region's facilities is quite broad. For example, two programs in Orlando and Jacksonville train more than 1,500 officers each month, with at least 40 percent coming from departments outside Florida. Their 1999 calendars boasted more than 100 tactical, criminal investigation, and management courses open to local, state, and federal officers.

Florida training schools have also become places where officers can keep current with rapidly changing technologies and tactical issues that directly impact their jobs. Some of the region's latest new training topics include:

- Female Officer Survival Techniques, designed to increase physical and psychological confrontational skills. Defensive tactics and live fire response drills are included.

- Cyber Crime Investigations, including an overview of the Internet and online crimes, hacking and cracking, bank and credit card fraud, information warfare, network intrusion, child exploitation, terrorism, software piracy, and hardware theft.

- Harnessing the Internet Pedophile, which explores the types of child molesters, child pornography, collectors of child porn, techniques of child porn used by computer pedophiles, and investigative methods.

Increasingly, the region's facilities are structuring weapons and other tactical training events as highly popular "police sports" competitions, such as Sniper Week and the SWAT Round-Up and Trade Show. Organized by Fort Lauderdale-based Sniper Craft, Sniper Week draws police and military sharpshooters from across the U.S. The week culminates in the Sniper Challenge, in which two-member teams get their abilities tested and scored by mock missions.

Special operations teams from across the continents gather for the SWAT Round-Up and Trade Show. Held at the Orange County Sheriff's Office firing range, the event is the largest of its kind in the world, with teams vying for trophies in hostage and officer rescue, tower scrambles, and obstacle course runs worthy of the Marines. In 1998, 69 five-member law enforcement, military, and correctional special reaction teams from 12 states and six countries, such as Germany, Bosnia, Kuwait and Hungary, attended. "Even though it began as a way for local teams to come together and compete, it has evolved into a major training opportunity for teams from around the world," said Lt. Matt Weathersby, SWAT team coordinator for the Orange County Sheriff's Office.

Sharpening practical skills and procedures is also a major focus of a large swath of sessions. For example, what are the latest methods for dealing with high-risk people and places, vehicles stops, and street gang control? A three-day tactics course offered by Calibre Press in Orlando aims to provide officers with a broad base of practical survival tactics for tricky situations.

—Adapted from an APBNews.com article by Michele Tirado, April 16, 1999

CHAPTER FIVE
Reading Comprehension

The POST test will require you to read short passages and answer questions about the content. In this chapter, as in the chapter on grammar and spelling, you'll see two sets of questions. The first develops your skills, the next prepares you for the specific format on the POST test.

Even if you're confident of your reading skills, I suggest you go over this chapter and work on the practice tests anyway. Under pressure, it's easy to freeze up: Why take the chance? And if you're not confident of your skills—spend some serious time here. Beyond the test, honing your reading comprehension skills will boost your day-to-day effectiveness, in the police department or anywhere else.

BASIC READING TECHNIQUES

Here are some basic tips for focusing on the important aspects of a written passage. As you prepare for your test, try applying these techniques to everything you read—from the morning paper to your sports magazine to the novel.

Prereading

You can often get a pretty good idea of what a story or article is about by just *observing* it. Before you read the entire thing, put it through a quick prereading survey:

- Is there a title? If so, what does it tell you about the article?
- Are there pictures, charts, illustrations? What information do they give you?
- What does the first sentence say?

Based just on your prereading, you often can make a pretty good prediction about the content of the text itself.

Active Reading

Most of us had it drilled into our heads that we weren't supposed to mark up books as we read them. I can understand that rule when you're talking about textbooks that have to survive more than one kid's onslaught. But you're a grownup now, and you can mark up your books, magazines, and newspapers. And you *should* mark them up. That's part of active reading, which will help you focus on the meaning of the text. Mark words that are repeated. Write down any questions you have as you read, or circle words you don't understand. Underline the sentence, or sentences, that introduce or sum up the author's main point. This will help you spot the building blocks of any essay or article, which are:

The Purpose

Why did the author write the material you're reading? To inform you? Persuade you? Motivate you? What particular issue does the text cover? In the margin, write down what you think the author's purpose is. It will be related to, but not exactly the same as. . .

The Main Idea

The main idea is a specific idea that supports the author's broader purpose. Often, the first sentence clues you in to the main idea, or topic; sometimes, the first sentence is a straightforward statement of the topic. However, don't count on that. A writer may choose to leave the main idea unstated, expecting you to draw your own conclusions from the evidence and arguments assembled in the essay.

Think of the main idea as the spine of the essay; it's the long line that holds everything together.

Look for a statement of the main idea; underline it, if you find it. If there doesn't seem to be a sentence that sums up the topic, write your own statement of the main idea in the margin.

Paragraph Topics

If the main idea is the spine of the essay, the paragraph topics are the bones; they provide the underlying structure. Each paragraph adds something slightly different to the author's argument; the supporting element contained in a paragraph is the paragraph topic. As with the main idea, paragraph topics may or may not be directly stated.

After you finish each paragraph, look for its topic sentence and underline it. If you can't find one topic sentence, write your own statement in the margin.

Details

So far, we've got the skeleton of an essay, with the basic substructure of main idea and paragraph topics in place. But it's still a bit flimsy. That's why the author adds *details*. The details are the muscle attached to that skeleton, making it stronger and more stable. These details can be examples or logical arguments, but they have to be directly connected to the paragraph topic they flesh out.

The details are always directly stated; otherwise, they wouldn't be very useful. Number the details the author gives to build up the paragraph topics. You'll always have more details than anything else. After all, there can be only one main idea, and one paragraph topic per paragraph. But within a single paragraph, the author may provide several supporting details.

Keywords

Okay, now we've got a fairly functional organism here: a stable structure made up of the main idea and the paragraph topics, fleshed out with details. We can complete things with *keywords,* which will provide the skin and connective tissue that keep everything working together.

Keywords link the sentences within and between paragraphs; they also guide the reader smoothly through the author's argument. There are six types of keywords, depending on their function in the paragraph.

- *Continuation keywords* tell you that you're getting more of the same kind of information. The new detail builds on the earlier one. The commonest continuation keywords are *and, also, moreover,* and *furthermore.*

  The U.S. team won the gold medal in the 400-meter relay. Furthermore, it established a new world record.

- *Illustration keywords* let you know that the author is about to give you an example of an idea or concept. *For example* and *for instance* are the two most common illustration keywords.

  Psychology has many practical uses. For example, it is used regularly in advertising research.

- *Contrast keywords* tell you that author is about to change direction in his or her argument, or mention an opposing idea. The most common keywords are *but, however, although, otherwise, nevertheless,* and *by contrast.*

  Yesterday was rainy and cold. However, today it's sunny and warm.

- *Conclusion keywords* let you know that the author is about to summarize or restate an important idea. Conclusion keywords often signal that the author is wrapping up the argument. Pay attention to conclusion keywords, because they often relate directly to the main idea. The most common conclusion keywords are *therefore, thus, in conclusion,* and *consequently.*

  The score was tied after nine innings. Therefore, the game went to extended innings.

- *Evidence keywords* tell you that the author is going to offer a piece of evidence that supports an idea that was just stated. Often, the evidence has a cause-and-effect relationship with the idea it supports. The most common evidence keywords are *because* and *since.*

  In today's job market, it's a good idea to know a second language, because many employers demand bilingual skills.

- *Importance keywords* let you know that the author thinks a particular idea or fact is very important. The most common importance keywords are *especially, above all, most of all, primarily,* and *particularly.*

  The crowd at Atlanta was especially pleased when Americans won the first women's Olympic team gold medal in the nation's history.

After Reading

Before you move on, think about what you've just read and make sure you fully understand it.

- *Identify the key points.* What are the most important statements the author made? List them.
- *Summarize.* Try to shrink these statements down to one or two sentences.
- *Any questions?* If you wrote down questions that remain unanswered when you finish reading, take another look. Focus on the specific sentences or passages that prompted the questions.

Unfamiliar Words: Using Context

It's a good idea to read unfamiliar material with a dictionary close by. That way, you can easily look up any words you don't understand. But what if you aren't allowed to use a dictionary? In those situations, which include just about all standardized tests, you need to be able to make a good guess about the meaning of a word based on its context. Here's what I mean:

Even though they give her nightmares, Joyce likes gruesome movies.

Let's say you don't know exactly what "gruesome" means. But the sentence tells you that gruesome movies give Joyce nightmares, so it's a good bet that "gruesome" doesn't mean "romantic" or "funny." What kind of movies would give someone nightmares? Just using context and your own common sense, you can figure out that "gruesome" means something close to "scary" or "violent."

Unfamiliar Words: Prefixes and Suffixes

Taking a word apart can help you determine its meaning. Prefixes, additions to the beginning of words, and suffixes, additions to the end of words, can point you in the right direction when you're trying to figure out what an unfamiliar word means. How? Because different prefixes and suffixes have different meanings.

For instance, someone was telling me the other day that she was working on an intranet system. I was sure I hadn't heard her correctly, so I said something about how easy it was to do research on the Internet. She shook her head. "No, I said intra-net." No mistaking her that time. The system she was working on operates within a company—and the prefix "intra-" means within, or inside. "Inter-" means—you guessed it—outside.

Here are tables of several common prefixes and suffixes and what they indicate. Knowing their meaning can help you make an educated guess at the meaning of an unfamiliar word.

Prefix	Meaning	Example
a-, ab-	from	*avert, away, abstain*
a-, an-	without, not	*atheist, anarchist*
ant- , anti-	against	*antonym, antipathy*
ante-	before	*antedate*
ex-	out of	*external*
hyper-	above, over	*hypercritical*
hypo-	under	*hypodermic*
in-	not	*inactive*
im-, in-	within	*implode, internal*
ir-	not	*irresponsible*
post-	after	*postpone, posterity*
pre-	before	*predict, precede*
re-	back, again	*recall, revive, retreat*
sub-	under	*subordinate*
super-	over, above	*supervise*

Suffix	Use	Meaning	Example
-able, -ible	adjective	capable of	*flammable*
-ac, -al, -ial	adjective	pertaining to	*maniac, bestial*
-acy	noun	pertaining to	*bureaucracy*
-ance, -ence	noun	state of being	*tolerance*
-ant, -ent,			
-er, -or	noun	one who does	*lieutenant, worker*
-ion	noun	act of	*comprehension*
-ive	adjective, noun	state of being	*festive, collective*
-ish	adjective	the quality of	*foolish*
-ity	noun	the quality of	*serenity*
-ful	adjective	filled with	*hopeful*
-less	adjective	without	*pointless*
-ly	adjective, adverb	like, in a specified way	*brotherly, quickly*
-ness, -ry	noun	state of	*happiness, bravery*

In the final section of the POST test, you'll have to read a couple of paragraphs with certain words blanked out; you'll be asked to write in the missing words. To do this well, you'll have to use your reading comprehension skills, your knowledge of grammar, and your ability to use context as a source of information.

- Don't panic. The first time you look at the paragraph, you'll be convinced you can't figure out any of the missing words. That's not so. All the clues are there, right there in the paragraph. It's just that you've probably never seen a test that looked like this before.
- What are you looking for? Is the missing word a verb, a noun, or some other part of speech? Can you get the answer just knowing that? For instance, if the missing word appears just after, "As well. . .", you know it's got to be "as."
- Look at the context. What's the writer's tone? If it's formal, you're going to be looking for different kinds of words than if the writing is more casual. Are there any other sentences that seem to be dealing with the same idea? Often, writers repeat words. The answer may be right in front of you.
- Be flexible. If the answer you come up with doesn't have the same number of letters they're looking for, start thinking of as many other synonyms as you can. (Synonyms are words with the same or very similar meanings, like "frigid" and "arctic.") Start writing down everything you can think of that might fit.

When You Hit a Wall

In a testing situation, it's natural to panic. Sometimes, you'll just go blank on a reading comprehension section. You won't be able to make heads or tails out of what you're supposed to be reading. Relax—here are some ways to break through that wall.

- **Reread.** Sometimes all it takes is another run through a sentence to make its meaning clear.
- **Stop and think.** Make notes to yourself. Look at sentences just above and just below the difficult passage.
- **Paraphrase.** If a sentence is especially baffling, try putting it into your own words.

APBnews.com
CRIME JUSTICE SAFETY

Suspect Gives Up After 12-Hour Manhunt

A massive 12-hour manhunt for a double-murder suspect ended on May 18, 1999 with a cry from the bushes. "It's me. I'm Larry Lavell. I give up!" the 41-year-old slaying suspect shouted as he emerged from the underbrush near a police check at about 2 A.M., authorities said.

Larry Roman Lavell had been the object of a 130-man search through the hills of Los Gatos, a northern California town, since 2 P.M. the day before, when he escaped from a sheriff's deputy who spotted him near a pay phone and tried to arrest him. The tattooed survivalist was wanted for his role in the killing of his estranged wife, Suzanne Snyder, 35, and her new boyfriend, Howard Beiderman, 36, in Los Gatos, police said.

When he was sighted at the phone near Summit Road and Route 17, the Santa Clara County sheriff's deputy pulled her gun, ordered him to the ground and called for backup. While she waited for other officers to arrive, Lavell allegedly had other ideas.

"She was talking to him, trying to calm him, tell him that everything would be all right if he just stayed calm," said Sheriff's Department spokesman Sgt. Luther Pugh. "But he became more and more incoherent, and he got up and ran away."

That escape led police to create a 10-square-mile perimeter centering on the area of nearby Mt. Charley Road. Seven law enforcement agencies from the local police to the California Highway Patrol searched until nightfall with an airplane, helicopter, and team of dogs. After several hours, the search was suspended, and a series of checkpoints were set up to keep watch overnight.

As the temperature fell from the 70s to the high 30s, however, the shorts- and T-shirt-clad Lavell approached the checkpoint near the pay phone where he first escaped and surrendered.

Pugh said officers later found a rough campsite the suspect made in the woods. There they uncovered clothes stained with a substance that is being tested to see if it is blood. Officers also found a police scanner Lavell apparently used to monitor his pursuers.

Lavell is being held in the Santa Clara County jail without bail pending the filing of formal charges, officials said.

—Adapted from an APBNews.com article by Todd Venezia, May 18, 1999

SECTION 1—READING COMPREHENSION REVIEW

Exercise 1—Using Context to Fill in the Blanks

This first exercise will get you used to coming up with accurate answers based on the context of missing words. Give yourself fifteen minutes to go through these 15 questions. Fill in the blank with any word that makes sense within the sentence. If you can't think of a single word, write down a phrase. Answers appear at the end of this exercise.

1. Since I'm a loyal Republican, I _____ with the Republican senators on most issues.

2. When I went shopping for earrings, I realized I couldn't afford a pair with _____ diamonds, so I bought earrings with imitation diamonds.

3. Unlike the more experienced members of the team, the _____ kept making obvious errors.

4. Joe had to stop practicing with the team after his injury; once the injury had healed, he _____ practicing.

5. The movie was so _____ that everyone left the theater before the movie was even half over.

6. Stores are _____ from selling cigarettes to children; they may, however, sell cigarettes to adults.

7. When Jamie had a part-time job, she was able to go to the gym regularly. But ever since her promotion, she's been extremely busy. She's only been able to get to the gym _____.

8. Danny had underestimated his favorite band's _____. Even though he was in line at 6:00 A.M. on the first day concert tickets went on sale, the entire stadium was sold out by the time he got to the ticket window.

9. Buying the ticket with the winning numbers in the $10 million jackpot was lucky; losing the ticket was _____.

10. Jane wanted to make sure the audience could understand her, so when she stepped up to the microphone, she spoke very _____.

11. The student's excuse for not turning in his homework—his dog ate it—was especially _____, considering he didn't even have a dog.

12. Strangely enough, Alison felt no _____ when she saw the deadly rattlesnake inches away from her.

13. When John moved from his parents' spacious house to his first apartment, a small studio, he had to be very _____ about the belongings he took with him.

14. The two horses crossed the finish line _____, so the race was declared a tie.

15. After I replaced the broken lamp, my bedroom was much _____.

Explanations for Exercise 1—Using Context to Fill in the Blanks

1. *Agree* or *vote*. A "loyal Republican" would tend to agree with other Republicans.

2. *Real* or *genuine*. If you could only afford imitation diamonds, you wouldn't be able to buy real ones.

3. *Rookie* or *new player*. The missing word has to contrast with "more experienced members" who don't make obvious mistakes.

4. *Resumed* or *went back to*. If he's stopped because of the injury, he can start again once it's healed.

5. *Bad* or *boring*. These are the most obvious reasons why an audience would walk out of a movie. Maybe you thought about using "long." That's not as good an answer. If a movie is interesting enough, people will stay for the whole thing, no matter how long it is.

6. *Forbidden* or *banned* or *outlawed*. "However" signals that there's a contrast between what stores can do with adults and what they can do with children. If they can sell cigarettes to adults, then they must be forbidden from selling them to children.

7. *Occasionally* or *rarely*. Once Jamie's schedule became "very busy," she could no longer go to the gym regularly.

8. *Popularity*. If the tickets sell out so quickly, the band must be popular.

9. *Disaster* or *tragedy* or *nightmare*. Think about how you'd feel if that were *your* lottery ticket.

10. *Slowly* or *clearly* or *loudly*. These words describe how you would speak if you wanted to make sure you'd be heard.

11. *Unbelievable* or *far-fetched*. "The dog ate it" is already a doubtful excuse, but if the guy doesn't even have a dog. . . .

12. *Fear* or *panic*. These are emotions you'd expect someone to feel if she spotted a rattlesnake nearby.

13. *Selective* or *careful*. Because John can't take everything, he has to be careful how he chooses what he moves to the new apartment.

14. *Simultaneously* or *at the same time*. That's what a tie means.

15. *Brighter* or *lighter*. After you replace a broken lamp with one that works, you'd expect the room to be brighter.

Exercise 2—Using Context to Choose the Answer

This set of questions trains you to look at the context to figure out the meaning of unfamiliar words.

1. Strict vegetarians <u>eschew</u> not only meat, but also products that come from animals, such as eggs and cheese.
   A. sell
   B. like
   C. avoid
   D. grade

2. At his funeral, Malcolm X was <u>eulogized</u> by admirers such as Ossie Davis.
   A. praised
   B. rescued
   C. delighted
   D. forgotten

3. He didn't like his birthday present from his aunt, but <u>feigned</u> excitement to avoid hurting her feelings.
   A. hid
   B. suppressed
   C. pretended
   D. felt

4. The buzzing and biting of mosquitoes <u>vexed</u> the campers as they tried to sleep.
   A. soothed
   B. annoyed
   C. pleased
   D. lulled

5. Western accounts of Buddhism are often inaccurate. They tend to <u>distort</u> Buddhist thought by exaggerating some aspects of it and ignoring others.
   A. analyze
   B. explain
   C. praise
   D. misrepresent

6. Flooding is <u>anticipated</u> in the Brazos River valley, so sensible residents in the area are moving to higher ground.
   A. moderate
   B. expected
   C. rare
   D. beneficial

7. Because the instructor was so <u>verbose</u>, the explanation took much longer than necessary.
   A. serious
   B. intelligent
   C. wordy
   D. experienced

8. She was a <u>recluse</u>, living by herself and avoiding other people.
   A. loner
   B. adventurer
   C. fool
   D. homemaker

9. Members of the scouting patrol faced the greatest chance of being injured or killed; only the most <u>intrepid</u> soldiers volunteered for the assignment.
   A. careful
   B. clever
   C. polite
   D. brave

10. At home, the child was obedient and well behaved, but at school her teachers found her <u>intractable</u>.
    A. uncontrollable
    B. puny
    C. curious
    D. absentminded

11. The art collector has <u>eclectic</u> taste; she owns paintings and sculpture from all over the world, in many different styles.
    A. crude
    B. wide-ranging
    C. sturdy
    D. old-fashioned

12. The governor's opponents searched for evidence of wrongdoing in her background, but her record was <u>immaculate</u>.
    A. unbroken
    B. conclusive
    C. popular
    D. spotless

13. Judge Connor was known for his <u>placid</u> temperament; his colleagues, and even his subordinates, felt comfortable speaking to him directly, even criticizing him when necessary.
    A. peaceful
    B. violent
    C. gloomy
    D. lucky

14. The light that came through the windows was <u>fleeting</u>. It faded before anyone could examine the scene carefully.
    A. moving
    B. blinding
    C. bright
    D. brief

15. She generally paints in an abstract style, using patterns and colors. The lifelike portrait of her cat was <u>uncharacteristic</u> of her work.
    A. drab
    B. fashionable
    C. unusual
    D. inspiring

FLORIDA RECRUITS COPS WITH SCHOLARSHIPS

Call it the G.I. Bill for police officers.

Police agencies across western Florida are trying to recruit community patrol officers by offering $30,000 toward their education, much the way the U.S. Army recruits college students.

The only catch: The prospective police officers must pledge to spend four years fighting crime on street patrols or lose their tuition reimbursement. Florida Police Corps officials say the program is designed to ensure that police departments receive applicants who are serious about getting a college education and who want to strengthen community police initiatives with their degrees.

The recruits will begin their police training only after they receive a four-year college education in any major. The first class of recruits is expected to graduate this year.

"We want the best educated officers we can get," said Lew Elliott, a civilian who will train the recruits on police tactics. "We feel that we will get kids who are more mature, who have a four-year degree under their belt and are more tuned in to societal problems and community policing."

The Florida Police Corps program, which is being run by the Florida State University School of Criminology and Criminal Justice in Tallahassee, is part of a national bill signed by President Clinton in 1994. The Police Corps program exists in 19 states, but Florida officials boast that the state is the first to implement the program.

—Adapted from an APBNews.com article by Michelle Gotthelf, May 7, 1999

Explanations for Exercise 2—Using Context to Choose the Answer

1. The correct answer is **C**. Vegetarians probably don't like meat, and they may or may not sell or grade it, but they always *avoid* it.

2. The correct answer is **A**. An admirer would probably *praise* the someone at his funeral.

3. The correct answer is **C**. If he didn't like the present, the best way to avoid hurting the giver's feelings is by pretending to like it.

4. The correct answer is **B**. When's the last time you were *pleased* or *lulled* or *soothed* by mosquito bites?

5. The correct answer is **D**. If the accounts of Buddhist thought are inaccurate, then they must *misrepresent* the religion.

6. The correct answer is **B**. Moving to higher ground is sensible if flooding is expected. If the flooding is *moderate, beneficial,* or *rare,* leaving the area probably wouldn't be necessary or sensible.

7. The correct answer is **C**. The word *verbose* has to describe a quality that would make an explanation take longer than necessary. Being *serious, intelligent,* or *experienced* wouldn't necessarily have this effect; being wordy would.

8. The correct answer is **A**. Someone living by herself and avoiding others is a *loner.*

9. The correct answer is **D**. A soldier would have to be *brave* to volunteer for an especially risky task.

10. The correct answer is **A**. The word "but" signals a contrast between the girl's behavior at home and her behavior at school. The word that contrasts with "obedient and wellbehaved" is *uncontrollable.*

11. The correct answer is **B**. Collecting art from all over the world, in many different styles, indicates *wide-ranging* tastes.

12. The correct answer is **D**. The word *but* lets you know the opponents didn't find what they were looking for. If they couldn't find wrongdoing, then the governor's record must be *spotless.* A record may be *unbroken, popular,* or *conclusive* and still contain incidents of wrongdoing.

13. The correct answer is **A**. If people are comfortable criticizing the judge to his face, he must be a *peaceful* person.

14. The correct answer is **D**. If the light faded "before anyone could examine the scene carefully," that means the light didn't last long.

15. The correct answer is **C**. If the artist generally paints in an "abstract style, using patterns and colors," a lifelike painting would be unusual for her.

Exercise 3—Identifying Main Ideas, Paragraph Topics, and Details

Give yourself thirty minutes to complete the following test, which has two sections. For the first section, read the following three passages and answer the questions based on each one.

Passage A

Many people mistakenly believe that the average police officer often uses his or her firearm on duty. While all officers are trained in the use of firearms and are expected to be able to use a weapon when necessary, gunfire plays little role in the everyday duties of a law enforcement officer. It's not surprising that this misunderstanding exists; the media pays more attention to situations in which a suspect or bystander is shot by an officer than they do to any other police action. This widespread media coverage focused on relatively rare incidents has led to an exaggerated idea about officers' use of firearms. In fact, most officers rarely draw their weapons, and many officers retire after never having fired a shot for 20 years.

1. Select the paragraph's topic from the following choices:

    A. newspaper and television headlines

    B. people's beliefs about police officers' use of guns

    C. the increase in the use of weapons among police

    D. the reckless use of weapons

2. Which of the following best states the author's main idea?

    A. Newspapers shouldn't write about the police.

    B. News stories lead people to think police officers use their weapons more often than they actually do.

    C. Officers need to be better trained in the use of firearms.

    D. More stories are written about the use of firearms than any other police action.

Passage B

The early Dutch settlers on the island of Manhattan organized the formal security operations that eventually became New York Police Department. In the early 1600s, New Amsterdam, as New York was then known, had only one formal peace keeper, a "schout-fiscal," or "sheriff/attorney." As New Amsterdam grew, the colonists decided they needed better protection from wild animals, hostile tribes and law-breakers. The settlers constructed a gated wall from river to river, across the northern end of the colony, at the site of today's Wall Street. In 1658, the first "night watch" was formed as a group of volunteer colonists, who were soon replaced by a paid force of eight men. The night watch patrolled the settlement, carrying wooden noisemakers to awaken the colonists to fight fires, invasions, or other common threats. These clanking noisemakers let colonists to refer to the men as the "Rattle Watch." Each member of the Rattle Watch also carried a lantern with inserts of green glass. This distinctive lantern lit the watchman's way on the dark paths and streets, and also identified him to any passersby. Eventually, watch houses were built to shelter the watchmen on duty; a man returning from his rounds hung his lantern by the front door, showing he was in the watch house in case anyone needed his help. Even today, every NYPD precinct house has green lights at its doors, what the department calls a "symbol that the Watch is present, and vigilant."

3. What is the main idea of this passage?
    A. The first police officers in New York City were volunteers.
    B. Early colonists were most concerned about fire.
    C. New York City's law enforcement operations were first set up by Dutch colonists.
    D. Colonial cities needed only one peace keeper.

4. List four supporting details mentioned by the author.

    _____

    _____

    _____

    _____

Passage C

Public safety professionals—a group that includes firefighters, paramedics and law enforcement officers—deal with tremendous amounts of stress simply because of the nature of their work. However, police officers face added levels of stress because of the power of the badge and the dangers that go with it. A police officer is entrusted with powerful weapons such as firearms, batons, and Tasers. The officer can arrest citizens on his own authority; short of arrest, an officer can make traffic stops, write tickets, and in other ways inconvenience and intimidate others. Officers must have this authority and autonomy in order to uphold their duty of protecting life and property; however, a good officer is always careful not to abuse his authority, and this can lead to second-guessing. The constant need for independent decision making in high-stakes situations creates further stress. Civilians may disagree with an officer's actions; they can become hostile and suspicious of the police, which causes problems for individual officers. Officers know that, at any time, they may be targeted by individuals seeking revenge, expressing hatred of authority, or acting from deranged motives. All these factors create stress unique to law enforcement.

5.   State the author's main idea in your own words.

   _____

   _____

6.   List four supporting details mentioned by the author.

   _____

   _____

   _____

   _____

The second portion of the exercise contains a longer reading passage. See if you can identify the main idea, the paragraph topics, and the details.

Passage D

The first detective stories were written by Edgar Allan Poe and Arthur Conan Doyle in the mid-1800s, a time of great public interest in science and scientific progress. Newspapers continually ran articles describing the latest scientific discoveries, and scientists were often treated like national heroes. Like the rest of the public, Poe and Conan Doyle were fascinated with the systematic, logical approach used by scientists in their experiments. Poe and Conan Doyle both endowed their detective heroes with outstanding powers of scientific reasoning.

The character of Sherlock Holmes illustrates Conan Doyle's admiration for the scientific mind. In every case that Holmes agrees to investigate, he is able to use the most unlikely pieces of evidence to track down and identify the criminal. Relying on his restless eye and phenomenal reasoning powers, Holmes pieces together the solution to the crime from details like the type of cigar ash left at a crime scene, or the kind of ink used to write a letter. In fact, Holmes's careful attention toe detail reminds the reader of Charles Darwin's scientific method in *Origin of Species,* the revolutionary book on natural history published twenty years earlier.

7. Mark the following choices, indicating whether each is a main idea (MI), paragraph topic (PT) or detail (D).

    A. cigar ash _____

    B. Poe and Conan Doyle endowed their characters with great powers of scientific reasoning. _____

    C. Sherlock Holmes had an eye for detail. _____

    D. Sherlock Holmes had the mind of a scientist. _____

    E. Scientists use a methodical, step-by-step approach to thinking. _____

    F. Holmes can be compared to Charles Darwin. _____

    G. The detective story was created in the mid-1800s. _____

Explanations for Exercise 3—Identifying Main Ideas, Paragraph Topics, and Details

1. The correct answer is **B.** The first and last sentences of almost all paragraphs provide very important information. In this case, the first sentence of this paragraph tells you that the author will be discussing common beliefs about police officer's use of firearms.

2. The correct answer is **B.** At the beginning of the paragraph, the author states that police use their weapons less often than people believe. Then, the author says that this is because incidents involving shootings by officers receive more media coverage out of proportion to their occurrence. Choice B is the best statement of this. Note that Choice D is a supporting detail.

3. The correct answer is **C.** The author begins by stating that the Dutch first set up the law enforcement system in what became New York City; the rest of the paragraph supplies supporting details. Choice C supplies the best summary of that idea.

4. *List four supporting details mentioned by the author.*

   The exact wording you use doesn't matter, but here are some of the details you might have mentioned:

   - New Amsterdam's first law enforcement official was a "schout-fiscal" or "sheriff/attorney."
   - The settlers built a gated wall where Wall Street is today.
   - In 1658, a group of patrolmen was formed; the first volunteers were replaced by paid patrolmen.
   - The patrolmen guarded against common threats such as fires and attacks on the settlement.
   - These patrolmen carried green lanterns, which they hung outside their watch house when not on patrol; today, the green lights at NYPD precinct houses are a reminder of those early patrolmen.

5. *What is the main idea of this passage?*

   Your wording may be different, but the author's main idea is this: While all public safety professionals face stress in their jobs, law enforcement officers face stresses that are unique to their job.

6. *List four supporting details mentioned by the author.*

   Here are some of the details you might have mentioned:

   - Police officers have authority that no one else is allowed.
   - This authority includes carrying weapons, right to arrest anyone, right to inconvenience citizens.
   - A conscientious officer will always try to make sure he or she isn't abusing his authority.
   - Some citizens will always disagree with the way officers exercise their authority.
   - Officers are a target for people who have an argument against authority or police in general.

7. *Which of the following choices refer to main ideas, paragraph ideas, or details?*

   A. Cigar ash

   Detail—Illustrates Holmes's outstanding reasoning powers.

   B. Poe and Conan Doyle endowed their characters with great powers of scientific reasoning.

   Main idea—The rest of the passage tries to show this is true, using Holmes as an example.

   C. Sherlock Holmes had an eye for detail.

   Detail—Illustrates Holmes's outstanding scientific reasoning powers.

   D. Sherlock Holmes had the mind of a scientist.

   Paragraph topic—All of paragraph two seeks to illustrate this.

   E. Scientists use a methodical, step-by-step approach.

   Detail—Introduces discussion of Poe and Conan Doyle.

   F. Holmes can be compared to Charles Darwin.

   Detail—Illustrates Holmes's reasoning skills.

   G. The detective story was created in the mid-1800s.

   Detail—Introduces discussion of Poe and Conan Doyle.

POLICE BADGES SOLD ON INTERNET

Police are accusing an Internet businessman with trafficking in phony police badges, some of which bore authentic serial numbers and would have made an impostor virtually indistinguishable from a real officer.

Thomas Gunther, 54, of Schaumburg, Illinois was found with 200 badges, including shields for security officers in Walt Disney World and several Nevada casinos and 82 Chicago Police Department stars, Officer Cesar Guzman said. According to reports, Gunther had been selling the illegal identification for between $150 and $1,200, when officers surfing the Internet happened upon the site. Guzman said Gunther had been trying to draw customers to his site with the tag line "Authentic Chicago Gang Crimes Police Stars, Make Your Bid," and that some of the Chicago stars looked incredibly authentic.

Guzman said Gunther has been released on $1,000 bond on charges of impersonating a police officer. Meanwhile, real cops continue to probe how he got the badges and if there is any link to the companies that manufacture the real thing for the Chicago police.

Meanwhile, Guzman warned people to beware of police impostors. "Whenever a police officer shows a badge, ask for some more identification to back it up," he said.

Gunther could not be reached for comment.

—Adapted from an APBNews.com article by Todd Venezia, November 20, 1998

Exercise 4—Identifying Keywords

Give yourself 15 minutes for this exercise. Each of the following statements ends with a keyword. Use the statement's main idea and the keyword to figure out which of the four choices makes the most sense.

1. Many scientific studies have shown that regular physical exercise helps people deal with psychological stress. **Therefore,**
    A. people who frequently experience stress should make physical exercise part of their regular routine.

    B. one study has found that people who never exercise tend to be older than people who often exercise.

    C. without more information, beginning an exercise program could prove dangerous.

    D. many people who experience stress aren't physically fit.

2. A crime scene should be kept off-limits to bystanders and most police officers until the forensics experts have completed their work; **otherwise,**

    A. old-fashioned magnifying glasses will have to be used.

    B. the forensics team will have nothing to do.

    C. important evidence may be damaged or lost completely.

    D   the criminal may be among the bystanders.

3. The suspect benefited from the rookie officer's inexperience, **because**

    A. the officer had never handled a murder case before.

    B. the officer's flawed search warrant eventually led to the suspect's release.

    C. the suspect knew all the other officers at the precinct.

    D. the suspect had a lot of experience, judging from his criminal record.

4. It's very unlikely that two people will have the same genetic "fingerprint," **since**

    A. genetic research has made great advances in the last two decades.

    B. only identical twins, which are relatively rare, share the same DNA, or genetic material.

    C. practically all of the genetic research done has taken place in universities.

    D. man's genetic codes are so similar to those of the chimpanzee.

5. The city jail was built to serve a much smaller population, and crime rates keep going up. **Consequently,**

    A. the jail is always filled with far more inmates that it was designed to hold.

    B. the mayor has blocked every attempt to improve the situation.

    C. the police officers have a hard time finding parking places.

    D. the population figures must be going up as well.

6. The purpose of the new task force is to reduce the rate of gang activity. **Therefore,**

    A. gangs are expected to accumulate more firearms.

    B. a large part of the department's budget is set aside for new equipment.

    C. more research into gang membership should be done.

    D. the group's effectiveness will be judged on whether gang activity declines.

7. Some people seem to believe that stricter gun control would eliminate violent crime. **But**

   A. the causes of violent crime are too complicated for any one action, including gun control, to overcome by itself.

   B. gun control is favored by many law enforcement officers.

   C. these people really aren't part of the mainstream, since they tend to be vegetarians.

   D. many Americans feel that the Second Amendment guarantees an unrestricted right to gun ownership.

8. Many police officers find it difficult to maintain friendships and other relationships with people outside law enforcement, **because**

   A. other police officers compete with them for the most desirable assignments.

   B. people outside law enforcement always want to handle the officers' firearms.

   C. working in law enforcement makes it difficult to schedule get-togethers.

   D. other police officers readily understand the stresses of the job.

Explanations for Exercise 4—Indentify Keywords

1. The correct answer is **A**. *Therefore* is a conclusion keyword, so the answer must add a logical conclusion to the idea in the first sentence. Since exercise tends to help people handle stress, choice A makes sense. None of the other choices presents an idea that flows logically from the first sentence.

2. The correct answer is **C**. *Otherwise* is a contrast keyword, one that signals a change in direction, or a kind of warning—"Get in out of the rain, otherwise you'll get wet." The only logical connection is between protecting the crime scene and preserving evidence.

3. The correct answer is **B**. *Because* is an evidence keyword, something that provides proof of an idea or statement—in this case, the statement that the suspect gained something from the officer's mistake. The only choice that does this is B.

4. The correct answer is **B**. *Since* is another evidence keyword, something that gives support for the first statement. Go through the choices, and you'll see that B is the only one that would allow us to draw the conclusion that it's rare for two people to share identical genetic material.

5. The correct answer is **A**. *Consequently* is a conclusion keyword, which signals a logical conclusion that can be drawn from the first statement. Only one of the choices follows logically from the original sentence. If the jail was built when the population was smaller, and a larger percentage of that larger population is being arrested, then the jail must be chronically overcrowded.

6. The correct answer is **D**. *Therefore* is another conclusion keyword. You're looking for something that's logically connected to the original statement. If the whole point of creating a task force is to reduce gang activity, then its effectiveness will be measured by how much gang activity is reduced. Research, new equipment, or the gangs' weapons don't have the same direct connection with the task force's goals.

7. The correct answer is **A**. *But* is a contrast keyword, so you're looking for an idea that would cast some doubt on the original statement. The only choice that does this is A. You might have picked D, a statement which is undoubtedly true and seems to oppose the original statement. But look again. The first sentence isn't just about favoring gun control; it links gun control with an automatic reduction in crime. The only answer that directly addresses that is A.

8. The correct answer is **D**. *Because* is an evidence keyword. You're looking for evidence—an explanation for why police officers are most comfortable with other officers. Choice D is the only answer that makes sense.

Exercise 5—Summarizing Your Reading

Being able to sum up the material you've read is an important aspect of reading comprehension. It demonstrates that you've understood the argument well enough to state the author's main idea in your own words. Here's an example of how to summarize material:

Hollywood movies and television series tend to show criminal profiling as a mysterious, supernatural talent, something like mind-reading or predicting the future. In fact, criminal profiling consists of close analysis of crime scene evidence, using a large body of information gathered from other offenders to make reasonable assumptions about the offender in a particular case. Like any other human activity, some people have more of a "knack" for profiling than others, but anyone can learn the basic principles and techniques of criminal profiling.

An accurate summary of the paragraph's topic would be something like this:

Criminal profiling is not a mysterious talent, but a set of principles and techniques which can be taught.

This sentence sums up the author's argument; everything else in the paragraph provides details.

Now take 45 minutes to read the following short passages and answer the questions about each one.

Passage E

Though it's one of the most effective tools of forensic science, DNA testing can lead to delays in prosecuting—or clearing—suspects. While DNA testing is 99.99 percent accurate, it also is extremely time-consuming. A chemist in a crime lab can handle 75 to 100 drug tests a month; in that same period, an analyst can complete only one or two DNA tests. This lengthy processing time often causes a backlog in the lab. DNA testing also requires equipment and expertise that are too specialized and expensive for many smaller agencies; if the sample has to be sent out for analysis, the delays increase. For instance, it may take as long as a year to get DNA test results back from the FBI lab. While a DNA test can provide a highly accurate answer to the question of a suspect's guilt, everyone involved—the suspect, the victim, and the investigators—may have to wait a long time for that answer.

1. Write down a one- or two-sentence summary of the passage's main idea.

   _____

   _____

   _____

2. DNA testing is very accurate, but

   A. it's too expensive for many police departments to use.

   B. can only be done at the FBI lab.

   C. it's also time-consuming.

   D. takes too long to be widely useful.

Passage F

As disgusting as most people find them, maggots can help forensic entomologists solve murders. Forensic entomologists apply entomology, or the study of insects and other arthropods, to legal issues and investigations. In terms of this field, the most important aspect of arthropods is the fact that many varieties are carrion feeders; that is, they eat dead vertebrate bodies, including human corpses. A forensic entomologist classifies and analyzes the flies and larvae found on a body. Using his or her expertise in the life cycles of these creatures and the variables affecting the timing of each stage, the analyst can then estimate when the person died. By comparing the insects commonly found near the body with those on the body itself, a forensic entomologist also can help determine whether the corpse has been moved after death. In some instances, movement of suspects, goods, victims, or vehicles can be traced with the help of insects. Insect parts or whole insects can caught in automobile headlights or radiators. By identifying these insects and plotting the distribution and biology of species, the forensic entomologist can create a map of where the suspect has been.

3. Summarize the passage in one or two sentences.

_____

_____

_____

_____

4. The author would agree with all of the following statements about forensic entomology EXCEPT

   A. Forensic entomology applies the study of insects and arthropods to legal issues.

   B. Forensic entomology can be used to estimate the time of death of a body.

   C. Forensic entomology relies on the fact that many arthropods are carrion feeders.

   D. Forensic entomology has no application in cases that lack a body.

Passage G

Private security firms are growing, despite a falling crime rate, as smaller law enforcement agencies "privatize" and more affluent communities demand the round-the-clock presence no police force can offer. These private security officers must handle many of the same tasks as police, and many citizens mistake uniformed security officers for police. However, there is a big difference between private officers and the public force. While an applicant to a city or state police force must undergo a thorough background check, most private security firms lack the resources for the same kind of screening; this makes it easier for truly dangerous people to take on the authority of a gun and badge. In California, the serial killer known as the Hillside Strangler was able to become a security guard after he had been turned down by the Los Angeles Police Department and Sheriff's Department. In other states, private security officers have been accused of a variety of crimes, from theft to rape, while on duty. Furthermore, most private security officers don't receive the same thorough training as police. While police spend several months in training, and often are required to continue training throughout their careers, private security officers may have as little as eight hours in training if they are unarmed, or 12 hours in training if they are armed.

5. State the main idea of the passage, in your own words.

   _____

   _____

   _____

   _____

6. More and more private security officers are being hired, although

   A. they are expected to assist the city police.

   B. they have to work around the clock.

   C. fewer applicants than ever pass the required background checks.

   D. the crime rates have been decreasing.

Passage H

The earliest European settlers in North America had no particular system of laws. The problems and disputes that arose between people were solved by using common sense. After England gained control over its colonies, however, the system based on common sense was gradually replaced by a formal system of laws, courts and judges. Today, America's legal system still closely resembles that of England.

7. Summarize the passage, stating the main idea.

_____

_____

_____

_____

8. The author would agree that

    A. America's legal system is still based on common sense.

    B. Many legal systems around the world resemble the English legal system.

    C. The American legal system has been strongly influenced by the English system.

    D. There were relatively few disputes among the earliest American settlers.

Passage I

When selecting dogs for narcotic detection training, the behavior of an individual dog is more important than the dog's breed or background. Trainers have identified several different categories of behavior that all dogs display; from a forensic standpoint, investigative behavior is the most important of these categories. A high degree of investigative behavior indicates a very inquisitive nature and a desire to examine objects closely and thoroughly. Both these qualities make the dog an excellent candidate for narcotic detection training. Several specific signs indicate investigative behavior in dogs. First, watch the dog in its kennel. Does it stop to look and listen when it hears an unusual sound? Then, introduce a new object. Does the dog investigate it thoroughly, sniffing and pawing it? When outside the kennel, other investigative behaviors include walking or running with nose to ground, sniffing; holding the head in air sniffing; holding the head raised, ears erect; nosing and sniffing urine or feces. Of course, all dogs display this behavior to some degree; the dog who's a good candidate for training will keep sniffing and investigating after other dogs have lost interest.

9. Summarize the passage, stating the main idea.

_____

_____

_____

_____

10. The passage implies which of the following about dogs' behavior?

    A. A dog's breed has a major impact on its behavior.

    B. Some dogs display no investigative behavior.

    C. Any dog who shows investigative behavior would be a good candidate for narcotic detection training.

    D. Dogs who show strong investigative behavior tend to be very inquisitive and examine objects closely.

Explanations for Exercise 5—Summarize Your Reading

1. Summary: Although DNA testing is accurate and important in investigating crimes, it can also create delays in those investigations.

2. The correct answer is **C**. The fact that DNA testing takes a long time to complete is central to the passage's explanation of why such an accurate method can actually delay investigations. Notice that this does not mean the same thing as choice D. The author says that DNA testing is useful, even though it is time-consuming.

3. Summary: Forensic entomology allows investigators to use insects in investigating crimes, such as murder and smuggling.

4. The correct answer is **D**. While much of the passage concerns the application of forensic entomology in murder cases, its application in cases of contraband, or smuggling, is also discussed.

5. Summary: While the number of private security officers is increasing, and their duties and appearance may be similar to those of police officers, their screening and training procedures are not as rigorous as those for police officers.

6. The correct answer is **D**. The author gives a couple of reasons for the growth of private security firms, but says specifically that the crime rate is decreasing.

7. Summary: While the earliest American colonists had no particular legal system, England eventually imposed its own system, which saved the American legal system that we still know today.

8. The correct answer is **C**. This choice is very close to the author's main idea.

9. Summary: A dog who shows strong investigative behavior is the best candidate for training in narcotics detection.

10. The correct answer is **D**. This sentence explains why dogs demonstrating high levels of investigative behavior tend to make good narcotics detection dogs.

Putting It All Together: Reading Longer Passages

As you've just learned, each paragraph is its own mini-argument, with a topic and supporting details. When several paragraphs are linked to make a single passage, each paragraph lends support to the author's topic.

Exercise 6

Give yourself 45 minutes to read and answer questions about the two longer passages that follow.

Passage J

Taking accurate and useful fingerprints is one of the most cost-effective investigative techniques a police officer can use. Three simple tools—fingerprint powder, a brush and some tape—will allow an officer to handle about 70 percent of the normal crime scene fingerprinting.

1. What's the author's primary topic?

    _____

    _____

2. Does the author believe that fingerprinting is a worthwhile investigative technique?

    _____

One thing inexperienced investigators often forget to keep in mind is the color of the print card. That's more important than the color of the surface you're printing. If you use a light powder, then lift the print and place it on a white or clear card, you'll make the print almost invisible, and therefore useless. Black powder is a better choice, and can be used even on black or dark surfaces. If you have trouble seeing the powdered print on the dark surface, use a high-powered flashlight and slant the beam at an angle until you can see the print clearly enough to lift it.

3. The author uses the second paragraph primarily to:
    A. discuss an important aspect of fingerprinting that is often mishandled.
    B. explain what light and dark fingerprint powders are made of.
    C. make an argument against using white or clear print cards.
    D. remind officers to put batteries in their flashlights.

Now read the two paragraphs together.

Taking accurate and useful fingerprints is one of the most cost-effective investigative techniques a police officer can use. Three simple tools—fingerprint powder, a brush and some tape—will allow an officer to handle about 70 percent of the normal crime scene fingerprinting. A few simple techniques will help you lift clear, useful fingerprints every time.

One thing inexperienced investigators often forget to keep in mind is the color of the print card. That's more important than the color of the surface you're printing. If you use a light powder, then lift the print and place it on a white or clear card, you'll make the print almost invisible, and therefore useless. Black powder is a better choice, and can be used even on black or dark surfaces. If you have trouble seeing the powdered print on the dark surface, use a high-powered flashlight and slant the beam at an angle until you can see the print clearly enough to lift it.

4. The most important function of the techniques discussed in the second paragraph is to:
    A. shorten the time needed to take fingerprints.
    B. discuss the different colors of powder available and what they're made of.
    C. make sure that the fingerprints are readable and useful once they're lifted.
    D. create a step-by-step procedure for fingerprinting.

5. The author describes fingerprinting as
    A. tricky and complicated.
    B. simple and cost-effective.
    C. troubling and useless.
    D. difficult but worthwhile.

6. Based on the passage, the author would be most likely to support which of the following statements about fingerprinting?
    A. It's an old-fashioned and outdated investigative technique.
    B. It's expensive, but well worth the cost.
    C. It can't be used at least 70 percent of crime scenes.
    D. It can be extremely useful, if it's done properly.

Explanations for Exercise 6—Passage J

1. The primary topic is fingerprinting. More specifically, the author's major purpose is to describe a method of getting clear prints.

2. Yes. The author calls it "cost-effective" and "useful."

3. The correct answer is **A**. The second paragraph spells out one way to keep from lifting unreadable prints.

4. The correct answer is **C**. Again, the second paragraph describes one common mistake and how to avoid it.

5. The correct answer is **B**. Although the second paragraph describes a common problem, the author never describes fingerprinting as difficult or complicated.

6. The correct answer is **D**.

Passage K

In 1996, the U.S. Department of Justice released a report entitled "Convicted by Juries, Exonerated by Science." The report contains case studies of 28 individuals convicted of sexual assaults and murders. These individuals were released when postconviction DNA testing proved they could not have committed. In 24 of the 28 cases, eyewitnesses identification was a significant factor in convicting these individuals. But in all 24 cases the eyewitnesses were wrong. This isn't uncommon; studies have shown that eyewitness identification is wrong almost 50 percent of the time. This doesn't mean witnesses are lying or deliberately concealing the truth; most often, they're trying to help solve a crime and make an honest mistake in their identification. Why do so many eyewitnesses make mistakes? To understand this, we need to know something about how memory works, and how it can change over time.

1. State the topic in your own words.

_____

_____

There's a common belief that the brain stores memories like a videotape stores images; the brain records events and, once recorded, the recollection of those events doesn't change. However, years of research have shown that memory is fluid, not static. First, no one remembers everything about an event. Instead, fragments are noticed and registered. Once stored, these fragments can be changed by information taken in later, as the person recalls the incident. All of this takes place on an unconscious level; the person believes that what he remembers seeing is what actually happened.

Psychological experts divide the process of memory into three stages. The first is the acquisition stage, which is the individual's immediate perception of the event, and the entry of the information into the memory system. This is followed by the retention phase, which covers the time elapsed before the witness tries to recall the event. The final stage is the retrieval stage, which occurs when the witness actually tries to retrieve the stored information. The memory can change at any point in this process.

2. The author uses the second paragraph primarily to

    A. describe the ways in which the brain is like a videotape.

    B. describe the fluidity of memory.

    C. argue that faulty eyewitnesses are consciously lying.

    D. convince the reader of the accuracy of memory.

3. In the third paragraph, the author

    A. describes the biological structure of the human brain.

    B. describes three ways in which memory is erased.

    C. lists three stages of memory.

    D. gives three reasons to suspect the accuracy of memory.

The acquisition stage is influenced by both "event factors" and by "witness factors." "Event factors" are related to the incident itself: how well-lit the environment was, how long the event lasted, how far away the witness was, and how much violence occurred. "Witness factors" include personal qualities that can affect a witness's memory. These are internal factors such as fear, any previous experience with similar situations, or expectations the witness has of his or her own behavior or the behavior of those he or she is witnessing. These factors, and many others, influence what bits of information the witness first notices and remembers.

4. Based on this paragraph, the author probably would agree with which of the following statements?

    A. The acquisition stage is most strongly affected by the qualities of the event itself.

    B. Both event factors and witness factors have little effect on a witness's expectations.

    C. Dim lighting often frightens witnesses, especially witnesses who often work in badly lighted rooms.

    D. As memories are formed, they can be affected by factors that are both internal and external to the witness.

The retention or storage phase also is influenced by two sets of factors. The first is "retention interval," or the length of time between when the memory is acquired and when it is retrieved. Research indicates that as the retention interval increases, the accuracy and details of the memory decrease. The second factor at this stage is "postevent information," or information learned after an event takes place, which is then integrated into the memory of the event. Once witnesses have blended postevent information into memory, it's nearly impossible to separate what information came from the event itself and what was learned later. Because the witness doesn't consciously add postevent information, there is no way for him or her to distinguish between original memory and later revision. Witnesses can gather postevent information from sources such as leading questions, talking with other witnesses about the event or hearing other witnesses' conversations, reading or watching stories about the event in the media.

5. The retention interval is:

    A. relatively unimportant in the process of memory.

    B. always more than thirty days.

    C. the period before the event takes place.

    D. the period between acquiring and retrieving a memory.

External factors can have a tremendous influence on memory during the third stage, the retrieval of information. Sociologists and psychologists describe the Experimenter Expectancy Effect: the interviewer unintentionally and unconsciously signals the subject, encouraging the desired response. The subject, also unintentionally and unconsciously, tailors his or her responses to fit the interviewer's expectations. The only way to prevent the interviewer from affecting the outcome of the interview is to create a "double blind" situation, in which the interviewer is not aware of the desired outcome. The Experimenter Expectancy Effect is so strong that scientific experiments generally must be double-blind for their results to be accepted by the scientific community.

The responses a witness receives after recalling a memory also can affect the memory itself. The witness can become more confident in the accuracy of a memory—and less likely to recall conflicting information—if he or she receives positive feedback. On the other hand, people become less sure if given negative feedback or no feedback at all. This feedback can come from repeated questioning, or even casual conversation with others. A witness who is strongly confident seems more credible than a witness who is more tentative; however, studies demonstrate that confidence is a poor indicator of accuracy.

None of this suggests that eyewitness testimony has no value, or shouldn't be used. It does suggest that investigators should be aware of its potential weaknesses, and seek as much supporting evidence as possible.

6. Based on the paragraphs above, which of these statements would the author DISAGREE with?
    A. Once memory is recalled, it remains fixed.

    B. An interviewer's expectations can affect the reposes of the interviewee.

    C. Scientists feel that double-blind experiments provide more accurate results than those in which the experimenter is aware of the desired outcome.

    D. A confident witness may be no more accurate than a witness with less confidence.

Now read the entire passage again.

In 1996, the U.S. Department of Justice released a report entitled "Convicted by Juries, Exonerated by Science." The report contains case studies of 28 individuals convicted of sexual assaults and murders. These individuals were released when postconviction DNA testing proved they could not have committed. In 24 of the 28 cases, eyewitnesses identification was a significant factor in convicting these individuals. But in all 24 cases the eyewitnesses were wrong. This isn't uncommon; studies have shown that eyewitness identification is wrong almost 50 percent of the time. This doesn't mean witnesses are lying or deliberately concealing the truth; most often, they're trying to help solve a crime and make an honest mistake in their identification. Why do so many eyewitnesses make mistakes? To understand this, we need to know something about how memory works, and how it can change over time.

There's a common belief that the brain stores memories like a videotape stores images; the brain records events and, once recorded, the recollection of those events doesn't change. However, years of research have shown that memory is fluid, not static. First, no one remembers everything about an event. Instead, fragments are noticed and registered. Once stored, these fragments can be changed by information taken in later, as the person recalls the incident. All of this takes place on an unconscious level; the person believes that what he remembers seeing is what actually happened.

Psychological experts divide the process of memory into three stages. The first is the acquisition stage, which is the individual's immediate perception of the event, and the entry of the information into the memory system. This is followed by the retention phase, which covers the time elapsed before the witness tries to recall the event. The final stage is the retrieval stage, which occurs when the witness actually tries to retrieve the stored information. The memory can change at any point in this process.

The acquisition stage is influenced by both "event factors" and by "witness factors." "Event factors" are related to the incident itself: how well-lit the environment was, how long the event lasted, how far away the witness was, and how much violence occurred. "Witness factors" include personal qualities that can affect a witness's memory. These are internal factors such as fear, any previous experience with similar situations, or expectations the witness has of his or her own behavior or the behavior of those he or she is witnessing. These factors, and many others, influence what bits of information the witness first notices and remembers.

The retention or storage phase also is influenced by two sets of factors. The first is "retention interval," or the length of time between when the memory is acquired and when it is retrieved. Research indicates that as the retention interval increases, the accuracy and details of the memory decrease. The second factor at this stage is "postevent information," or information learned after an event takes place, which is then integrated into the memory of the event. Once witnesses have blended postevent information into memory, it's nearly impossible to separate what information came from the event itself and what was learned later. Because the witness doesn't consciously add postevent information, there is no way for him or her to distinguish between original memory and later revision. Witnesses can gather postevent information from sources such as leading questions, talking with other witnesses about the event or hearing other witnesses' conversations, reading or watching stories about the event in the media.

External factors can have a tremendous influence on memory during the third stage, the retrieval of information. Sociologists and psychologists describe the Experimenter Expectancy Effect: the interviewer unintentionally and unconsciously signals the subject, encouraging the desired response. The subject, also unintentionally and unconsciously, tailors his or her responses to fit the interviewer's expectations. The only way to prevent the interviewer from affecting the outcome of the interview is to create a "double blind" situation, in which the interviewer is not aware of the desired outcome. The Experimenter Expectancy Effect is so strong that scientific experiments generally must be double-blind for their results to be accepted by the scientific community.

The responses a witness receives after recalling a memory also can affect the memory itself. The witness can become more confident in the accuracy of a memory—and less likely to recall conflicting information—if he or she receives positive feedback. On the other hand, people become less sure if given negative feedback or no feedback at all. This feedback can come from repeated questioning, or even casual conversation with others. A witness who is strongly confident seems more credible than a witness who is more tentative; however, studies demonstrate that confidence is a poor indicator of accuracy.

None of this suggests that eyewitness testimony has no value, or shouldn't be used. It does suggest that investigators should be aware of its potential weaknesses, and seek as much supporting evidence as possible.

6. The word "tentative" in the next-to-last paragraph means:

    A. severe

    B. eager

    C. careful

    D. uncertain

7. The author suggests that

    A. witnesses must be interrogated repeatedly and severely in order to weed out liars.

    B. witnesses should be protected as much as possible from exposure to outside influences that, consciously or not, could taint their memories.

    C. witnesses consciously try to give investigators the answers they want because they crave the investigators' approval.

    D. witnesses who "block out" portions of their memory could retrieve these portions under hypnosis.

8. Based on this passage, which of these statements would the author be likely to agree with?

   A. Eyewitness testimony can be very persuasive to a jury, and is estimated to be accurate in over 80 percent of the cases in which it is used.

   B. Police officers and other investigators often make deliberate efforts to manipulate witnesses' recollections of an event.

   C. While juries consider eyewitness testimony extremely strong evidence, a witness's memory of an event can be flawed, even if the witness honestly believes the memory is accurate.

   D. The common image of memory as a faithful recording of an event, like a videotape, is a good representation of the way memory works; flaws in memory can be compared to tracking problems when playing a videotape.

Explanations for Exercise 6—Passage K

1. The general topic is eyewitness testimony. More specifically, the author is arguing that eyewitness testimony is less reliable than most people believe.

2. The correct answer is **B.** In the second paragraph, the author argues that the image most of us have of memory as a kind of recording is not accurate, and memory is subject to change.

3. The correct answer is **C.** The author divides the process of memory into three steps or stages.

4. The correct answer is **D.** "Event factors" and "witness factors" are external and internal to the witness, and affect the witness's initial memory of an event.

5. The correct answer is **A.** These paragraphs are intended to show that memory can be affected even as it is recalled, and afterwards. In other words, it's *not* fixed.

6. The correct answer is **D.** The author is comparing a confident witness with a tentative one; "uncertain" is the only word that contrasts with "confident."

7. The correct answer is **B.** The author never actually recommends this, but protecting witnesses from outside influences is a logical extension of his or her arguments.

8. The correct answer is **C.** This is a good summary of the author's argument.

SECTION 2—POST FORMAT

Exercise 1—Using Context

This exercise is almost exactly like the second exercise in the first section above. For each of the following sentences, select the word or the phrase that has most nearly the same meaning as the underlined word.

1. The teacher's lesson was underline{instructive} to her students, who all felt they'd learned something new.

    A. boring

    B. educational

    C. exciting

    D. ingrown

2. The teacher suspected the student was underline{feigning} illness and ordered him to bring in a doctor's note.

    A. seeking

    B. developing

    C. faking

    D. feeling

3. Hurricanes are <u>generated</u> far out to sea, where the deep ocean currents feed their power as they move toward land.

   A. found

   B. chased

   C. formed

   D. heard

4. Frightened witnesses can be <u>reluctant</u> to testify in court.

   A. eager

   B. hesitant

   C. challenged

   D. dared

5. Repetitive tasks often are <u>monotonous</u>, but that does not mean they are not important.

   A. difficult

   B. meaningless

   C. varied

   D. boring

6. An undercover officer has to be able to think on her feet and act <u>spontaneously</u> as situations change.

   A. unafraid

   B. quickly

   C. visibly

   D. quietly

7. Although he had good references and no police record, the <u>rogue</u> emptied his employer's cash register after one week on the job.

   A. scoundrel

   B. man

   C. convict

   D. fugitive

8. The hideout was reached through a twisting <u>labyrinth</u>, and the officers nearly got lost several times

    A. sewer

    B. cave

    C. maze

    D. tunnel

9. The <u>devout</u> woman didn't care about her rings, but she refused to allow the burglar to steal her rosary beads.

    A. cunning

    B. religious

    C. former

    D. limber

10. Many people were killed and many more were <u>maimed</u> as a result of the earthquake.

    A. disappeared

    B. homeless

    C. uninsured

    D. injured

11. The <u>prevailing</u> opinion was that the schools should remain closed, though a substantial minority disagreed.

    A. majority

    B. risky

    C. loudest

    D. wisest

12. After spending hours in <u>deliberation</u>, the jury returned with a verdict.

    A. consideration

    B. absence

    C. testimony

    D. deposition

13. After many disagreements between the district attorney and the defense lawyer, the <u>atmosphere</u> in the courtroom was tense.

    A. temperature

    B. mood

    C. space

    D. audience

14. It took only a few minutes for the lieutenant to make her <u>determination</u> that this was a probable homicide.

    A. accusation

    B. appointment

    C. decision

    D. announcement

15. Although no one became hostile, there was a definite <u>schism</u> in the community between those who favored the law and those who did not.

    A. wall

    B. fight

    C. plan

    D. division

16. Officer Meyers recognized the suspect, who was a(n) <u>veteran</u> burglar.

    A. experienced

    B. elderly

    C. military

    D. valiant

17. The city's <u>disintegration</u> made longtime residents very sad and nervous.

    A. increased wealth

    B. disagreement

    C. busing

    D. decay

18. Those who believed that the man was innocent hoped that he would be <u>exonerated</u>.

    A. executed

    B. cleared

    C. found guilty

    D. paid

19. After several meetings and little progress, the problems in the community began to seem <u>insoluble</u>.

    A. expensive

    B. solid

    C. unsolvable

    D. unmentionable

20. The practice exercise <u>replicated</u> the events of a real hostage rescue.

    A. duplicated

    B. referenced

    C. deleted

    D. corrected

21. The training officer outlined a <u>scenario</u> in which they would have to respond quickly.

    A. city

    B. scandal

    C. situation

    D. responsibility

22. Because Officer Fisher was trusted by both sides, she was asked to <u>mediate</u> the argument.

    A. deliver

    B. settle

    C. stir up

    D. complicate

23. Trying to cross the freeway, the boys were <u>flustered</u> by the heavy traffic.

    A. calmed

    B. amused

    C. encouraged

    D. upset

24. Her explanation <u>encapsulated</u> the procedure for the trainees.

    A. performed

    B. enlarged

    C. summarized

    D. confused

25. After descending the castle's sweeping staircase, the <u>aristocrat</u> took his place at the long, candlelit table.

    A. nobleman

    B. captain

    C. chef

    D. architect

26. The scientist was tremendously excited, because he was sure he was on the <u>verge</u> of a great discovery.

    A. committee

    B. brink

    C. payroll

    D. recess

27. Because of his expertise in firearms, he was assigned to inventory the base's <u>ordnance</u>.

    A. finances

    B. medical supplies

    C. roster

    D. artillery

28. Talk of the officer's resignation was only <u>conjecture</u>; the officer hadn't confirmed anything.

    A. speculation

    B. lies

    C. weakness

    D. argument

29. She thought her husband's new jacket was <u>hideous</u>, but said nothing because she didn't want to hurt his feelings.

    A. attractive

    B. ugly

    C. oversized

    D. itchy

30. He's a <u>dynamic</u> leader, which is one reason he's so effective.

    A. well-paid

    B. jealous

    C. powerful

    D. sympathetic

31. It began as a normal day; they took their <u>customary</u> route to work.

    A. long

    B. usual

    C. secret

    D. personal

32. He runs the company like a(n) <u>tyrant</u>, so none of his employees dare to offer any ideas of their own.

    A. dictator

    B. idiot

    C. general

    D. intellectual

33. He earned a reputation for kindness because he's been so <u>generous</u> with his time and his money.

    A. concerned

    B. giving

    C. stingy

    D. playful

34. The bright little girl always had a(n) <u>inquisitive</u> look on her face.

    A. frightened

    B. angry

    C. curious

    D. insulted

35. With its sweeping terraces and ornate stonework, the <u>grandeur</u> of the governor's mansion is unequaled.

    A. size

    B. magnificence

    C. height

    D. view

36. He <u>prizes</u> his rare book collection and has it fully insured.

    A. sizes up

    B. views

    C. values

    D. wins

37. Sylvia's boyfriend tries to control every move she makes, as if he wants to <u>possess</u> her.

    A. appreciate

    B. squander

    C. support

    D. own

38. Hours passed, and Mrs. Wills grew more and more <u>fretful</u> as she waited for her son to return from the party.

    A. worried

    B. stiff

    C. understanding

    D. quiet

39. Saving the small pond from developers became his personal <u>crusade</u>, and he worked on it night and day.

    A. fear

    B. mission

    C. guilt

    D. amusement

40. They were told to <u>batten</u> the windows and doors to prepare for the hurricane.

    A. secure

    B. break

    C. remove

    D. avoid

41. The <u>paraphernalia</u> at the scene suggested to the officers that drugs were involved.

    A. dust

    B. fingerprints

    C. animals

    D. equipment

42. When she answered the question, she was so <u>subdued</u> that no one heard her at first.

    A. rude

    B. cheerful

    C. quiet

    D. hoarse

43. The manufacturer <u>sponsored</u> the track and field event, in exchange for large displays of the company logo around the track.

    A. financed

    B. boycotted

    C. competed in

    D. attended

44. Because the office gets almost no natural light, the designer recommended <u>artificial</u> plants.

    A. inexpensive

    B. green

    C. flowering

    D. fake

45. He complained to the doctor about his <u>recurrent</u> headaches, which occurred at least twice a month.

    A. severe

    B. repeated

    C. brief

    D. new

Explanation for Exercise 1—Using Context

1. You're looking for a word that's connected to learning. The best answer is **B**, educational.

2. If the teacher wants confirmation of the illness from a doctor, then the illness may not be real. The best answer is **C**.

3. The only answer that makes sense is **C**. The others refer to actions that aren't taking place in this sentence.

4. The answer is **B**. A frightened witness isn't likely to be eager to testify, and it wouldn't be a good idea to challenge or dare them to take the stand.

5. The best answer is **D**. Repetitive tasks can't be varied, and the statement says that they may be meaningful. There's no information about the level of difficulty.

6. The correct answer is **B**.

7. The best choice is **A**. The keyword "although" signals that you're looking for a contrast, the opposite of what you'd expect from good references and no record.

8. The best answer is **C**. "Maze" matches most closely with getting lost on a twisting path.

9. The best answer is **B**. She may be a cunning and limber woman, or even a former woman. But all we know from this sentence is that she cares more about her rosary beads than her jewelry.

10. The best answer is **D**. Again, all the other answers make some sense, but "injured" is the only one that offers a clear connection to "killed."

11. The correct answer is **A**. The keyword "though" tells you to look for contrast.

12. The answer is **A**. You're looking for what the jury does; they don't testify and they don't depose. "Absence" makes some sense, but "consideration" provides the most logical connection to the verdict.

13. The answer is **B**. You've probably seen "atmosphere" used in reference to air or space, but in this context it refers to the mood of a scene.

14. The best answer is **C**. She's not accusing or appointing anyone, and before she can announce anything, she's got to make a decision. You've probably also seen "determination" used to talk about willpower, or stick-to-itiveness. This is a more specialized use of the word.

15. The answer is **D**.

16. **A** is the best answer. The burglary may have had something to do with the military, but that wouldn't explain why Officer Meyers recognized him.

17. **D** is the best answer. This has nothing to do with busing; "integration" simply means assembled or put together as one, and can be applied to many, many situations.

18. **B** is the correct answer.

19. **C** is the correct answer.

20. **A** is the best answer. Don't get confused by the "re" in both "referenced" and "replicated." The prefixes are actually "ref-" and "rep-" so there's no relationship.

21. **C** is the correct answer.

22. **B** is the correct answer.

23. **D** is the correct answer.

24. **C** is the best answer. Think about the prefix "en-" or "within." The explanation is wrapped up within a small space, or capsule; that's a pretty good figure of speech describing a summary.

25. **A** is the best answer. None of the others would be likely to make themselves at home in this way.

26. **B** is the best answer. This is the only answer that would explain tremendous excitement.

27. **D** is the best answer. Which of the answers if the closest synonym to "firearms"?

28. **A** is the best answer. If nothing had been confirmed, we can't know if the talk was lies; "weakness" doesn't make sense; "argument" sort of works, but only sort of.

29. **B** is the correct answer.

30. **C** is the correct answer.

31. **B** is the best answer. When you've got two sentences linked with a semicolon like this, it means they're very closely connected. Often, as in this case, the second sentence expands upon or adds detail to the first one. "Usual" has the closest relationship to "normal."

32. **A** is the best answer. Only a dictator would be likely to cause that kind of fear.

33. **B** is the best answer. "Because" means you're about to get an explanation. Someone who shares his time and money would be thought of as kind.

34. **C** is the best answer. "Curious" connects with "bright."

35. **B** is the best answer. The first phrase doesn't say much about the mansion's size or view, so "magnificence" is all that's left.

36. **C** is the best answer. "Values" has the most logical connection with insurance.

37. **D** is the most logical answer.

38. **A** makes the most sense.

39. **B** is the best answer. Only "mission" clearly connects to "worked on it night and day."

40. **A** is the correct answer.

41. **D** is the most logical answer.

42. **C** is the only answer that explains why the woman couldn't be heard.

43. **A** is the most logical answer.

44. **D** is the best answer. Only fake plants would be suitable in the setting described. Inexpensive real plants would soon be just as dead as expensive ones.

45. **B** makes the most sense in context.

Exercise 2—Reading Comprehension and Context

Read the following paragraphs and write the missing word in the appropriate blank. The first number, at the front of the blank, is the question number; the number in parentheses tells you the number of letters in the word.

Homicides can be classified by number of victims, type _____ (3) style. A single homicide is defined as one victim and _____ (3) homicidal event. A double homicide is defined as two _____ (7) who are killed at one time in one location. A _____ (6) homicide is defined as three victims who are _____ (6) at one time in one location. Any single event, _____ (6) location homicide involving four or more murders is classified _____ (2) mass murder.

There are two subcategories of mass murderer: classic mass _____ (6) and family mass murder. A classic mass murder involves _____ (3) person operating in one location at one period of _____ (4). The time period could be minutes, hours or even _____ (4). The prototype of a classic mass murderer is a _____, (8) disordered individual whose problems have increased to the point _____ (4) he acts out against groups of people _____ (9) to him or his problems, unleashing his hostility through _____ (9) or stabbings. A classic mass murderer was Charles Whitman, _____ (3) in 1966 barricaded himself in a tower at the University _____ (2) Texas at Austin and opened fire for 90 minutes, _____ (7) sixteen people and wounding more than 30 others. He _____ (3) stopped only when he was killed during an assault _____ (2) the tower.

The second type of mass murder is the _____ (6) mass murder. If four or more family members are _____ (6) and the perpetrator takes his own life, it is _____ (10) as a mass murder/suicide. Without the suicide and _____ (4) four or more victims, the murder is classified as _____ (6) mass murder. An example is John List, an insurance _____ (8) who killed his entire family in 1972. List disappeared _____ (5) the crime and his car was found at an airport _____ (7) lot. He was located 17 years later _____ (9) a television program describing the murders.

—adapted from *Crime Classification Manual: A Standard System for Investigating and Classifying Violent Crimes*, by John E. Douglas, Ann W. Burgess, Allen G. Burgess, and Robert K. Ressler

Remember, you are your dog's surrogate parent; you must _____ (3) your dog to respond to you. If your dog were _____ (6) with his real mother, he would follow her and _____ (6) to her totally and she would never speak even a _____ (6) word. To do this effectively, you must be yourself. _____ (4) copy the moves of a trainer or animal _____ (6) unless you want to be just like that person. Chances _____ (3) you don't. Your dog or puppy—age makes little _____ (10)—will pick up habits and respond to voice and _____ (4) language very quickly. It would be a good thing _____ (2) the language that your dog sees, hears, and learns is _____ (5).

It has taken you many years to develop your _____ (3) habit patterns, and those are the ones you should _____ (3) with your dog. If you're most comfortable telling your _____ (3) what you want him to do with a certain _____ (4) gesture, then that's the way you teach him. If _____ (3) have a habit of stuttering, talking fast, or _____ (5) your hands to express yourself, then teach him in _____ (4) way. Don't force yourself to use hand gestures or _____ (6) commands that are awkward or make no sense to _____ (3). You want the dog to understand that this is the _____ (4) you.

—adapted from *Smarter than You Think: A Revolutionary Approach to Teaching and Understanding Your Dog in Just a Few Hours,*
by Paul Loeb and Suzanne Hlavacek

The disorganized offender is likely to be of below _____ (7) intelligence and/or of low birth status in the family. _____ (4), harsh parental discipline is sometimes reported in childhood. The _____ (7) work history is unstable, and the disorganized offender _____ (5) to mirror this pattern with his _____ (3) inconsistent and poor work history.

Typically, this offender is _____ (10) by repeating obsessional and/or primitive _____ (8) and is in a confused and distressed state of _____ (4) at the time of the crime.

The disorganized offender is _____ (8) inadequate. Often he has never married, lives alone or _____ (4) a parental figure, and lives in close proximity to the _____ (5) scene. This offender is fearful of people and may _____ (4) developed a delusional system through which he interacts _____ (4) the world. He acts impulsively under stress, finding a _____ (6) usually within his own geographic area.

The offender is _____ (4) sexually incompetent, often never having achieved any level of _____ (6) intimacy with a peer. Although the offenders we interviewed _____ (7) to be heterosexual, there is a clear suggestion that the _____ (12) offender is ignorant of sex and may actually be _____ (8) or disgusted by it.

—adapted from *Sexual Homicide: Patterns and Motives,*
by Robert K. Ressler, Ann W. Burgess, John E. Douglas

Suppose someone in the year 1000 had _____ (8) up some items of everyday life and _____ (6) them in a time capsule to be opened at the _____ (3) of the millennium. If he tried to predict who _____ (5) end up opening it, the answer would be _____ (7): the Chinese, of course! China was then the world's _____ (7), most powerful, most technologically advanced empire. It had the _____ (6) biggest and best ships, equipped with Chinese _____ (10) such as magnetic compasses, stern-post rudders, and watertight bulkheads. The _____ (4) list of other Chinese firsts included canal lock gates, _____ (4) iron, deep drilling, gunpowder, bamboo guns, kites, porcelain, printing _____ (3) wheelbarrows. At the dawn of this millennium, China seemed _____ (5) to colonize and conquer the world—as well as to _____ (4) that time capsule sealed away 1,000 years before.

In _____ (4), as we know, China's preeminince didn't last. China was derailed by _____ (13) that we can recognize today only from a long _____ (10) perspective. Those disadvantages grew out of China's geography, which _____ (3) always made the country (unlike Europe) easy to _____ (5) politically. A smooth coastline, parallel-flowing rivers, a lack of _____ (5) peninsulas, big islands or uncrossable mountain ranges—all _____ (5) have led to the eventual downfall of every attempt to _____ (9) breakaway states within China since its unification in 221 BC. _____ (7) chronic fragmentation into separate states encouraged competition; China's chronic _____ (5) encouraged dictatorships. Whatever progress China had made in reaching _____ (3) to the world in the early years of the _____ (10) was undone by a few ignorant emperors, who in the 15th _____ (7) banned oceangoing ships, clocks and water-powered machines through China.

_____ (6) decline, only recently reversed, warns us that the West's _____ (10) for the last several centuries may also prove to be transient.

—adapted from "To Whom It May Concern," by Jared Diamond, in the *New York Times Magazine*, Dec. 5, 1999

Explanations for Exercise 2—Reading Comprehension and Context

Homicides can be classified by number of victims, type **and** style. A single homicide is defined as one victim and **one** homicidal event. A double homicide is defined as two **victims** who are killed at one time in one location. A **triple** homicide is defined as three victims who are **killed** at one time in one location. Any single event, **single** location homicide involving four or more murders is classified **as** mass murder.

There are two subcategories of mass murder: classic mass **murder** and family mass murder. A classic mass murder involves **one** person operating in one location at one period of **time**. The time period could be minutes, hours or even **days**. The prototype of a classic mass murderer is a **troubled**, disordered individual whose problems have increased to the point **that** he acts out against groups of people **connected** to him or his problems, unleashing his hostility through **shootings** or stabbings. A classic mass murderer was Charles Whitman, **who** in 1966 barricaded himself in a tower at the University **of** Texas at Austin and opened fire for 90 minutes, **killing** sixteen people and wounding more than 30 others. He **was** stopped only when he was killed during an assault **in** the tower.

The second type of mass murder is the **family** mass murder. If four or more family members are **killed** and the perpetrator takes his own life, it is **classified** as a mass murder/suicide. Without the suicide and **with** four or more victims, the murder is classified as **classic** mass murder. An example is John List, an insurance **salesman** who killed his entire family in 1972. List disappeared **after** the crime and his car was found at an airport **parking** lot. He was located 17 years later **following** a television program describing the murders.

—adapted from *Crime Classification Manual: A Standard System for Investigating and Classifying Violent Crimes*, by John E. Douglas, Ann W. Burgess, Allen G. Burgess, and Robert K. Ressler

Remember, you are your dog's surrogate parent; you must **get** your dog to respond to you. If your dog were **living** with his real mother, he would follow her and **listen** to her totally and she would never speak even a **single** word. To do this effectively, you must be yourself. **Don't** copy the moves of a trainer or animal **expert** unless you want to be just like that person. Chances **are** you don't. Your dog or puppy—age makes little **difference**—will pick up habits and respond to voice and **body** language very quickly. It would be a good thing if the language that your dog sees, hears, and learns is **yours**.

It has taken you many years to develop your **own** habit patterns, and those are the ones you should **use** with your dog. If you're most comfortable telling your **dog** what you want him to do with a certain **hand** gesture, then that's the way you teach him. If **you** have a habit of stuttering, talking fast, or using your hands to express yourself, then teach him in **that** way. Don't force yourself to use hand gestures or **verbal** commands that are awkward or make no sense to **you**. You want the dog to understand that this is the real **you**.

—adapted from *Smarter than You Think: A Revolutionary Approach to Teaching and Understanding Your Dog in Just a Few Hours*, by Paul Loeb and Suzanne Hlavacek

The disorganized offender is likely to be of below **average** intelligence and/or of low birth status in the family. **Also,** harsh parental discipline is sometimes reported in childhood. The **father's** work history is unstable, and the disorganized offender **seems** to mirror this pattern with his **own** inconsistent and poor work history.

Typically, this offender is **distracted** by repeating obsessional and/or primitive **thoughts** and is in a confused and distressed state of **mind** at the time of the crime.

The disorganized offender is **socially** inadequate. Often he has never married, lives alone or **with** a parental figure, and lives in close proximity to the **crime** scene. This offender is fearful of people and may **have** developed a delusional system through which he interacts **with** the world. He acts impulsively under stress, finding a **victim** usually within his own geographic area.

The offender is **also** sexually incompetent, often never having achieved any level of **sexual** intimacy with a peer. Although the offenders we interviewed **claimed** to be heterosexual, there is a clear suggestion that the **disorganized** offender is ignorant of sex and may actually be **offended** or disgusted by it.

—adapted from *Sexual Homicide: Patterns and Motives,*
by Robert K. Ressler, Ann W. Burgess, John E. Douglas

Suppose someone in the year 1000 had **gathered** up some items of everyday life and **stored** them in a time capsule to be opened at the **end** of the millennium. If he tried to predict who **would** end up opening it, the answer would be **obvious:** the Chinese, of course! China was then the world's **largest,** most powerful, most technologically advanced empire. It had the **world's** biggest and best ships, equipped with Chinese **inventions** such as magnetic compasses, stern-post rudders, and watertight bulkheads. The **long** list of other Chinese firsts included canal lock gates, **cast** iron, deep drilling, gunpowder, bamboo guns, kites, porcelain, printing **and** wheelbarrows. At the dawn of this millennium, China seemed **ready** to colonize and conquer the world—as well as to **open** that time capsule sealed away 1,000 years before.

In **fact,** as we know, China's preeminince didn't last. China was derailed by **disadvantages** that we can recognize today only from a long **historical** perspective. Those disadvantages grew out of China's geography, which **has** always made the country (unlike Europe) easy to **unify** politically. A smooth coastline, parallel-flowing rivers, a lack of **major** peninsulas, big islands or uncrossable mountain ranges—all **these** have led to the eventual downfall of every attempt to **establish** breakaway states within China since its unification in 221 B.C. **Europe's** chronic fragmentation into separate states encouraged competition; China's chronic **unity** encouraged dictatorships. Whatever progress China had made in reaching **out** to the world in the early years of the **millennium** was undone by a few ignorant emperors, who in the 15th **century** banned oceangoing ships, clocks and water-powered machines through China.

China's decline, only recently reversed, warns us that the West's **leadership** for the last several centuries may also prove to be transient.

—adapted from "To Whom It May Concern," by Jared Diamond,
in the *New York Times Magazine,* Dec. 5, 1999

CHAPTER SIX

Writing

You may or may not have to answer an essay question as part of your written test. POST doesn't require it, but some agencies do include an essay question as part of the screening process.

Even if you escape an essay on the written test, at some point in the application process, you're going to have to write something. The Personal History form asks for a couple of short descriptions, and you'll probably run into more.

No one is expecting Pulitzer Prize material here. You just need to get your point across clearly. If you've gone through the reading comprehension chapter, then you already know how to do that. Instead of looking for the structure, you have to put it together yourself.

Here are some suggestions for how to do that:

Write an Outline

This is worth doing, even when you're on a deadline. Developing a strong structure before you begin writing will save you time in the long run. It doesn't really matter what form you write your outline in—you're the only one who's going to see it. But you should always jot down some notes to help yourself get organized.

First, write down the most important thing you want to say. Don't worry about how you write it now; it doesn't even have to be a complete sentence at this point. Just summarize your main point. Think of it as the direct answer to the question.

Now you have to come up with some support for your main point. If your main point is the direct answer to the question, the supporting examples are the answers to the follow-up questions. The support material can be examples from your own experience or reasoning that you've worked out; they can be more or less separate, or one can build on top of another.

Finally, you need to wrap it up with a conclusion. You don't need to get fancy; you can just restate your original main point.

Be Clear

Once you've got your outline finished, you're over halfway there. All you have to do is flesh out the sentences, or sentence fragments, and you're done.

The big mistake people make here is they get a little too fancy. Remember, you're writing to express, not impress. No one reading a police report cares about the writer's literary craft. So skip the ten-dollar words and the mile-long sentences. Just say what you want to say, and stop.

Be Active

One of the ways of categorizing verbs is active and passive. Some people think that the passive voice is more formal; it's really just blander and more boring. You'll automatically sound like a better candidate if you just eliminate any passive verbs in favor of active verbs.

Here are some examples:

Passive

I was introduced to the importance of hard work by my grandfather.

Active

I learned the importance of hard work from my grandfather.

Passive

While a senior in high school, I was named to the All-Region football team as an offensive lineman.

Active

During my senior year in high school, I played offensive line for the All-Region football team.

Passive

My most difficult situation occurred shortly after my older brother was diagnosed with leukemia.

Active

I faced the most difficult period of my life after my older brother was diagnosed with leukemia.

Give It a Rest and a Reread

Once you're written your first draft, let it sit for a day or two and then come back to it. You'll be able to see mistakes or awkward sentences that seemed fine when you wrote them down.

Obviously, on a timed test you won't *have* a couple of days to mull over what you've written. But you should *always* reread your written material before turning in the test. Look for misspellings and grammatical errors, along with holes in your logic and other structural mistakes.

Well, good luck. Take the time to prepare; identify and work on your weak spots, and I'm sure you'll do fine.

I've got one more very important piece of advice for you as you prepare for these tests: read. If you're not in the habit of reading the daily paper, start—even if it's just the sports section. Set aside a half-hour or 45 minutes a day to read something. The POST test measures how well you understand what you read, and whether you can recognize and repair faulty grammar. I covered as much ground as I can here, but there's no way I can prepare you for every single possible question. Reading more is like your backup plan; the more familiar you are with the process, the better you'll be at it. That just makes sense.

San Diego to Study Racial Profiling

Minority drivers have long complained that police often target them in traffic stops because of their race—a practice called racial profiling—but police have consistently denied it's done.

In San Diego, Police Chief Jerry Sanders is teaming up with the American Civil Liberties Union (ACLU) to study if there's any validity to the charge. Sanders says to find out, his department will be the first in the nation to voluntarily collect race information on traffic stops.

It's a hot-button issue for law enforcement officials nationwide. O. J. Simpson prosecutor Christopher Darden, actors Wesley Snipes and Blair Underwood, and former San Diego Charger Shawn Lee are among those who say they've been pulled over simply because of their skin color. In New Jersey, the Justice Department is probing state police to determine if troopers regularly violate the civil rights of motorists. Documents made public after police shot three unarmed minority men in a traffic stop on the New Jersey Turnpike show that 75 percent of motorists arrested on the turnpike over a two-month period in 1997 were minorities.

Minority leaders in San Diego cite a study in Maryland that showed that although blacks represented only 14 percent of the drivers on a certain highway, they made up 72 percent of those pulled over.

"This type of complaint is not uncommon," said San Diego County Sheriff's Commander Bill Flores, a Latino community leader. "Any government agency perceived to be biased against any group of citizens, particularly by race, has a responsibility to determine if that bias exists."

San Diego officers will track the age, race, and gender of every motorist who is stopped—regardless of whether he or she is ticketed, arrested, or formally interviewed. The department will collect baseline information to determine whether people of color are stopped in higher percentages and decide whether more diversity training or other measures are needed. A committee, including the ACLU and the National Association for the Advancement of Colored People, will further interpret the data, which promises to be fairly complex, Sanders said.

During every stop, officers will record the reason for the stop, the suspect's name, age, race, and other pertinent information on laptop computers. The $30,000 cost of capturing the data will cover the cost of reprogramming computers that needed to be upgraded anyway, Sanders said.

—Adapted from an APBNews.com article by Karen S. Smith and Craig Miller, Feb. 26, 1999

Part Three

Practice POST Exams

The following four tests are based on the POST exam given to police officer applicants in California. The test administered by the department you're applying to might include other sections that are not represented here. Regardless of the actual form of the test you'll take, you can only help your chances by developing your skills at standardized test taking.

Give yourself a total of two hours for each of the following tests. Take the first test, then check your answers against the answer key following the test. Then look at the questions you have the most trouble answering and review that section before you take the next test. You should show improvement right away.

POST Practice Test 1

The following test is based on the POST exam given to police officer applicants in California. The test administered by the department you're applying to might include other sections that are not represented here. Regardless of the actual form of the test you'll take, you can only help your chances by developing your skills at standardized test taking.

Give yourself a total of two hours for the following test. An answer key and explanations follow the test.

Answer Sheet for Practice Test 1

Use the answer sheet to mark your choices for the multiple-choice questions. An answer key and explanations follow the test.

Clarity	Spelling	Context	Multiple-Choice Reading Comprehension
1. Ⓐ Ⓑ	1. Ⓐ Ⓑ Ⓒ Ⓓ	1. Ⓐ Ⓑ Ⓒ Ⓓ	1. Ⓐ Ⓑ Ⓒ Ⓓ
2. Ⓐ Ⓑ	2. Ⓐ Ⓑ Ⓒ Ⓓ	2. Ⓐ Ⓑ Ⓒ Ⓓ	2. Ⓐ Ⓑ Ⓒ Ⓓ
3. Ⓐ Ⓑ	3. Ⓐ Ⓑ Ⓒ Ⓓ	3. Ⓐ Ⓑ Ⓒ Ⓓ	3. Ⓐ Ⓑ Ⓒ Ⓓ
4. Ⓐ Ⓑ	4. Ⓐ Ⓑ Ⓒ Ⓓ	4. Ⓐ Ⓑ Ⓒ Ⓓ	4. Ⓐ Ⓑ Ⓒ Ⓓ
5. Ⓐ Ⓑ	5. Ⓐ Ⓑ Ⓒ Ⓓ	5. Ⓐ Ⓑ Ⓒ Ⓓ	5. Ⓐ Ⓑ Ⓒ Ⓓ
6. Ⓐ Ⓑ	6. Ⓐ Ⓑ Ⓒ Ⓓ	6. Ⓐ Ⓑ Ⓒ Ⓓ	6. Ⓐ Ⓑ Ⓒ Ⓓ
7. Ⓐ Ⓑ	7. Ⓐ Ⓑ Ⓒ Ⓓ	7. Ⓐ Ⓑ Ⓒ Ⓓ	7. Ⓐ Ⓑ Ⓒ Ⓓ
8. Ⓐ Ⓑ	8. Ⓐ Ⓑ Ⓒ Ⓓ	8. Ⓐ Ⓑ Ⓒ Ⓓ	8. Ⓐ Ⓑ Ⓒ Ⓓ
9. Ⓐ Ⓑ	9. Ⓐ Ⓑ Ⓒ Ⓓ	9. Ⓐ Ⓑ Ⓒ Ⓓ	9. Ⓐ Ⓑ Ⓒ Ⓓ
10. Ⓐ Ⓑ	10. Ⓐ Ⓑ Ⓒ Ⓓ	10. Ⓐ Ⓑ Ⓒ Ⓓ	10. Ⓐ Ⓑ Ⓒ Ⓓ
11. Ⓐ Ⓑ	11. Ⓐ Ⓑ Ⓒ Ⓓ	11. Ⓐ Ⓑ Ⓒ Ⓓ	11. Ⓐ Ⓑ Ⓒ Ⓓ
12. Ⓐ Ⓑ	12. Ⓐ Ⓑ Ⓒ Ⓓ	12. Ⓐ Ⓑ Ⓒ Ⓓ	12. Ⓐ Ⓑ Ⓒ Ⓓ
13. Ⓐ Ⓑ	13. Ⓐ Ⓑ Ⓒ Ⓓ	13. Ⓐ Ⓑ Ⓒ Ⓓ	13. Ⓐ Ⓑ Ⓒ Ⓓ
14. Ⓐ Ⓑ	14. Ⓐ Ⓑ Ⓒ Ⓓ	14. Ⓐ Ⓑ Ⓒ Ⓓ	14. Ⓐ Ⓑ Ⓒ Ⓓ
15. Ⓐ Ⓑ	15. Ⓐ Ⓑ Ⓒ Ⓓ	15. Ⓐ Ⓑ Ⓒ Ⓓ	15. Ⓐ Ⓑ Ⓒ Ⓓ
			16. Ⓐ Ⓑ Ⓒ Ⓓ
			17. Ⓐ Ⓑ Ⓒ Ⓓ
			18. Ⓐ Ⓑ Ⓒ Ⓓ
			19. Ⓐ Ⓑ Ⓒ Ⓓ
			20. Ⓐ Ⓑ Ⓒ Ⓓ

Book 1

Clarity

Choose the sentence that's most clearly and correctly worded.

1. A. The tourists left they're suitcases at the hotel.
    B. The tourists left their suitcases at the hotel.

2. A. Her new dress fit her perfect.
    B. Her new dress fit her perfectly.

3. A. The farmer hoped he would not lose his crops to a late frost.
    B. The farmer hoped he would not loose his crops to a late frost.

4. A. As he approached, he feels the tension increasing.
    B. As he approached, he felt the tension increasing.

5. A. Her horse performed good in the race.
    B. Her horse performed well in the race.

6. A. The salesman dropped his phone.
    B. The salesman, dropped his phone.

7. A. If her father were still alive, he could teach her how to drive.
    B. If her father was still alive, he could teach her how to drive.

8. A. He excepted her apology.
    B. He accepted her apology.

9. A. The gift-wrapped teapot was fore her.
    B. The gift-wrapped teapot was for her.

10. A. The longer we waited, the later it became.
    B. The longer we waited, the later it become.

11. A. Her favoritest movie is Alvin Johnson.

    B. Her favorite movie is Alvin Johnson.

12. A. He threw the ball to his brother.

    B. He throwed the ball to his brother.

13. A. The ditch was deep. And muddy.

    B. The ditch was deep and muddy.

14. A. Her appetite is much bigger than his.

    B. Her appetite is much more bigger than his.

15. A. After a heavy meal, I like to lie down.

    B. After a heavy meal, I like to laid down.

Spelling

For each question, select the correct spelling of the word from the four choices given below.

1. Tabloid magazines report sensational stories about _____ .

    A. selebrities

    B. cellebrities

    C. sellebrities

    D. celebrities

2. The townspeople had to make a _____ effort to clean up their streets.

    A. concerted

    B. conserted

    C. concertted

    D. conncerted

3. Both sides of the debate presented _____ arguments.

    A. pasionate

    B. passionate

    C. pasinate

    D. passonate

4. She responded _____ to his request.

   A. cooly
   B. coollie
   C. coolly
   D. cooley

5. The fire _____ the house to a pile of ashes.

   A. reduced
   B. redused
   C. redduced
   D. reddused

6. He liked _____ his muscles.

   A. flexxing
   B. flecksing
   C. flecsing
   D. flexing

7. Her mother was an _____ and sensitive woman.

   A. observent
   B. obzervant
   C. observint
   D. observant

8. The _____ dog strained against its chain.

   A. whilful
   B. wilfull
   C. willful
   D. willfull

9. If they lose, the football players will _____ their losing streak to ten games.

   A. extind
   B. extand
   C. axtend
   D. extend

10. The _____ is a beautiful instrument.

   A. voilin

   B. violin

   C. vilion

   D. viollin

11. He claimed that meeting her was a _____ .

   A. coincidence

   B. coinsidence

   C. coincidents

   D. coinsidense

12. The preacher encouraged his congregation to try to live a _____ life.

   A. riteous

   B. rightous

   C. righteous

   D. ritheous

13. The young _____ was an inspiration to children everywhere.

   A. jimnast

   B. gyminast

   C. jymnast

   D. gymnast

14. His _____ band was The Popards.

   A. favoret

   B. favorite

   C. faivorite

   D. faverite

15. The store offered a _____ on the oven.

   A. garantee

   B. guarrantee

   C. garanty

   D. guarantee

Context

For each question, choose the answer most similar in meaning to the underlined word in the sentence.

1. The brilliant surgeon worked with great <u>exactitude</u>, making small, neat incisions.
   A. speed
   B. excitement
   C. emotion
   D. accuracy

2. Her father was very <u>miserly</u>, and she rebelled by spending money as fast as she could.
   A. thoughtful
   B. stingy
   C. quiet
   D. humorous

3. Listening to the language tapes was a good way to <u>augment</u> her classes and homework, and her grades improved.
   A. develop
   B. counterbalance
   C. add to
   D. interfere with

4. After checking the outlet, which was fine, the electrician found <u>faulty</u> wiring in the air conditioner.
   A. defective
   B. fancy
   C. old
   D. complex

5. The park ranger takes his duties seriously, and keeps a <u>vigilant</u> eye on the preserve and the wildlife there.
   A. lacking
   B. watchful
   C. bloodshot
   D. resentful

6. She rarely asked for advice; in every decision, she let her <u>morals</u> guide her.

    A. parents

    B. emotions

    C. principles

    D. mobility

7. The man's behavior at his brother's wedding was <u>infantile</u> and embarrassing.

    A. immature

    B. youthful

    C. restrained

    D. uninformed

8. It was several days before other world leaders officially <u>recognized</u> the president-elect.

    A. spoke with

    B. acknowledged

    C. abdicated

    D. fought

9. Paris was their <u>eventual</u> destination, but they made several stops on the way.

    A. ideal

    B. most expensive

    C. foreign

    D. final

10. The plane somehow remained <u>intact</u> when it crashed into the sea.

    A. powered

    B. dry

    C. in one piece

    D. undetected

11. She was <u>melancholy</u> after the death of her cat.

    A. alone

    B. unfriendly

    C. furious

    D. sad

12. The riots resulted in a breakdown of civic order, followed by citywide <u>pandemonium</u>.

    A. fights

    B. chaos

    C. store closings

    D. poverty

13. The book is a(n) <u>anthology</u> of twenty new American short stories.

    A. summary

    B. criticism

    C. collection

    D. apology

14. She charmed everyone with her <u>scintillating</u> conversation.

    A. boring

    B. sparkling

    C. frank

    D. modest

15. Having studied abroad, he considered himself far more <u>worldly</u> and interesting than most of his coworkers.

    A. exiled

    B. sophisticated

    C. without a home

    D. European

Multiple-Choice Reading Comprehension

Read each paragraph or passage and choose the statement that best answers the question. Choose your answer solely on the basis of the material in the passage.

1. Chocolate is derived from the beans of the tropical New World tree *Theobroma cacao*. When chocolate arrived in Europe around 1500 it was consumed only as a hot drink. In the mid-1800s, however, the Swiss invented the first method for producing it in a solid edible form. Today, millions more pounds of chocolate are produced for eating than for drinking.

   Which one of the following can be inferred from the statements above?

   A. Today, *Theobroma cacao* is grown only in the tropical New World.

   B. When chocolate was introduced to Europe, it was most commonly used in a solid form.

   C. The number of pounds of chocolate made for eating today is greater than the number of pounds of chocolate that were made for drinking during the 1800s.

   D. Chocolate was not consumed in a solid form in the New World during the 1500s.

2. A free press always informs the public of all aspects of a country's current military operations except for cases in which the safety of troops or the success of a mission would be jeopardized by the public's right to know.

   Which one of the following adheres most closely to the principle set forth above?

   A. A free press would publish editorials supporting a current military campaign, but could repress dissenting opinions regarding the campaign.

   B. An unfree press would release information on the country's prisoners of war taken during a current military campaign, unless such information would hamper efforts to secure the prisoner's release.

   C. A free press would accurately report the number of casualties suffered on both sides of a battle, but could withhold information regarding the possible targets for a future military strike.

   D. An unfree press would print inflammatory accounts of an international event in order to garner public support for an unpopular war.

3. A passenger vehicle is defined as any fully enclosed four-wheeled vehicle with room to transport at least one other passenger in addition to the driver. A semitruck, though it may have enclosed room to transport one nondriving passenger, always has more than four wheels. A jeep, though it may have four wheels and room to carry a driver and additional passengers, is rarely fully enclosed. A postal van, though it may be enclosed and have four wheels, usually does not have room to transport passengers other than the driver.

    If the statements in the passage above are true, which one of the following must also be true?

    A. If an automobile is neither a semitruck, nor a jeep, nor a postal van, then it is not a fully enclosed four-wheeled vehicle.

    B. If an automobile is not a semitruck, or a jeep, or a postal van, then it is a passenger vehicle.

    C. If a jeep is fully enclosed with four wheels and room to carry nondriving passengers, then it is both a jeep and a passenger vehicle.

    D. Postal vans are more like passenger vehicles than are semitrucks.

4. Some individuals believe that attending cooking school located in southern France teaches one all there is to know about French cooking. All branches of La Terrelle Cooking Academy are located in southern France. Yet, a recent graduate of La Terrelle did not know how to make bechamel sauce, a sauce widely used in French gourmet cooking.

    If the statements above are true, which one of the following must also be true?

    A. Attending cooking school in southern France does not always teach one all there is to know about French cooking.

    B. No graduate of La Terrelle Cooking Academy has learned all there is to know about French gourmet cooking.

    C. At least one branch of La Terrelle Cooking Academy is located outside of southern France.

    D. La Terrelle Cooking Academy does not provide an effective education in French gourmet cooking.

5. Six months ago, a blight destroyed the cattle population in the town of Cebra, eradicating the town's beef supply. As a result, since that time the only meat available for consumption in Cebra has been poultry, lamb, and other nonbeef meats.

    If the above statements are true, which one of the following must also be true on the basis of them?

    A. Villagers in the town of Cebra consume only beef raised by Cebra farmers.
    B. Cebra villagers prefer lamb and poultry to beef.
    C. The town of Cebra has not imported beef for consumption during the last six months.
    D. Most of the residents of Cebra are meat eaters.

6. For healthy individuals who wish to improve their overall fitness, cross-training in several sports is more beneficial than training with a single activity. Cross-training develops a wide range of muscle groups, while single-sport training tends to isolate a select few muscles. Single-sport activities, especially those that target slow-twitch muscles, tend to increase the tonic muscle fibers in the body. Cross-training works instead to increase the body's phasic muscle fibers, which burn more calories than tonic muscle fibers.

    Which one of the following, if true, best supports the argument above?

    A. In healthy persons, overall fitness increases in proportion to the number of calories burned by the body.
    B. Overall fitness is most effectively improved through athletic training.
    C. Tonic muscle fibers are of greater value to overall fitness than are phasic muscle fibers.
    D. Strenuous physical exertion on a single sport is not recommended for those recovering from a serious illness.

7. Sarrin monks practice the Pran meditation technique only when extremely damaging weather conditions confront the farming villages surrounding Sarrin monasteries. Pran meditation is a more highly disciplined form of the ritual meditation that the monks practice daily, and involves unique practices such as isolation and fasting.

   Which one of the statements below does NOT follow logically from the passage above?

   A. Some meditation practices are less disciplined than Pran meditation.

   B. Pran meditation among Sarrin monks does not take place according to a precisely regulated schedule.

   C. The ritual meditation that a typical Sarrin monk practices daily does not take place in an atmosphere of isolation.

   D. The ritual meditation that Sarrin monks practice daily is largely undisciplined.

8. Movie pirating, the illegal videotaping of a new theater release and subsequent selling of the tape on the black market, is a major concern to the film studios that produce today's mainstream movies. When pirating sales are high, individual studios whose movies are being taped and sold illegally lose a large amount of revenue from black-market viewers who would otherwise pay the full theater price. A low level of pirating sales during a specific period, however, is a fairly reliable indicator of an economic downturn in the movie industry as a whole during that period.

   Which one of the following, if true, most helps to reconcile the discrepancy noted above?

   A. The film studios that produce today's mainstream movies occasionally serve as distribution outlets for smaller budget independent films that are also susceptible to pirating.

   B. Movie piraters exclusively target blockbuster hits, the existence of which is inextricably tied to the financial success of the movie industry during any given period.

   C. Most movie piraters use small, hand-held video cameras that are specially designed to record images in the darkened environment of a movie theater.

   D. The five largest film studios take in a disproportionate amount of movie revenue compared to hundreds of smaller and independent film studios, regardless of whether pirating activity during a specific period is high or low.

Questions 9–10

A consumer survey of independent feature films revealed that the percentage of action films that received the survey's highest rating was greater than the percentage of romance films that received the highest rating. Yet, the survey organizers were probably erroneous in their conclusion that subject matter determines a feature film's popular appeal, since the action films were all directed by filmmakers with at least one hit film to their credit, while the romance films were directed by newer filmmakers, many of whom had not produced a previous film.

9. The statements above, if true, support which one of the following inferences?

    A. Fewer romance films than action films received the survey's highest rating.

    B. There is no relationship between the popular appeal of the feature films evaluated in the survey and any previous successes of the directors of those films.

    C. If consumers were surveyed regarding their impressions of big-budget mainstream films, the percentage of romance films that would receive the survey's highest rating would be lower than the percentage of action films that would receive the highest rating.

    D. Among directors with the same number of hit films to their credit, differences in the subject matter of their feature films may not affect the way the films are popularly rated.

10. Each of the following, if true, supports the author's contention that the organizers misinterpreted the survey data EXCEPT:

    A. The fact that one has directed a previous hit film is a positive indicator of that director's filmmaking talent.

    B. Consumer ratings of a new film are influenced by the previous history of success of the film's director.

    C. Action films generally require larger budgets than romance films and are thus prohibitive for many first-time film directors.

    D. It is rare for the films of first-time directors to attain the popular appeal of films directed by filmmakers with at least one hit film to their credit.

11. The paintings of French painter Trianne Déjère sold best in the period following the production of *La Triumph*, now Déjère's most famous piece. In the twelve-month period preceding the unveiling of this piece, Déjère sold 57 percent of her works, a far greater percentage than in previous years. In the twelve-month period following a glowing review of *La Triumph* in a popular magazine, however, Déjère sold 85 percent of the paintings she produced. Interestingly, Déjère's revenue from painting sales was roughly the same in both periods, since she sold the same number of paintings in the twelve months before presenting *La Triumph* as she did in the twelve months following the favorable review.

Which one of the following statements can be concluded properly from the passage, if the information above is true?

A. Due to the positive review, Déjère was able to charge substantially more for the works produced after *La Triumph* than the works produced before it.

B. Déjère was more concerned with positive reviews than with increasing the prices of her paintings.

C. The positive review of *La Triumph* brought Déjère's work to the attention of more art collectors than were previously aware of her work.

D. Déjère painted fewer works in the twelve-month period following the review of *La Triumph* than she had in the twelve month period preceding its unveiling.

12. Many Maids, a well-known commercial cleaning franchise, has always relied heavily on income from its major clients and would have been forced to close down this year if any of its major clients had closed their accounts. However, Many Maids has not only been able to continue its operation throughout the year, but it has also announced the grand opening of its second office.

The above statements, if true, support which one of the following conclusions?

A. During this year Many Maids' clients have placed a larger than usual number of special cleaning orders.

B. Over the past few months, Many Maids developed many new small client accounts, which made the company less dependent on its major clients for income.

C. None of Many Maids' major clients closed its account with the company this year.

D. Corporate use of cleaning services like Many Maids has recently increased.

13. Without a fundraising specialist, foundations have trouble meeting their fundraising targets. Research shows that fundraising specialists help foundations raise the majority of their yearly funds. Financial planners serve a key organizing and advisory role, but financial planners raise only a small percentage of foundation funds, if they raise any funds at all. Therefore, _____ .

    The argument above can be best completed by which one of the following?

    A. a foundation interested in raising funds should entrust its fundraising activities to fundraising specialists rather than financial planners

    B. no foundation that does not employ fundraising specialists can raise the same amount of funds as a foundation that employs financial planners

    C. fundraising specialists lacking financial planning knowledge will provide less help to foundations than will financial planners with no fundraising knowledge

    D. foundations that employ fundraising specialists meet their annual fundraising targets

14. Until 1990, the results of the Reading Level Assessment Test given in junior high schools of school districts X and Y have indicated that the reading ability of students in the two districts was nearly identical. Since 1990, however, the average score on the test has been markedly higher in district Y than in district X. The Superintendent of district Y theorizes that the difference is due to the reinstatement of the minimum reading level requirement in all junior high schools in his district, which mandates students reading below grade level to attend after-school reading workshops one day a week.

    If the statements above are true, which one of the following must also be true?

    A. The average score on the Reading Level Assessment Test in district Y has risen dramatically since the reinstatement of the minimum reading level requirement.

    B. There was a minimum reading level requirement in the junior high schools of district X at some point before 1990.

    C. There was no minimum reading level requirement in the junior high schools of district Y at some point before 1990.

    D. There was no minimum reading level requirement in the junior high schools of district X at some point after 1990.

15. An economic or political crisis in a poor country can lead to a lack of faith in the country's leaders, which is often followed by violent behavior, dissent, and even revolt among specific segments of the population. In many cases, propaganda is immediately issued from media outlets that quells such reactions by downplaying the extent of the recent crisis, thereby helping to restore belief in the efficacy of the government. However, the habitual violence exhibited by certain groups of disaffected youths in such countries generally has nothing to do with a lack of faith in their leaders, but rather is the consequence of an endemic boredom and lack of any vision of a positive future for themselves.

    Which one of the following statements follows most logically from the statements in the passage above?

    A. It is easier to quell periodic revolts in poor countries than it is to solve the habitual problem of youth violence.

    B. In all poor countries, propaganda alone cannot entirely diffuse dissent stemming from an economic or political crisis.

    C. To the extent that propaganda may help to decrease youth violence in a poor country, it is probably not the result of restoring the youths' faith in their country's leadership.

    D. The effect that propaganda has in putting down revolts in poor countries is primarily related to its ability to alter people's fundamental beliefs.

16. If ad pages in *Fission* magazine have increased in December, then either ad rates have decreased or circulation has increased for the month, but not both. If circulation has increased in December, then the editors will receive year-end bonuses. If ad pages have not increased in December, then the editors will not receive year-end bonuses.

    If all of the above statements are true, which one of the following can be concluded from the fact that the editors of *Fission* will not receive year-end bonuses?

    A. Ad rates have not increased in December.

    B. Ad pages have increased in December.

    C. Ad pages have not increased in December.

    D. Circulation has not increased in December.

17. For exactly ten years, it has not been legal to bungee jump in state A. All of the members of the Rubberband Club must live in state A and have bungee jumped at least once in the last two years. The Rubberband Club is currently taking applications for new members.

    Which one of the following necessarily follows from the information provided above?

    A. Every current member of the Rubberband Club has bungee jumped outside of state A.

    B. No current applicant to the Rubberband Club has legally bungee jumped in state A.

    C. The current members of the Rubberband Club have bungee jumped illegally at least once.

    D. Current members of the Rubberband Club who have never bungee jumped outside of state A have broken the law in state A.

18. Fewer geniuses have emerged from the present era than emerged in previous eras. In the seventeenth century there were only about one one-hundredth as many people as today, and yet in Europe alone geniuses like Galileo, Descartes, Newton, and Shakespeare flourished. In the twentieth century, Einstein is the only accepted genius of that stature.

    Which one of the following, if true, provides the most support to the argument above?

    A. Geniuses are widely recognized during their lives or soon after their deaths.

    B. There are many different kinds of geniuses, some of which are not easily comparable.

    C. The very idea of genius has been questioned and seriously criticized.

    D. The twentieth century has seen the spread of education to a much greater proportion of the population, reducing the extremes in educational attainment present in previous centuries.

19. It is not illegal to use hairspray, air conditioners, or vacuum-pressurized aerosol food containers, but it is well known that the use of such products damages the ozone layer, which may in turn have serious negative ecological consequences for future generations. It is therefore incumbent upon us to stop using these products so as to preserve the environment as best we can, even though we believe these products may enrich our lives and there are no legal sanctions against them.

Which one of the following principles is most consistent with the line of reasoning presented above?

A. The legality of one's self-interested actions should be determined in light of the moral quality of that action.

B. The morality of one's self-interested actions should be judged in light of the legal ramifications of performing those actions.

C. The legality of one's self-interested actions should be determined based on the consequences such actions had on previous generations.

D. The morality of one's self-interested actions should be judged in light of the consequences those actions may have for others.

20. The Fines Museum has a totem pole that was too tall to be stored in the museum's temperature-controlled storage vault. Fortunately, the totem pole can now be stored in the temperature-controlled vault, thanks to the efforts of restoration artists who have discovered a way to separate the pole into two parts for storage purposes while allowing it to be reassembled later without any noticeable change in the appearance of the artifact.

The conclusion in the passage above depends on which one of the following assumptions?

A. Neither of the separated parts of the totem pole is too tall to fit into the vault.

B. The totem pole can be separated into two equal-sized parts.

C. The procedure for separating the parts of the totem pole will not cost more than it would cost to replace the totem pole if it deteriorated.

D. Placing the two parts of the totem pole into the vault would not require removing other key artifacts from the vault.

Book 2

Reading Comprehension and Context

In the following two passages, certain words have been deleted. Write the missing word in the appropriate blank. The number in parentheses indicates the number of letters in the missing word. Note: A word may be used in your answers more than once.

Passage 1

An indiscriminate felony murder is a homicide that is _____ (7) in advance of committing the felony without a specific _____ (6) in mind.

The victim of an indiscriminate felony murder _____ (2) a potential witness to the crime. The victim offers _____ (2) apparent threat to the offender but is killed anyway. The _____ (6) is one of opportunity: walking into a store or _____ (5) at the wrong time, or having a work shift _____ (8) with a robbery.

There are occupations, shifts, and environments _____ (4) elevate a victim's risk factor. Working the night shift _____ (5) at a 24-hour gas station or convenience store is _____ (3) example. This situation elevates the chance of a person _____ (8) a victim of felony murder, compared with the department _____ (5) clerk who works days among many coworkers. Environmental factors that _____ (7) the victim risk factor are: being in locations within _____ (4) crime areas and working in environments that enhance crime _____ (10). Crime-enhancing environments may have any or all of the _____ (9) characteristics: views obstructed by advertising or product shelves, _____ (4) lighting, no alarms or intercom systems linking the establishment to _____ (5) law enforcement stations, one-clerk staffing, especially at _____ (5), and quantities of cash readily available.

It is also _____ (8) for a victim to elevate his or her risk _____ (2) attitude and behavior. A careless, naïve, or flippant approach to _____ (8) safety heightens the chance of being targeted for robbery and _____ (10) felony murder.

—adapted from *Crime Classification Manual: A Standard System for Investigating and Classifying Violent Crimes*, by John E. Douglas, Ann W. Burgess, Allen G. Burgess, and Robert K. Ressler

Passage 2

_____ (2) have believed for many years that there is no group of _____ (6) more versatile, durable, and attractive than perennials, or plants _____ (4) continue growing year after year. The _____ (5) of colors, heights, bloom times, flower forms, leaf colors, and _____ (7) requirements is so broad that practically _____ (3) desired effect can be brilliantly realized. _____ (7) it's a formal flower bed, a solid planting of _____ (3) or two varieties, or a wild garden at the _____ (4) of the woods, you can have your dream if you _____ (6) with care. It is, of course, an added benefit that a well-prepared _____ (9) planting will perform reliably for many years, repaying your _____ (6) and investment, while developing your gardening skills.

In pursuit of _____ (4) belief, and for our own _____ (8), we have collected as large, fresh, and varied a _____ (9) offering as can be found in this country. We _____ (4) you will take the time to explore it in detail. _____ (4) just a few exceptions, we have chosen to draw a _____ (11) between "hardy" perennials, which can survive the _____ (4), or overwinter, in Zone 7 and colder, and "tender" perennials, which _____ (6). Be aware that distinctions of this kind are _____ (8) to serve as guides in selection, not as absolute _____ (5). Gardeners in colder climates can achieve delightful results by the timely use of _____ (6) perennials, just as their peers in milder _____ (8) can often tease a year of color from plants whose natural preferences _____ (7) a proper northern winter.

—adapted from *The White Flower Farm Garden Book,* by Amos Pettingill

POST Practice Test 1 Answers and Explanations

ANSWER KEY

Clarity	Spelling	Context	Multiple-Choice Reading Comprehension
1. B	1. D–celebrities	1. D	1. D
2. B	2. A–concerted	2. B	2. C
3. A	3. B–passionate	3. C	3. C
4. B	4. C–coolly	4. A	4. A
5. B	5. A–reduced	5. B	5. C
6. A	6. D–flexing	6. C	6. A
7. A	7. D–observant	7. A	7. D
8. B	8. C–willful	8. B	8. B
9. B	9. D–extend	9. D	9. D
10. A	10. B–violin	10. C	10. C
11. B	11. A–coincidence	11. D	11. D
12. A	12. C–righteous	12. B	12. C
13. B	13. D–gymnast	13. C	13. A
14. A	14. B–favorite	14. B	14. C
15. A	15. D–guarantee	15. B	15. C
			16. D
			17. D
			18. A
			19. D
			20. A

EXPLANATIONS

Book 1

Clarity

1. The correct answer is **B**. The possessive form of the pronoun "they" is "their." In **A**, "they're" is a contraction of "they are."

2. The correct answer is **B**. Remember—adverbs describe verbs or adjectives. Turn an adjective into an adverb by adding the suffix "ly." Since "perfect" refers to the verb "fit," you need to use the adverb form—"perfectly."

3. **A** is the correct answer. To "loose" something is to set it free or unleash it.

4. The correct answer is **B**. You have to stick with same verb tense throughout the sentence. The first verb is past tense ("approached") so you have to use past tense for the second verb as well—"felt."

5. The correct answer is **B**. Okay, this is one of those exceptions to the rule. In sentence **A**, "good" describes "performed," so you know you have to use an adverb instead of the adjective. But how do you turn "good" into an adverb? "Goodly?" Actually, "goodly" *was* used, around the time of the Pilgrims, but people will look at you funny if you use it now. Just memorize this one: "Good" is an adjective; "well" is the corresponding adverb.

6. **A** is the correct answer. You don't need the comma in **B**.

7. **A** is the correct answer. The writer is talking about a situation that isn't true; the woman's father *isn't* alive. In this case, you don't use ordinary past tense ("was"). Instead, you use the subjunctive tense, "were." Don't worry about remembering the name of that tense, as long as you know how to use it.

8. The correct answer is **B**. This is a common mistake. Because the words sound alike, people often get them confused. "Excepted" means to omit or exclude, while "accepted" means to take something that's offered

9. The correct answer is **B**. You need the preposition "for" to indicate direction. "Fore" is an old-fashioned adjective that means "towards the front," as in "The dog injured its forepaw."

10. **A** is the correct answer. Stick to the same verb tense. "Waited" is past tense, so you need to use the past tense verb "become."

11. The correct answer is **B**. Unlike most adjectives, "favorite" doesn't have a comparative ("favoriter") or a superlative ("favoritest") form. "Favorite" is like "unique." Both words describe something that's one-of-a-kind, different from or better than everything else like it. In a sense, they're already superlatives.

12. **A** is the correct answer. I've heard people use "throwed" in casual conversation, and you probably have too. But the correct past tense form of the verb is "threw."

13. The correct answer is **B**. The first answer, **A**, contains a sentence fragment. "And muddy"—huh? Where's the verb? Where's the noun?

14. **A** is the correct answer. You don't need "more" in the sentence.

15. **A** is the correct answer. Remember, "lie" is an action that's *done*, while "lay" is an action that's *done to*. You *lie* on the sofa, but you *lay* tiles.

Context

1. **D** is the best answer. This is the only answer that corresponds with "small" and "neat."

2. **B** is the correct answer. Even though the conjunction "and" signals a link, the verb tells you a different story. When you're rebelling, you're going *against* something. "Stingy" is the only answer that contrasts with "spending money."

3. **C** is the most logical answer.

4. **A** makes sense in context.

5. **B** is the correct answer. Only "watchful" describes the actions of someone who "takes his duties seriously."

6. **C** is the most logical answer.

7. **A** is the correct answer. "Restrained" and "uninformed" don't connect with "embarrassing," so they're out. If you picked "youthful," you're close, but no cigar. "Youthful" has positive connotations: "She retained her youthful enthusiasm," or "He has such a youthful face for his age." On the other hand, "infantile" means acting like a baby. For anyone other than a baby, that is embarrassing.

8. **B** is the correct answer. "Spoke with" makes some sense, but logically you have to acknowledge someone before you have a conversation with them.

9. **D** is the best answer. "But" signals a contrast. The only contrast with "made several stops" would be "final."

10. **C** is the best answer.

11. **D** is the most logical answer.

12. **B** is the correct answer. After a breakdown of civic order, you'd expect something much bigger and more dramatic than any of the other three answers.

13. **C** is the best answer. The only other answer that seems possible is **A**, "summary," but why would you summarize short stories?

14. **B** is the correct answer. If you're saying, "But conversation can't sparkle!" you're absolutely right, in literal terms. But in this case, the writer is using a little poetic license to emphasize the liveliness and charm of the woman's conversation.

15. **B** is the best answer.

Multiple-Choice Reading Comprehension

1. **D**

   Once you've grasped the story in the passage, check out the answer choices. **A** is wrong because the passage tells us that *Theobroma cacao* is a tropical New World tree, but that doesn't mean that this tree only grows in the tropical New World. The tree might very possibly exist in other countries. **B** contradicts the passage, which tells us that chocolate was introduced to Europe as a liquid. **C** makes an unsupported comparison. We do know that more pounds of chocolate today are produced for eating than drinking, but we have no idea how the amount of drinkable chocolate in the 1800s compares to the amount of solid edible chocolate produced today. **D** is valid: If the Swiss invented the first way to produce solid edible chocolate in the 1800s, then solid edible chocolate wasn't consumed anywhere in the 1500s.

2. **C**

   We're asked for a situation that conforms to a principle, so your best bet is to understand the principle thoroughly, and then test the choices against this understanding. The rule: A free press always reports all information about a country's military operations. There are only two cases in which this might not be true. First, if such information would jeopardize the safety of the troops. Second, if such information would jeopardize the success of a mission. We'll be looking for the answer choice that follows the rules faithfully.

   For **A** to work, you'd have to assume that dissenting opinions would jeopardize the troops and/or the success of the mission. This choice is not consistent with the principle. **B** and **D** discuss unfree presses. The rules pertain only to a free press, and we can't infer how an unfree press would behave in regard to these issues. **C** is correct because according to the principle, a free press could withhold information that endangers the troops or mission, and it's reasonable to say that the info discussed in **C** could fall into that category.

3. **C**

    This passage presents us with a list of different transportation vehicles and their definitions. With so much rather disconnected information, be prepared to refer to the passage as you comb the answer choices for a proper inference. Choice **C** is the right answer, since any jeep meeting such criteria would also fulfill all of the criteria listed in the definition of a passenger vehicle. The author never says that a vehicle can't belong to more than one category.

    A is wrong because if the automobile in question were a passenger vehicle, then it would be fully enclosed with four wheels. **B** knocks out three of the vehicles described in the passage, and chooses the fourth, but that's only valid if there aren't any other vehicle options. Nowhere does the author say that these are the only four vehicles in existence. **D** makes an unsupported comparison among the vehicles. Even if the definitions of two of these vehicles are more similar, that doesn't suggest that the vehicles themselves are necessarily more alike.

4. **A**

    Some people believe that the cooking schools in Southern France teach all there is to know about French cooking. And yet one recent graduate of a cooking school in southern France did not know how to make the ever-popular bechamel sauce. The Keyword *yet* clearly suggests the author's belief that this piece of evidence undermines the first stated conclusion. The author doesn't actually make her own conclusion. She provides evidence that would weaken the first conclusion, thereby implying her conclusion that cooking schools in southern France do not necessarily teach a student all that there is to know about French cooking. Since the author doesn't directly state her conclusion, the right answer choice will likely state that implied conclusion, as **A** does. Since the author provides an exception to the first conclusion, then it must not always be true.

    B is too extreme. All we know is that one graduate didn't know everything, so La Terrelle doesn't necessarily teach all that there is to know about French cooking. Still, some graduates could have learned everything. **C** contradicts the passage which clearly states that all of La Terrelle's branches are in southern France. As for **D**, just because La Terrelle may not teach all that there is to know about French cooking to every student, it might still provide an effective education. Incomplete does not mean ineffective.

5. **C**

The author concludes that no beef has been available in Cebra for the past six months. The evidence is the first sentence: A blight wiped out all of the town's beef supply six months ago. If we interpret **A** to mean that Cebra folks consume nothing but Cebra beef (i.e., no fruits, veggies, etcetera), then **A** is easy to dismiss—there's been no Cebra beef for six months, and these people must eat something. The more plausible reading of **A** is that the only type of beef Cebra residents consume is that raised by Cebra farmers. Still, this is going too far: Although for the past six months no non-Cebra beef has been brought into town, for all we know there was plenty of outside beef consumed in Cebra prior to the blight.

B is out because it discusses the issue of preferences. According to the author, lamb and poultry are available for consumption while beef is not. What's available is clear; what's preferred is not. **C** must be true: If the elimination of the town's beef supply means that no beef is available, then the town must have no external beef provider during the last six months. As for **D**, technically, we don't even have enough information to infer that one resident is a meat eater, although since they do have meat available for consumption, it's likely that someone's eating it. However, we certainly can't infer that most people eat the stuff—that's just going too far.

6. **A**

The author begins by concluding that cross-training is more beneficial than single-sport training for those who wish to improve their overall fitness. The author assumes a link between developing a wide range of muscles/burning calories and overall fitness, so we can check to see if any answer choice strengthens the argument by asserting that assumption. We can stop at choice **A**, since it establishes the connection between burning calories and overall fitness.

B is out since the author contrasts the benefits of two different kinds of athletic training. The fact that athletic training in general is the best way to improve overall fitness doesn't strengthen an argument that cross-training is better for fitness than single-sport training. **C** would actually weaken the argument. Tonic muscle fibers are exercised by single-sport training, so increasing their value would weaken the author's argument in support of cross-training. **D** is out because the author only considers which type of training works better to improve overall fitness in healthy people, so the danger of one type of training for those recovering from serious illness is beside the point.

7. **D**

Understanding the differences between Pran meditation and ritual meditation will be key to getting this question right. Pran meditation is different than ritual meditation because it's more highly disciplined and uniquely involves isolation and fasting. **D** is correct because, even though the author implies that ritual meditation is less disciplined than Pran, that doesn't mean that it's undisciplined.

A is out since the author states that Pran meditation is more disciplined than ritual meditation, so **A** must be true. Remember that "some" means "one or more." We have one example of less disciplined meditation and that means that some practices are less disciplined. This is a valid inference, so it's not the answer. As for **B**, the monks practice Pran meditation only when there's severe weather and, since weather isn't precisely scheduled, then Pran meditation must not be precisely scheduled either. Sure, that's an inference. As for **C**, if Pran meditation involves the unique practice of isolation, then no other meditation, including ritual meditation, involves isolation.

8. **B**

The author tells us that a high volume of pirating sales causes studios to lose a great deal of money. *However* (a Keyword that signals the discrepancy in the passage), a low volume of pirating sales generally indicates a period of economic weakness in the movie industry. Why does a low level of pirating sales, which would seem to benefit the industry, actually signal a period of economic weakness in the industry? This is the question that we need to answer, so let's look at the answer choices.

A doesn't address the issues involved in the discrepancy, focusing as it does on whether these studios distribute smaller films.

B is correct because it creates a direct connection between pirating and the financial success of the entire industry. If pirating is related exclusively to big hits, then a low level of pirating signals a lack of blockbuster hits, in which case it's more understandable how a low level of pirating would correspond to periods of economic downturns in the industry.

C is off base, focusing as it does on the methods of pirated tape production and not on the connection between pirating and the economic health of the movie industry.

D is similarly off base, since it offers a comparative analysis between the largest and not-so-large studios, which isn't a comparison relevant to the original discrepancy.

9. **D**

A survey showed that, as a group, action films were rated higher than romance films. Viewpoint number one comes from the survey organizers, who concluded from this that subject matter of popular movies must determine their appeal. Seems reasonable, but the author, making use of the contrast keyword *yet*, states that this conclusion is probably wrong and offers an alternative explanation. She notes that the producers of the action films were more experienced in successful film production. Notice that the author doesn't disagree that actions films receive better ratings, but rather supports a different explanation for that superiority; the effect is the same in both viewpoints, but the causes differ.

A confuses percentages and numbers. The survey is based on the percentage of films in each category to receive the highest rating, not on the actual number of films to receive the top rating. A lower percentage doesn't necessarily mean a lower number. **B** contradicts the author's argument: The author does suggest a relationship between previous directorial successes and the popular appeal of the survey films. As for **C**, the argument is about independent feature films. We can't infer anything about what a survey of big-budget mainstream films would show.

D's all that's left. The author suggests that having a previous hit film to the director's credit is more important than subject matter in determining ratings, so it logically follows that subject matter may not be a significant factor in the popular ratings of films made by directors with an equal number of previous hits.

10. **C**

The question asks us to locate the one answer choice that doesn't strengthen the author's argument. So we want to eliminate choices that strengthen the connection between the popular appeal of a director's film and that director's having a past hit film, as well as those that strengthen the connection between lack of a hit film and less popular appeal.

A is out. If previous hits indicate talent, then the author's theory of the link between previous hit films and popular appeal of the survey films seems more plausible, and we're more likely to believe that the organizers are wrong, as the author maintains, about the effects of subject matter. **B** and **D** strengthen the argument by tying past experience of success to present cinematic successes. **B** links previous experience to ratings directly. **D** takes it from another angle and explains that the films of first-timers do not often achieve the same popular appeal as that attained by previous hit-makers. Like **A**, these choices make it seem more reasonable to argue that the organizers have misunderstood the role of subject matter in the survey ratings. That is, they all support the author's alternative explanation.

C is correct because the reason many first-time directors don't make action films has no impact on this argument. The fact remains that of the films in this particular survey, the action films were made by more experienced directors while the romances were made by novices, and the author uses this fact to counter a previous conclusion. **C** gives us one possible explanation for this fact, but has no effect on how this fact is used by the author.

11. **D**

If 57 percent equals the same number of paintings before the unveiling as 85 percent equals after the unveiling, then Déjère must have produced more paintings in the period before the unveiling—that's the only way that the numbers could work out. **D** states this from the other angle: Déjère must have painted fewer paintings after the unveiling.

A is out because the author tells us that revenue from both periods is equal since Déjère sells the same number of paintings in both. Therefore, if she had charged more in the second period, she would have made more money than she had in the first, which would contradict the passage. Because this is inconsistent with the passage, it certainly can't be inferred from it.

B is outside of the scope since the author never mentions Déjère's motivations behind painting. Since there's no information about this, we can't reasonably concluding anything pertaining to it. If anything, **C** might suggest that Déjère sells more paintings in the second period, which the passage explicitly contradicts. Further, the passage provides no information about how art collectors might have responded to the review, giving us no basis to make a conclusion about those collectors.

12. **C**

You can view this question from a logic angle: If a client had pulled out, the company would have closed. The company didn't close, so you can infer that no major client closed his or her account. **C** takes you exactly where you want to go.

There's no information in the passage that would support **A**. It could be true, but it might not be, so we really can't infer it. **B** and **D** suggest ways in which the business might have increased in the past year. But nothing in the passage suggests that business must have increased in these particular ways.

13. **A**

The passage begins by explaining that fundraising specialists help foundations to raise much of their money, unlike financial planners who raise much less money but serve an important function as organizers. Before the blank, we see the ever-important keyword *therefore*. That means that the right answer choice will provide a conclusion based on the information thus far provided.

A is perfectly consistent with the argument and represents a logical conclusion for it. If fundraising specialists raise more funds, then it is certainly logical that a foundation seeking to raise funds should entrust such activities to those specialists. **B** is too extreme. The passage never states or supports the notion that companies lacking fundraising specialists can't still raise lots of money. **C** ranks fundraising specialists based on what knowledge they do or don't possess. The author never breaks the specialists into these groups, or provides information about the specialists in terms of their knowledge of financial planning, so the passage as it stands provides no direct support for this conclusion. **D** is out because, based on the passage, we can't tell if foundations can actually reach their goals by using specialists.

14. **C**

The author tells us that two school districts were running neck and neck until about 1990 as far as their junior high school students' reading scores were concerned. After 1990, district Y consistently took the lead. The superintendent of district Y proposes an explanation for this occurrence, attributing it to her district's reinstatement of a minimum reading requirement in the junior high schools.

A is more than we know. All we know is that district Y's average score is higher than district X's, but we were given no information to suggest that the actual average score in district Y has been increasing. **B** deals with minimum reading requirements in district X before 1990, which isn't a subject that the passage even addresses. **C** is inferable. The superintendent attributes her district's successes to the reinstated reading requirement, and these successes began in 1990. This strongly suggests that the program must have been reinstated sometime around when the change in relative average scores occurred. Otherwise, it couldn't account for the district's post-1990 achievements. This leads to **C**: If the requirement was reinstated around 1990 when district Y began to outpace district X, then it must be true that the requirement was not in effect at some point in district Y before 1990.

D discusses the possibility that there was no reading requirement in district X at some point in time. But we know nothing about district X's history with the reading requirement, so we can't infer this answer choice.

15. **C**

Follow the steps of the argument: A crisis (step 1) can lead to a decrease in people's faith in their country's leaders (step 2), which can in turn lead to violence in unspecified segments of the population (step 3). Propaganda limits the perception of the crisis, thereby keeping the first domino from falling, and so favorably impacting at least the second step in the chain. This is the author's first explanation for violence, and the propaganda solution refers only to it. The author then gives an entirely different explanation for violence, this time more specifically explaining youth violence: Youth violence is caused by boredom and lack of vision regarding a promising future. We have two paths explaining violence. Let's look at the answer choices, keeping the distinctions in mind.

A is out. While the author offers us one potential antidote to the first type of violence without making any such reference in regards to the second, that doesn't mean that there is no solution for the second type. Because something isn't mentioned, that doesn't mean it doesn't exist, so we have no way of inferring which type of violence is easier to quell.

As for **B**, propaganda alone may be enough to entirely diffuse dissent in some poor countries, possibly those without disaffected youth, or even those with disaffected youth who are not driven to dissent by such crises.

C looks good. Since the author does not directly link habitual youth violence to economic or political crises, or to the decrease in faith, which such crises create, propaganda probably doesn't decrease that violence by restoring faith in the country's leaders. The author says that habitual youth violence is not caused by a loss of such faith, so restoring the faith probably wouldn't help matters any. If propaganda helps to quell habitual youth violence, then it probably does it in some other way.

D goes too far out on a limb. The author mentions two effects of the propaganda—it downplays the extent of the crisis and restores faith in the government. However, we don't know that an alteration in people's "fundamental beliefs" is inherent in either one of these cases; we simply know that the propaganda has an effect on their immediate actions at the time of the crisis.

16. **D**

The question stem gives us the first half of an if-then statement; the correct answer will likely be the second half. So, if the editors don't receive year-end bonuses, then what do we know? Scoping out the part of the passage that deals with bonuses, we come to sentences 2 and 3. Let's see if sentence 2 helps: If circulation has increased, then editors get their bonuses. We form the opposite of an if-then statement by reversing and negating the terms, so the opposite of sentence 2 will read "if editors DO NOT get bonuses, then circulation has NOT increased." We're given the first part, the "if" clause in the stem; the second part, the "then" clause that must follow is found in correct choice **D**.

A deals with ad rates, about which we can make no inferences based on what we're told about bonuses. **B** and **C** offer the two options regarding ad pages, but neither is right because, according to what we know, ad pages might have increased or not. There's no accurate inference that we can draw on this subject based on the information we're given.

17. **D**

This question is an exercise in keeping track of the many little pieces of information given to us through the passage. Everyone in the Rubberband Club lives in state A. Everyone in the Rubberband Club has bungee jumped at least once in the past two years. The club's still chugging along, despite the fact that it's been illegal to bungee jump in state A for the past ten years. Even though it may seem like there's a possible contradiction in the passage, don't seek to resolve the seeming discrepancy; rather, remain faithful to the four primary pieces of information while searching for a proper inference.

A is too extreme. The passage doesn't tell us that they can't bungee jump in state A, but that it's illegal to do so. While each current member must have jumped in the last two years, some of them may have broken the law and jumped away in state A anyway. **B** takes us too far also: It's quite possible that one or more of the current applicants or current members took the plunge legally in the state A ten or more years ago, before the ban was enacted. **C** is too extreme. As mentioned above, while each must have jumped at least once in the last two years, they needn't have jumped in state A; perhaps they're getting all of their kicks in another state where jumping is legal.

D is perfect. If they didn't jump outside of state A, then they must have jumped within state A sometime in the last two years to fulfill the club's requirements. And if they did that, then they must have bungee jumped illegally. There are no unsupported steps in this chain of reasoning, so it's a logical inference.

18. **A**

The author states that there are fewer geniuses nowadays than there were in the seventeenth century. Despite the fact that the population was so much smaller then, the author identifies four geniuses from the period and identifies only one from the modern era who would be comparable. The argument is pretty flimsy, based primarily on assumption that it's legitimate to compare the two periods. To strengthen this argument, we'll want a choice to demonstrate that this comparison is more likely to be valid. This is where **A** works. If people are indeed able to recognize geniuses while they're alive or soon after they die, then it's more valid to compare modern genius production to seventeenth-century genius production. After all, in order to make a valid comparison about the number of geniuses by period, the author must assume that we can count them accurately, and if it took, say, a hundred years or more to recognize genius stature, then the comparison wouldn't allow the author to form the conclusion in the first sentence; we'd just have to wait and see. Maybe in the year 2100, Howard Stern will grace the genius list too.

B doesn't help the argument since the author concerns himself only with the geniuses of one certain (though undefined) stature. If anything, **B** might weaken the argument by suggesting the author's comparison is not valid. Maybe there's only one twentieth-century genius (Einstein) who's in the same category as the seventeenth-century geniuses listed, but if there are other types of geniuses besides scientists and writers to consider, the author's conclusion may be a bit hasty.

C also does nothing to help the author's case, since the author relies on a stable definition of the term genius in his argument. Throwing that definition into question would only weaken his argument.

D would only be relevant if it could be shown that extremes in educational attainment were somehow related to the development of geniuses. We have no support to make such a leap, so **D** can't assist our author here.

19. **D**

The author argues against a course of action by stressing our obligation to consider the consequences of those actions on future generations. Thus we shouldn't do something now because it'll hurt people later on. According to **D**, the morality, or rightness, of an action depends on its future consequences, which is entirely in line with the logic underlying the author's argument.

In **A** and **C**, the author doesn't suggest what should determine the legality of one's actions. According to the passage, it's legal to use the mentioned products, so what determines legality isn't the issue. **B** goes against the grain of the argument. It's legal to use the products but the author argues that they still shouldn't be used, therefore arguing that the legality of an action does not necessarily determine its morality.

20. **A**

The author here begins by explaining a certain problem that the Fines Museum had: Its totem pole was too tall to fit into the storage vault. The author argues that dividing the totem pole into two pieces will enable its storage in the vault, thereby overcoming the problem with the height of the pole. Size offered the only barrier to putting the pole in the vault, so if the pole can presently fit into the vault, it must have overcome the size problem. Accordingly, the author assumes that each piece of the separated pole can fit into the storage vault, as **A** states.

B says too much. In order for the divided totem pole to fit into the storage vault, it just needs to be short enough to fit. That may not require that it be divided into equal pieces. **C** focuses on the issue of expense, which the author never discusses. **D** strays from the main points of size and storage. The author really only cares about this particular totem pole. How its storage would affect the other pieces doesn't matter. The argument is concerned only with this pole fitting into the vault.

Book 2

Reading Comprehension and Context

An indiscriminate felony murder is a homicide that is **planned** in advance of committing the felony without a specific **victim** in mind.

The victim of an indiscriminate felony murder **is** a potential witness to the crime. The victim offers **no** apparent threat to the offender but is killed anyway. The **victim** is one of opportunity: walking into a store or **house** at the wrong time, or having a work shift **coincide** with a robbery.

There are occupations, shifts, and environments **that** elevate a victim's risk factor. Working the night shift **alone** at a 24-hour gas station or convenience store is **one** example. This situation elevates the chance of a person **becoming** a victim of felony murder, compared with the department **store** clerk who works days among many coworkers. Environmental factors that **elevate** the victim risk factor are: being in locations within **high** crime areas and working in environments that enhance crime **commission**. Crime-enhancing environments may have any or all of the **following** characteristics: views obstructed by advertising or product shelves, **poor** lighting, no alarms or intercom systems linking the establishment to **local** law enforcement stations, one-clerk staffing, especially at **night**, and quantities of cash readily available.

It is also **possible** for a victim to elevate his or her risk **by** attitude and behavior. **A** careless, naïve, or flippant approach to **personal** safety heightens the chance of being targeted for robbery and **subsequent** felony murder.

—adapted from *Crime Classification Manual: A Standard System for Investigating and Classifying Violent Crimes*, by John E. Douglas, Ann W. Burgess, Allen G. Burgess, and Robert K. Ressler

We have believed for many years that there is no group of **plants** more versatile, durable, and attractive than perennials, or plants **that** continue growing year after year. The **range** of colors, heights, bloom times, flower forms, leaf colors, and **growing** requirements is so broad that practically any desired effect can be brilliantly realized. **Whether** it's a formal flower bed, a solid planting of one or two varieties, or a wild garden at the **edge** of the woods, you can have your dream if you **choose** with care. It is, of course, an added benefit that a well-prepared **perennial** planting will perform reliably for many years, repaying your **effort** and investment, while developing your gardening skills.

In pursuit of **this** belief, and for our own **pleasure**, we have collected as large, fresh, and varied a **perennial** offering as can be found in this country. We **hope** you will take the time to explore it in detail. **With** just a few exceptions, we have chosen to draw a **distinction** between "hardy" perennials, which can survive the **cold**, or overwinter, in Zone 7 and colder, and "tender" perennials, which **cannot**. Be aware that distinctions of this kind are **intended** to serve as guides in selection, not as absolute **rules**. Gardeners in colder climates can achieve delightful results by the timely use of **tender** perennials, just as their peers in milder **climates** can often tease a year of color from plants whose natural preferences **include** a proper northern winter.

—adapted from *The White Flower Farm Garden Book,* by Amos Pettingill

POST Practice Test 2

The following test is based on the POST exam given to police officer applicants in California. The test administered by the department you're applying to might include other sections that are not represented here. Regardless of the actual form of the test you'll take, you can only help your chances by developing your skills at standardized test taking.

Give yourself a total of two hours for the following test. An answer key and explanations follow the test.

Answer Sheet for Practice Test 2

For each question, select the best answer choice. Use the answer sheet to mark your choices. An answer key and explanations follow the test.

Clarity	Spelling	Context	Multiple-Choice Reading Comprehension
1. Ⓐ Ⓑ	1. Ⓐ Ⓑ Ⓒ Ⓓ	1. Ⓐ Ⓑ Ⓒ Ⓓ	1. Ⓐ Ⓑ Ⓒ Ⓓ
2. Ⓐ Ⓑ	2. Ⓐ Ⓑ Ⓒ Ⓓ	2. Ⓐ Ⓑ Ⓒ Ⓓ	2. Ⓐ Ⓑ Ⓒ Ⓓ
3. Ⓐ Ⓑ	3. Ⓐ Ⓑ Ⓒ Ⓓ	3. Ⓐ Ⓑ Ⓒ Ⓓ	3. Ⓐ Ⓑ Ⓒ Ⓓ
4. Ⓐ Ⓑ	4. Ⓐ Ⓑ Ⓒ Ⓓ	4. Ⓐ Ⓑ Ⓒ Ⓓ	4. Ⓐ Ⓑ Ⓒ Ⓓ
5. Ⓐ Ⓑ	5. Ⓐ Ⓑ Ⓒ Ⓓ	5. Ⓐ Ⓑ Ⓒ Ⓓ	5. Ⓐ Ⓑ Ⓒ Ⓓ
6. Ⓐ Ⓑ	6. Ⓐ Ⓑ Ⓒ Ⓓ	6. Ⓐ Ⓑ Ⓒ Ⓓ	6. Ⓐ Ⓑ Ⓒ Ⓓ
7. Ⓐ Ⓑ	7. Ⓐ Ⓑ Ⓒ Ⓓ	7. Ⓐ Ⓑ Ⓒ Ⓓ	7. Ⓐ Ⓑ Ⓒ Ⓓ
8. Ⓐ Ⓑ	8. Ⓐ Ⓑ Ⓒ Ⓓ	8. Ⓐ Ⓑ Ⓒ Ⓓ	8. Ⓐ Ⓑ Ⓒ Ⓓ
9. Ⓐ Ⓑ	9. Ⓐ Ⓑ Ⓒ Ⓓ	9. Ⓐ Ⓑ Ⓒ Ⓓ	9. Ⓐ Ⓑ Ⓒ Ⓓ
10. Ⓐ Ⓑ	10. Ⓐ Ⓑ Ⓒ Ⓓ	10. Ⓐ Ⓑ Ⓒ Ⓓ	10. Ⓐ Ⓑ Ⓒ Ⓓ
11. Ⓐ Ⓑ	11. Ⓐ Ⓑ Ⓒ Ⓓ	11. Ⓐ Ⓑ Ⓒ Ⓓ	11. Ⓐ Ⓑ Ⓒ Ⓓ
12. Ⓐ Ⓑ	12. Ⓐ Ⓑ Ⓒ Ⓓ	12. Ⓐ Ⓑ Ⓒ Ⓓ	12. Ⓐ Ⓑ Ⓒ Ⓓ
13. Ⓐ Ⓑ	13. Ⓐ Ⓑ Ⓒ Ⓓ	13. Ⓐ Ⓑ Ⓒ Ⓓ	13. Ⓐ Ⓑ Ⓒ Ⓓ
14. Ⓐ Ⓑ	14. Ⓐ Ⓑ Ⓒ Ⓓ	14. Ⓐ Ⓑ Ⓒ Ⓓ	14. Ⓐ Ⓑ Ⓒ Ⓓ
15. Ⓐ Ⓑ	15. Ⓐ Ⓑ Ⓒ Ⓓ	15. Ⓐ Ⓑ Ⓒ Ⓓ	15. Ⓐ Ⓑ Ⓒ Ⓓ
			16. Ⓐ Ⓑ Ⓒ Ⓓ
			17. Ⓐ Ⓑ Ⓒ Ⓓ
			18. Ⓐ Ⓑ Ⓒ Ⓓ
			19. Ⓐ Ⓑ Ⓒ Ⓓ
			20. Ⓐ Ⓑ Ⓒ Ⓓ

Book 1

Clarity

For each question, select the sentence that is worded most clearly and correctly.

1. A. She sweared that her story was true.

   B. She swore that her story was true.

2. A. For her birthday, she asked for, a bicycle.

   B. For her birthday, she asked for a bicycle.

3. A. After they had waited for hours, he finally arrived.

   B. Finally, he arrived. After they had waited for hours.

4. A. She looked really tired.

   B. She looked real tired.

5. A. Everybody has the right to be involved.

   B. Everybody have the right to be involved.

6. A. Later that night, they danced and listened to music.

   B. Later that night, they danced and listen to music.

7. A. The water is too shallower for diving.

   B. The water is too shallow for diving.

8. A. I, was overcharged for my cappuccino.

   B. I was overcharged for my cappuccino.

9. A. There were fewer attendees at this year's luncheon than were expected.

   B. There were less attendees at this year's luncheon than were expected.

10. A. The restaurant serves regional dishes.

    B. The restaurant serve regional dishes.

11. A. Neither of them wants to go.

    B. Neither of them want to go.

12. A. Walking, is good exercise.

    B. Walking is good exercise.

13. A. The turtle seemed to change its mind, and ducked back into its shell.

    B. The turtle seemed to change it's mind, and ducked back into it's shell.

14. A. Rejection is the harder thing to take.

    B. Rejection is the hardest thing to take.

15. A. That department store is the onliest one that offers discounted prices.

    B. That department store is the only one that offers discounted prices.

Spelling

For each question, choose the correct spelling from the four answers given.

1. The professor taught _____ to a large class of freshmen.

    A. filosophy

    B. phillosphy

    C. phillosophy

    D. philosophy

2. Visiting the zoo provided an _____ lesson in ecology.

    A. interesting

    B. intresting

    C. intereseting

    D. intreseting

3. She said his beard made him look even more _____ .

   A. masculene

   B. masculine

   C. maskuline

   D. masculin

4. The former senator published all her _____ when she retired.

   A. corespondence

   B. correspondance

   C. correspondence

   D. corespondance

5. Spicy foods always burned his _____ .

   A. stomech

   B. stomack

   C. stommach

   D. stomach

6. She swore a _____ oath to tell the truth.

   A. solemn

   B. sollem

   C. solemm

   D. salom

7. His teachers complained that he was too _____ .

   A. impacient

   B. empatient

   C. impatient

   D. impatent

8. Unfortunately, the important _____ was lost in the fire.

  A. doccument

  B. dockumint

  C. dockument

  D. document

9. The meeting was _____ and successful.

  A. brief

  B. breef

  C. brefe

  D. brieph

10. They kept an air _____ in their car at all times.

  A. freshner

  B. freshiner

  C. freshener

  D. freshenar

11. Everything on the table _____ over during the earthquake.

  A. tappled

  B. toppled

  C. topled

  D. toppeled

12. People say that he is a _____ with small engines.

  A. wizzard

  B. wezard

  C. wizerd

  D. wizard

13. They were surprised by the _____ cost of their new computer.

    A. actuel

    B. actual

    C. actuil

    D. acktual

14. He is lucky to have such a _____ sense of smell.

    A. kean

    B. kene

    C. keen

    D. keane

15. The vase was the perfect _____ for carrying water from the spring to the house.

    A. vessel

    B. vesel

    C. vessell

    D. vessele

Context

For each question, select the answer closest in meaning to the underlined word in the sentence.

1. She though of their affair as <u>transitory</u>, but he wanted something permanent.

    A. permanent

    B. difficult

    C. busy

    D. short-term

2. He watched the spider <u>ascend</u> the stovepipe, toward the ceiling.

    A. circle

    B. hang from

    C. climb

    D. slide down.

3. Her pearls were <u>luminous</u> in the moonlight.
   A. large
   B. hidden
   C. tiny
   D. radiant

4. The town council had the <u>vision</u> to anticipate the possibility of flooding and make plans to prevent it.
   A. foresight
   B. time
   C. hallucination
   D. visual aid

5. She loved sitting in the rose arbor, surrounded by the flowers' strong, almost <u>tangible</u> fragrance.
   A. fragile
   B. touchable
   C. drifting
   D. rare

6. He's so <u>truculent</u> that no one can work with him for more than a few months.
   A. organized
   B. truthful
   C. soft-spoken
   D. obnoxious

7. Despite his lawyer's reassuring advice, Clarence seemed <u>troubled</u> when he left.
   A. worried
   B. pursued
   C. peaceful
   D. suspected

8. In the standard superhero story, a madman hatches a <u>diabolical</u> scheme to take over the world.

    A. fancy

    B. chemical

    C. evil

    D. space-age

9. The zoo's policy is to provide natural-seeming <u>habitats</u> for the animals, so that they feel as comfortable as possible.

    A. surroundings

    B. names

    C. vegetation

    D. meals

10. She was <u>optimistic</u> about her chances for a full recovery and began to make plans for the coming year.

    A. curious

    B. upbeat

    C. unsure

    D. apathetic

11. Because the judge ruled in Ms. Clancy's favor, Mr. Frankel must <u>compensate</u> her for the wages she lost after she was fired.

    A. calculate

    B. forgive

    C. pay

    D. multiply

12. Volunteers <u>disseminate</u> literature about the site, trying to increase attendance.

    A. distribute

    B. explain

    C. destroy

    D. fabricate

13. Because of upstream pollution, the river water is no longer <u>potable</u> and must be treated with chemicals.

    A. cool

    B. drinkable

    C. murky

    D. crossable

14. Living alone in the cabin for so long helped her develop her <u>idiosyncratic</u> style of painting.

    A. individual

    B. trained

    C. idiotic

    D. arid

15. The explosions, one at each end of the battleship, were triggered by the same device and occurred <u>simultaneously</u>.

    A. shockingly

    B. dangerously

    C. within a few feet

    D. at the same time

Multiple-Choice Reading Comprehension

Read each paragraph or passage and choose the statement that best answers the question. Choose your answer solely on the basis of the material in the passage.

1. People who play chess as a hobby should not be discouraged by the recent record-breaking season of Anatoly Krupnik, the great Russian master. By far the most important factor in determining the quality of one's game is the amount of time one puts into practicing the basics. Even Anatoly Krupnik was once an uninitiated beginner.

   Which one of the following best expresses the author's main point?

   A. Practicing the basics of chess is the best way to become a quality chess player.

   B. Although time and effort spent mastering the fundamentals is of some importance, it will not train one to play as well as Anatoly Krupnik.

   C. If one puts in enough time practicing the basics of chess, one will eventually play the game as well as Anatoly Krupnik.

   D. Regardless of how much time and effort one has put into practicing the game of chess, luck is the most important factor in determining one's eventual success.

2. There can be little doubt that electoral suffrage is power. Of course, power must be wielded with reason, and in our present society there appears to be no way to achieve this except by giving a vote to everyone. But when all have votes, it will be both just in principle and necessary in fact that some mode be adopted of giving greater weight to the suffrage of the more educated voter, some means by which the one who is more capable and competent in the general affairs of life and who possesses more of the knowledge applicable to the management of the affairs of the community, could be singled out and allowed a superiority of influence proportional to his higher qualifications.

   The author's primary purpose is to argue that

   A. not everyone should be allowed to vote

   B. not all men are equal

   C. a dictatorship is preferable to a democracy

   D. the more knowledgeable members of society should have more power at the voting booth

3. In his *History of Oracles,* de Fontanelle maintained that it was not the obvious and true facts, for which we lack a cause or explanation, that had convinced him of our ignorance, but rather the obvious falsities we take for facts, and for which we have elaborate causes and explanations. He felt the greatest indication of our foolishness was not that we lack principles and methods to arrive at what is true, but that we possess others that coexist so peacefully with what is false.

   Which one of the following can most reasonably be inferred as an opinion de Fontanelle would hold?

   A. Facts are more important than explanations or causes.

   B. We are ignorant of the true nature of the oracles of ancient Greece and Rome.

   C. The truth can be arrived at if, and only if, we have principles and methods.

   D. It is better to be ignorant of a fact, and aware of this ignorance, than in error about a fact, and unaware of this error.

Questions 4–5

One of the most striking facets of the history of jazz in America is the relationship between improvisation and band arrangement. Starting with New Orleans jazz, almost totally improvised, we come to Chicago in the thirties, where only one soloist at a time had any real freedom. In the forties, the band arrangers reigned supreme, as the big bands relied on their intricate arrangements, even for soloists. Then the pendulum swung back with bebop, and improvisation returned to the fore. In the seventies and eighties jazz pieces once again came increasingly to be written down, and performers again found themselves in a period of complicated but confining arrangements.

4. Which one of the following is probably the conclusion toward which the author is moving?

   A. Apparently, then, the history of jazz does not conform to any coherent progression of styles.

   B. These written arrangements of jazz therefore result in an unfortunate lack of freedom for the soloists.

   C. Thus, the history of jazz seems to take the shape of a cyclical movement from improvisation to arrangement and back again.

   D. It would seem, then, that jazz has been fraught with inconsistencies such as these throughout its history.

5. The author would probably argue that the next style in jazz history will be characterized by

    A. extensive improvisation

    B. intricate big band arrangements

    C. freedom for one soloist at a time

    D. written scores for soloists only

6. State legislators Peter and Jerome are sponsoring separate bills, and each is attempting to win the support of fellow legislator Harold. If Harold votes against Peter's bill, Jerome will consider withdrawing his own bill from the docket. If Harold votes for Peter's bill, then Jerome will not withdrawn his own bill but will leave it on the docket for further consideration. Harold will vote for Peter's bill only if Peter opposes Jerome's bill.

    Given the information in the passage, which one of the following must be false?

    A. Harold votes against Peter's bill, and Jerome does not withdraw his bill from the docket.

    B. Peter does not oppose Jerome's bill, and Harold votes for Peter's bill.

    C. Harold votes for Peter's bill, and Jerome does not withdraw his bill from the docket.

    D. Peter opposes Jerome's bill, and Jerome votes for Peter's bill.

7. Hypnotic drugs, which are meant to restore normal sleep patterns, sometimes accumulate in the blood and lead to insomnia. Opioid drugs, which are used to blunt sensory awareness, occasionally result in heightened tactile sensations. Stimulants designed to decrease appetite and combat fatigue can cause both fatigue and ravenous hunger.

    Which one of the following conclusions can be most reasonably drawn from the passage above?

    A. The three major categories of drugs are hypnotics, opioids, and stimulants.

    B. Regardless of their stated purpose, very few drugs have a single, easily defined effect.

    C. Hypnotic and opioid drugs tend to have effects which are the opposite of those of stimulants.

    D. Some drugs can actually have effects roughly the opposite of their usual, expected effects.

8. So long as we must offer remedial programs in our doctoral courses we cannot say that the open admissions programs in our colleges have succeeded. In fact, were our high schools more successful, we would have no need for open admissions in our colleges. We must admit that the practice of passing more people farther along into higher education has merely delayed their realization of their disadvantages rather than equalized their advantages.

    Which one of the following educational reforms would the author probably consider most beneficial?

    A. elimination of the open admissions program

    B. elimination of remedial programs at the doctoral level

    C. improvement of practices in secondary education

    D. a higher teacher-student ratio in low income areas

9. Once thought to be extinct for tens of millions of years, the coelacanth is a large, predatory fish with limblike fins. In recent years, however, a number have been found in the Indian Ocean around the Comoro Islands. Last month, a team of marine biologists found a large fish with limblike fins in the Indian Ocean.

    Solely on the basis of the statements above, it would be most reasonable to conclude that

    A. the fish found by the marine biologists may be a coelacanth

    B. if the fish the marine biologists have found is predatory, then it is a coelacanth

    C. we will never know if the fish the marine biologists have found is a coelacanth

    D. the marine biologists have either found a coelacanth or another supposedly extinct fish

10. The principal of a public elementary school complained bitterly when his school was included on a list of the fifty most academically troubled in the state. "Look around," he told reporters. "There's no graffiti in the hallways; no one is selling drugs; and math and reading scores have been going up for every grade except the fifth. Everyone on the staff here thinks it's very unfair, especially when you consider that this school didn't even have the lowest fifth-grade achievement scores in the city."

Based on the passage above, the principal most likely believes which one of the following?

A. The school in question had never been included on the list before.

B. The school in question made the list primarily because of its low fifth-grade achievement scores.

C. Students at the school in every grade except the fifth can read and do math well above their grade level.

D. Drug problems at other elementary schools in the state are much worse than those of the school in question.

11. The recent uproar against awarding Artistic Landmark status to the 19th-century courthouse on which the infamous Tweed Administration spent so much of the public's money has revealed a widespread misconception. The misdeeds of its builders—even the corrupt billing practices that so spectacularly inflated its cost—should no more keep us from honoring this magnificent example of Anglo-Italianate civic architecture than should the crimes of those tried within its walls.

With which one of the following would the author of the passage above be most likely to agree?

A. The value of a work of art is independent of the character of its creators.

B. Spending freely to create a lasting monument is no vice.

C. Monumental corruption can itself constitute an enduring work of art.

D. The lofty ethical purpose of a courthouse makes its external appearance unimportant.

12. The recent dramatic drop in nationwide unemployment has been hailed by a relieved public, but skepticism, according to informed financial experts, is the proper reaction. Yes, in the short term, reduced unemployment will benefit families, stimulate retail trade and encourage the housing industry. Experienced analysts note, however, that low unemployment over the long run can produce a competition for credit that will drive up interest rates to dangerous levels and thus cause widespread economic stagnation.

In the passage above the author argues that

A. the recent dramatic drop in nationwide unemployment is probably the most significant threat to economic stability we are likely to encounter

B. it is prudent to view declines in unemployment with caution because they can produce economic disadvantages in the long run

C. the housing industry's growth, along with stimulation of retail trade, is more significant for the overall economy than changes in unemployment statistics

D. financial experts tend to be unduly skeptical about the effects of reduced unemployment upon the national economy

Questions 13–14

The opposition party is making a blatantly sentimental and completely nonsensical appeal. They ask us to support Governor Stoppard's senatorial campaign, after his six previous unsuccessful attempts, because, "even if Stoppard is not Thomas Jefferson, he has clearly tried harder than anyone else in U.S. politics today." The Ford Motor Company tried hard to construct the Edsel, but that does not mean that we should all rush out to purchase this structurally unsound automobile.

13. Which one of the following best describes the main point of the passage above?
    A. Governor Stoppard's senatorial campaign is doomed to failure.
    B. Jefferson is superior to Stoppard as a political leader.
    C. The opposition party is confusing effort with achievement.
    D. Stoppard has not been very effective in his pursuit of a Senate seat.

14. In the author's analogy, a vote for Stoppard would correspond to
    A. a vote for Jefferson
    B. the purchase of an Edsel
    C. the Ford Motor Company
    D. the construction of an Edsel

15. Now that the holiday season has arrived there will be much more activity in our building. Thus, it is more important than ever for employees to keep an eye on their valuables and personal belongings.

    The argument above encourages the employees to make which one of the following inferences?

    A. Most thefts occur during the holiday season.

    B. Increased activity in the building will result in a greater risk of theft.

    C. The arrival of the holiday season leads most thieves to start working indoor locations.

    D. The arrival of the holiday season inevitably leads to a greater increase in the number of thefts.

16. Many a proposed economic solution to Third World payment problems can immediately be recognized as sound on purely theoretical grounds. We have found, however, that other proposals prove themselves to be beneficial only when tested in operation in a country's actual economy.

    Which one of the following can logically be inferred from the passage above?

    A. There are proposed economic solutions to Third World payment problems that can be identified as beneficial only when they are actually put into practice.

    B. Many proposed economic solutions to Third World payment problems are too purely theoretical to work in actual practice.

    C. It is likely that there are economic solutions to Third World payment problems that have not yet been conceived.

    D. Third World payment problems are less likely to be solved by purely theoretical proposals than by proposals that have been tested in operation.

17. The nuclear family, unlike society's institutional constructs in business, politics, and the military, does not derive its meaning from the written contract or the shared ideal. It is an organic institution that survives on trust and love rather than by means of legal restraint. It is a spiritual unit, not a social integer defined for the convenience of bureaucratic administration. To circumscribe family relationships, therefore, in terms more accurately applicable to the description of socioeconomic relationships is to deny the family its fundamental rights. To constrain the actions of family members toward each other, purely upon the basis of society's needs, is to attack the very existence of the family as an autonomous institution.

    The main point of the argument above is that

    A. the nuclear family is no longer able to compete as an institution with the institutions of business, politics, and the military

    B. those who attack the existence of the family are unlikely to believe in spiritual attachments or in the importance of trust and love

    C. legal restraint is likely to be necessary when family members deny each other a fundamental right

    D. the institution of the family should not be defined or dealt with as if it were a socioeconomic institution set up for society's convenience

18. Alaska, Wyoming, North Dakota, and South Dakota, all states with cold climates, have small populations. Nevada, a state with a warm climate, has a small population. Massachusetts, a state with a cold climate, has a large population. The state of Florida, which has a warm climate, has a large population.

    Which one of the following best expresses the main point of the statements made above?

    A. Large populations are a result of neither warm nor cold climates.

    B. Large populations are not a result of warm climates.

    C. Large populations are a result of cold climates.

    D. Large populations are not a result of cold climates.

19. Music should achieve much more than mere stimulation of the emotions or evocation of the pictorial. Melody, harmony, and instrumentation do, of course, satisfy the esthetic sense, but, in order to be more than mere entertainment, they must appeal to the listener's innate sense of order and capacity for intellectual play. If a composition truly deserves the name "masterpiece," it will answer the demands of logic and architectural construction, speaking with precision to the brain before pandering to the vaguer needs of the heart.

Which one of the following is implied by the passage above?

A. The importance of melody, harmony, and instrumentation as components in the composition of great music has been overrated.

B. Music cannot stimulate the emotions and the intellect simultaneously.

C. An esthetic sense is best described as an appropriate combination of an innate sense of order and a capacity for intellectual play.

D. Truly great music appeals first and foremost to the intellect.

20. Politicians who believe that the graduated income tax is needlessly complex and expensive to administer in its present form are strongly urging the adoption of a flat-rate tax, a more manageable system which would involve taxing all citizens at the same rate regardless of their income level. Opponents of this demonstrably regressive scheme argue that, since such a system would be inherently unjust to people at the lower end of the economic scale, who are forced to devote a larger portion of their income to life's necessities than those who are more affluent, it would not serve the aims of taxation in a democracy—namely, the sharing of the costs of society on the basis of one's ability to pay.

Which one of the following is the main point of the opponents' argument?

A. A demonstrably regressive system of taxation is unlikely to be more efficient in operation than a graduated system.

B. It is more important that a system of taxation in a democracy be just than that it be inexpensive to administer.

C. Although it is desirable to have society's wealthiest members shoulder a greater share of the tax burden, it is also needlessly complicated.

D. It is impossible to devise a system of taxation that would be fairer and more democratic than the graduated income tax system.

Book 2

Reading Comprehension and Context

In the following two passages, certain words have been deleted. Write the missing word in the appropriate blank. The number in parentheses indicates the number of letters in the missing word. Note: A word may be used in your answers more than once.

Passage 1

On September 3, 1821, a hurricane moving up the _____ (5) from Cape Fear made landfall near New York City, and _____ (9) north well into New England. Soon after the _____ (5) a thirty-two-year-old man named William Redfield, _____ (3) of a long-dead sailor, took a trip on horseback _____ (7) Connecticut and happened to notice something unusual in the _____ (9) around him. Near Canaan, in northernmost Connecticut, the trees _____ (3) fallen in a direction exactly opposite that of the toppled trees he had seen _____ (7) south.

After his return _____ (4), Redfield made a careful study of the hurricane. He _____ (9) fragments of detail about the storm from newspapers, letters, _____ (5) logs, and other sources, and in the process became the _____ (5) man to track a hurricane from first sighting to _____ (4). His interest expanded to include other hurricanes, which he _____ (7) with equal zeal. His first paper, "On the Prevailing _____ (6) of the Atlantic Coast," appeared in 1831 in the *American Journal* _____ (2) *Science*, and quickly became a classic of meteorology. He _____ (9) that there could be only one explanation for the _____ (8) patterns of damage he had encountered: "This storm was exhibited in the form of a great whirlwind."

Redfield's careful research _____ (6) the attention of a British naval officer, Lt. Col. William Reid, _____ (3) had been dispatched to Barbados to supervise reconstruction _____ (5) in the wake of a disastrous 1831 hurricane which _____ (6) over fifteen hundred people. Reid too became obsessed with _____ (10).

—adapted from *Isaac's Storm: A Man, a Time, and the Deadliest Hurricane in History,* by Erik Larson

Passage 2

Victimology is often one of the most beneficial investigative _____ (5) used in classifying and solving a violent _____ (5). It is also a crucial part of crime analysis. _____ (7) victimology, the investigator tries to evaluate why this particular _____ (6) was targeted for a violent crime. Very often, just _____ (9) this question will lead the investigator to the motive, _____ (5) will lead to the offender.

Was the victim known _____ (2) the offender? What were the victim's chances of _____ (8) a target for violent crime? What risk did the _____ (8) take in perpetrating this crime? These are some of _____ (3) important questions investigators should keep in mind as _____ (4) analyze the crime.

One of the most important aspects of classifying an _____ (7) and determining the motive is a thorough understanding of all offender _____ (8) with the victim (or, in the case of arson, the targeted _____) (8). With a sexual assault, this exchange between the victim _____ (3) offender would include verbal interaction as well as _____ (8) and sexual activity.

The tone of exchange between an offender and a _____ (6) of sexual assault is extremely helpful in directing the _____ (12) to an appropriate classification. Excessively vulgar or abusive_____ (8), scripting, or apologetic language: Each of these is common _____ (2) a certain type of rapist.

Victimology is the *complete history* of _____ (3) victim. (If the crime is an arson, that victimology _____ (8) targeted property.) A comprehensive victimology should include as much information _____ (2) possible on the victim.

—adapted from *Crime Classification Manual: A Standard System for Investigating and Classifying Violent Crimes,* by John E. Douglas, Ann W. Burgess, Allen G. Burgess, and Robert K. Ressler

POST Practice Test 2 Answers and Explanations

ANSWER KEY

Clarity	Spelling	Context	Multiple-Choice Reading Comprehension
1. B	1. D–philosophy	1. D	1. A
2. B	2. A–interesting	2. C	2. D
3. A	3. B–masculine	3. D	3. D
4. A	4. C–correspondence	4. A	4. C
5. A	5. D–stomach	5. B	5. A
6. A	6. A–solemn	6. D	6. B
7. B	7. C–impatient	7. A	7. D
8. B	8. D–document	8. C	8. C
9. A	9. A–brief	9. A	9. A
10. A	10. C–freshener	10. B	10. B
11. A	11. B–toppled	11. C	11. A
12. B	12. D–wizard	12. A	12. B
13. A	13. B–actual	13. B	13. C
14. B	14. C–keen	14. A	14. B
15. B	15. A–vessel	15. D	15. B
			16. A
			17. D
			18. A
			19. D
			20. B

EXPLANATIONS

Book 1

Clarity

1. The correct answer is **B**. The past tense form is "swore." "Sweared" might cut it in conversation—maybe—but never in writing.

2. The correct answer is **B**. You don't need that second comma in **A**.

3. The correct answer is **A**. There's a sentence fragment in **B**: "After they had waited for hours . . ." what? You need to connect it to the guy's arrival.

4. The correct answer is **A**. The writer wants to emphasize how tired the woman appears to be. To do that, you need to use an adverb. You remember adverbs—they modify or add details to adjectives or verbs. Generally speaking, you change an adjective to an adverb by adding the suffix "-ly." "Real" becomes "really."

5. The correct answer is **A**. Even though "everybody" may mean "a whole bunch of people," it's considered a singular noun, so it takes the singular verb form—"has." Remember that the pronouns containing "body" or "one" are singular: *anyone, no one, anybody, everybody.*

6. The correct answer is **A**. Both verbs need to agree in tense.

7. The correct answer is **B**. You use the endings "er" and "est" only when you're comparing things. There's no comparison here.

8. The correct answer is **B**. There's no reason for that comma after the "I" in **A**.

9. The correct answer is **A**. Use "fewer" when you're talking about individual units: in this case, attendees. Use "less" when you're talking about something that's presented as a whole: "There was less involvement at this year's luncheon." So you'd have fewer drops, but less water; fewer quarters, but less money. Got it?

10. The correct answer is **A**. Because the subject, "restaurant," is singular, the correct verb form is "serves."

11. The correct answer is **A**. "Neither" is always singular. Don't get thrown off by the plural "them" just before the verb.

12. The correct answer is **B**. Why use that comma in **A**?

13. The correct answer is **A**. The possessive form of "it" is "its." No apostrophe. "It's" is a contraction of "it is."

14. The correct answer is **B**. When you're making comparisons, use the "-er" ending when you're talking about two specific things: "Rejection is harder to take than indifference." Here, the author is comparing rejection to all other possible things, so the superlative, with "-est" ending, is correct.

15. The correct answer is **B**. The correct form of the adjective is "only." Maybe you hear "onliest" and maybe you say it, but don't ever write it.

Context

1. **D** is the best answer. The conjunction "but" signals a contrast. The best contrast to "permanent" is "short-term."

2. **C** is the only answer that indicates movement toward the ceiling

3. **D** is the best answer. Only "radiant" relates to moonlight.

4. **A** is the correct answer. Only "foresight" indicates anticipation.

5. **B** is the correct answer. Of course, you can't really touch a fragrance; that's why the writer used "almost," to show it's a deliberate exaggeration, not reality.

6. **D** makes sense in context.

7. **A** is the best answer. "Despite" tells you to look for a contrast to "reassuring." The best one is "worried."

8. **C** is the correct answer.

9. **A** is the correct answer.

10. **B** is correct.

11. **C** is the best answer.

12. **A** makes sense in context.

13. **B** is the correct answer. Treating water doesn't make it cooler, or clearer, or easier to get across.

14. **A** makes sense in context.

15. **D** is most logical.

Multiple-Choice Reading Comprehension

1. **A**

   The author is making the point in **A**, that practicing the basics is what will improve your chess game. **B** says that no matter how much you practice, you'll never be as good as Krupnik, the master. There is no hint of that pessimism in the argument. **C** reverses **B** and implies that enough practice guarantees skills as good as those of Krupnik. Again, no such claim is made. And **D** completely contradicts the author's point. The author considers practice the most important factor, not luck.

2. **D**

   The author argues that not all votes should be weighed equally. Those who are most knowledgeable should be entrusted with greater decision-making power. So **D** provides the author's primary purpose. **A** is incorrect because the author says that everyone in this society should be given a vote, but **A** suggests that not everyone should be allowed to vote. **B** is an assumption of the argument, rather than something the author tries to prove. By advocating a weighted voting system on the basis of how "capable" and "competent" an individual is, the author assumes that these people are not equal. The author never discusses the benefits of dictatorship, **C**.

3. **D**

   De Fontanelle's conclusion is that we human beings are ignorant and foolish. If the possession of false ideas is his ground for judging us foolish, rather than our not possessing certain truths, de Fontanelle must assume choice **D**, that humble ignorance is better than unknowing error. Since he assumes **D** in his argument, it is an opinion he is likely to hold. Choices **A** and **C** are too strong. Nowhere does he stress the importance of either facts or explanations over the other, as in **A**. **C** makes a claim that the author actually contradicts in the last sentence. **B** draws a conclusion about his view on oracles, but nowhere does the passage mention this view.

4. **C**

   The author's first statement in the paragraph contains the essence of his argument, that there is a relationship between improvisation and band arrangement (or written music) in American jazz. The most probable conclusion for this argument must be **C**, which involves the cyclical movement of improvisation and arrangement that the author has noted. **A** is the opposite of **C** and denies the author's evidence. **B**, with the word "unfortunate," is outside the argument because the author is not commenting on the merits of improvisation versus arrangements. **D** contains the word "inconsistencies," whereas our author points to a relationship that shifts, not one that contains internal contradictions.

5. **A**

We are asked here about what the author would probably predict for the next period of jazz. Since his point is about the cyclical nature of jazz, and the last period of jazz has been characterized by "confining arrangement," we can conclude that we are probably entering a period of improvisation. Choice **A**, then, is correct. **B** is the same thing as "complicated but confining arrangements," the same style that is in vogue now. We are asked what the author believes will be the *next* style, and we have no evidence to support the conclusion that the next style will be the same as the present one. **C** was only one aspect of the arranged music emanating from Chicago in the '30s. Besides, this style was said to follow a period of total improvisation, not total arrangement. **D** comes out of left field. The author mentions no such phenomenon in his survey of jazz history.

6. **B**

You're looking for the statement that "must be false," which means inconsistent with, contradictory to, the statements. The three wrong choices, then, can or must be true. Sentences 2 and 3 tell us the outcome if Harold votes against Peter's bill and if he votes for it, whereas Sentence 4 gives us a condition necessary (note the "only if") for Harold to vote for Peter's bill. It can be translated as "If Harold votes for Peter's bill *then* Peter will oppose Jerome's bill," and the contrapositive would read "If Peter doesn't oppose Jerome's bill, then Harold will not vote for Peter's bill"—something that's directly contradicted by **B**. You might've found that directly, or just recognized that the other four choices are consistent with the paragraph. **A** is trickiest: If Harold votes against Peter, then (says Sentence 2) Jerome will consider withdrawing his bill; but in the end he could, as **A** suggests, decide against withdrawing. **C** is simply Sentence 3 in action. **D** brings in Jerome's vote, and that's not mentioned in the paragraph.

7. **D**

The most reasonable conclusion is choice **D**, which pretty much just says that some drugs can have effects the opposite of those intended. We can't conclude, as **A** says, that these three types of drugs are the three major types. **B** is out since for all we know, most drugs may have such a single effect, and only these three types do not. **C** wants us to conclude that since opioid drugs are used to blunt sensory awareness, they tend to have the effects of increasing appetite and inducing sleep (that is, the opposite effects of stimulants). Well, not necessarily. If you chose **C**, you were using outside information. It could be that opioids are used to decrease appetite, just like stimulants.

8. **C**

Which reform would the author think *most* beneficial? In the passage, the author says "were our high schools more successful, we would have no need for open admissions," so presumably he or she would like to see an improvement in secondary education, and that's the reform in **C**. **C** is correct. **D** is the second-best answer, since it has to do with improving education at the precollege level, but there's nothing in the passage to show that the author thinks a "higher teacher-student" ratio will necessarily result in improvement. **A** and **B** recommend harsh measures that might cover up the problem, but not solve it. **C** would solve it.

9. **A**

The passage says that coelacanths still exist, and gives us a general description of this fish. It is large, predatory, and has limblike fins. We're told that a number have been found around some islands in the Indian Ocean. We're not told, though, that all the coelacanths have been found there. Neither are we told that only coelacanths meet this description. We are also told that a team of biologists has found a fish in the Indian Ocean. This fish has some of the attributes of the coelacanth, but we aren't told whether it is predatory. The most reasonable conclusion is choice **A**. The description of the newly found fish doesn't contradict that of the coelacanth; there's no reason why it can't be a coelacanth. But since we don't know if it is predatory, and we don't know about other traits of coelacanths that haven't been discussed, we have no way of knowing that it is a coelacanth. So this fish might be a coelacanth. Choice **B** is incorrect because it just matches the newly found fish to the description of the coelacanth. But there may be many other types of fish that fit this general description, and the newly found fish may be one of those other types. Choice **C** is too pessimistic. Just because we can't tell from the bare facts given whether or not the fish is a coelacanth does not mean that we will never know. And **D** is wrong because the fish could be something other than a coelacanth, yet not a fish that is thought to be extinct.

10. **B**

The principal makes it clear that he feels his school was listed as academically troubled because of its low fifth-grade test scores. He points out that achievement scores for all the other grades have been going up, and other schools in the city have lower fifth-grade scores. So the answer is **B**. Whether the school had ever made the list before is irrelevant, since the principal's point is that the school does not deserve to be listed now. So **A** is incorrect. As for **C**, the principal may very well believe that students not in fifth grade are exceeding expectations for their grade level; but he may not. He says only that their reading and math scores are going up. We can't reasonably infer that he believes his students are performing "well above their grade level." Nor can we reasonably infer from the principal's statement about the lack of drugs in his school that the principal thinks drug problems at other elementary schools are much worse than at his school, as in **D**.

11. **A**

The author argues here for landmark status for a building that has corrupt associations. In his view, the "magnificent" architecture should be preserved no matter how the edifice was built or what has taken place there over the years. In other words, as stated in **A**, the esthetic value of the Tweed courthouse is something to be respected no matter who created the building. Choice **B** goes too far; just because corruption has in this instance resulted in the building of an architectural wonder is not reason to decide that "free spending" that results in the creation of magnificent architecture is always a moral activity. For choice **C**, there is no justification in the passage. The author sees no art in the corruption that produced the courthouse, only in the courthouse itself. Choice **D** is contradicted by the passage. It's the external appearance of the courthouse that the author finds important. And he mentions its purpose in a negative light, by emphasizing that it is a place associated with the trials of criminals.

12. **B**

The passage argues that, as experts advise, we should react skeptically toward the recent nationwide drop in unemployment despite its short-term benefits. **B** is the correct answer because the author argues against too much optimism: he agrees with the experts who say that declines in unemployment can cause other problems in the long run. The author's caution is a far cry from the alarms sounding in choice **A**. The author isn't saying that a decline in unemployment could be the worst thing that ever happened to us. **C** distorts the second sentence of the passage. The author mentions growth in the housing industry and the retail trade as being caused by the drop in unemployment. But **C** attempts to persuade us that the author is arguing that the growth in housing and retail is separate from the drop in unemployment, and more important to the overall economic picture. If the author were arguing choice **D**, he or she would be trying to convince us that the experts are wrong. Just the opposite is true.

13. **C**

The opposition argues that Stoppard should be elected senator because, even if he's no Jefferson, he's tried harder to be elected than anyone else. The author's main point is that the fact that Stoppard has put a lot of effort into becoming a senator doesn't prevent him from being a lousy choice. So **C** is correct. The main point isn't choice **A**, because he never says that Stoppard's campaign is doomed, just that it's idiotic. While the author probably believes choice **B**, that Jefferson was a superior political leader, it's not his main point. The same goes for **D**. No one would dispute that Stoppard is a six-time loser. But the author's point is that his present campaign's appeal is nonsensical.

14. **B**

The author is making the point that no one should vote for Stoppard just because he works hard to get elected. The analogy used is that you wouldn't go buy an Edsel simply because Ford put a lot of time into constructing the car. So a vote for Stoppard corresponds to choice **B**, buying an Edsel. Choice **A** is wrong because the comparison of Stoppard to Jefferson is made by the opposition, not the author. Choice **C**, the Ford Motor Company, might correspond to Stoppard or his campaign, but the Company itself does not correspond to a vote for Stoppard. Constructing an Edsel, choice **D**, and the Edsel itself, choice (E), correspond to Stoppard's campaign and Stoppard himself, respectively. Neither corresponds to a person's voting for Stoppard; only purchasing an Edsel does this.

15. **B**

The argument concludes that it is now more important for employees to keep an eye on their possessions. The evidence presented is that the holiday season has arrived and there will be more activity in the building. The author must be assuming choice **B**. **B** says that an increase in building activity entails a greater risk of theft. The greater risk of theft implies that possessions should be watched more closely, which is the conclusion. The wrong choices all confuse the importance of the onset of the holidays. The argument doesn't imply that most thefts occur during the holiday season, choice **A**, just that the threat of theft is greater than usual. Neither is **C** assumed. Maybe the potential thieves have always worked indoors, just not in this building. In that case, the increased activity could reflect some of these thieves moving to this particular building.

As for **D**, it's not the holiday season that increases the risk of thefts; it's the increased activity that the holiday season brings with it.

16. **A**

According to the passage, there are at least two types of sound economic solutions to Third-World payment problems—those recognizable as such on theoretical grounds, and those proved to be sound only when put into practice. It is reasonable to infer choice **A**, which rephrases the second point: Solutions do exist whose soundness can be demonstrated only when they are actually tried out. Choice **B** is out. It's possible that this statement could be true, but on the basis of the information in the passage, we can reasonably infer only that some proposed economic solutions may be found unworkable when tested in actual practice. We have no reason to assume that many proposals fail or that they fail because they are "too purely theoretical." **C** seems reasonable enough. But the idea is not suggested by the passage, which focuses on the two types of solutions that have existed without addressing the possible existence of other solutions. Choice **D** also adds an element not found in the passage. The passage distinguishes between the two types of economic proposals without saying that one is better.

17. **D**

Every sentence of the passage is concerned with describing the nuclear family and distinguishing it from other socioeconomic institutions. The family is a spiritual unit surviving on love and trust, while military and political institutions depend on legal contracts and bureaucratic administration. The point is that the family shouldn't be defined in the same terms, choice **D**. Nowhere does the passage describe the family as being in competition with other institutions; so **A** is incorrect. **B** is wrong, since the passage is mainly about the undesirability of applying institutional terms and criteria to the family, not about the possible beliefs of people who do so. And **C** twists around information in the passage by saying that legal restraints should be applied to families, rather than restricted to other socioeconomic institutions.

18. **A**

The paragraph presents evidence concerning seven states. The evidence concerns the relationship, or lack thereof, between size of population and climate. We're given examples of states with cold climates and low populations (Alaska); we're given an example of a state with a cold climate and high population (Massachusetts); we're given an example of a state with a warm climate and low population (Nevada); and we're given an example of a state with a warm climate and a high population (Florida). So the best conclusion from this information, the main point that it is working towards, is that there isn't a causal relationship between climate and population. Large populations are not the result of either type of climate. This is expressed in choice **A**. Choice **C** is wrong because Massachusetts disproves it. Choices **B** and **D**, each express half of the main point—that large populations aren't due to warm climates, choice **B**, or cold climates, choice **D**. The main point is that large popuations aren't due to either climate, which is expressed in **A**.

19. **D**

The last sentence of this passage clues you in to the idea that this author believes that, while good music should appeal to both the brain and the heart, it should speak first to the intellect and then to the emotions. Melody and harmony are all right for "mere entertainment," but the use of "mere" indicates that this author believes there is a higher, prior function of music. So **D** is correct. **A** is wrong because it is not the importance of melody, harmony, and instrumentation *per se* that has been overrated; it's the importance of the *esthetic appeal* of these that's been overrated. **B** is contrary to the passage. The author feels that good music should stimulate both the emotions and the intellect simultaneously. **C** misdefines "esthetic sense," for the passage contrasts an esthetic sense, which appeals to the emotions, with an innate sense of order, which appeals to the intellect.

20. **B**

These opponents are arguing against a flat-rate income tax. Their complaint is that such a tax would be unjust, since it would shift an unfair burden of the costs of society onto the poor. Proponents of the flat-rate tax argue that it is less complex and more manageable to administer. The proponents talk about convenience; the opponents respond by talking about justice. Clearly the opponents believe, choice **B**, that justice is a more important factor in assessing a tax system than is convenience. **A** is an argument that opponents could make, but it's not one that these particular opponents make. **C** is an argument that the proponents, not the opponents, might make. **D**'s too strong. The opponents are not saying that the graduated income tax system is the most democratic system around; they're only saying that it is more democratic than a flat-rate tax.

Book 2

Reading Comprehension and Context

On September 3, 1821, a hurricane moving up the **coast** from Cape Fear made landfall near New York City, and **continued** north well into New England. Soon after the **storm** a thirty-two-year-old man named William Redfield, **son** of a long-dead sailor, took a trip on horseback **through** Connecticut and happened to notice something unusual in the **landscape** around him. Near Canaan, in northernmost Connecticut, the trees **had** fallen in a direction exactly opposite that of the toppled trees he had seen **farther** south.

After his return **home**, Redfield made a careful study of the hurricane. He **collected** fragments of detail about the storm from newspapers, letters, **ships'** logs, and other sources, and in the process became the **first** man to track a hurricane from first sighting to **last**. His interest expanded to include other hurricanes, which he **pursued** with equal zeal. His first paper, "On the Prevailing **Storms** of the Atlantic Coast," appeared in 1831 in the *American Journal of Science*, and quickly became a classic of meteorology. He **concluded** that there could be only one explanation for the **changing** patterns of damage he had encountered: "This storm was exhibited in the form of a great whirlwind."

Redfield's careful research **caught** the attention of a British naval officer, Lt. Col. William Reid, **who** had been dispatched to Barbados to supervise reconstruction **there** in the wake of a disastrous 1831 hurricane which **killed** over fifteen hundred people. Reid too became obsessed with **hurricanes**.

—adapted from *Isaac's Storm: A Man, a Time and the Deadliest Hurricane in History*, by Erik Larson.

Victimology is often one of the most beneficial investigative **tools** used in classifying and solving a violent **crime**. It is also a crucial part of crime analysis. **Through** victimology, the investigator tries to evaluate why this particular **person** was targeted for a violent crime. Very often, just **answering** this question will lead the investigator to the motive, **which** will lead to the offender.

Was the victim known to the offender? What were the victim's chances of **becoming** a target for violent crime? What risk did the **offender** take in perpetrating this crime? These are some of **the** important questions investigators should keep in mind as **they** analyze the crime.

One of the most important aspects of classifying an **offense** and determining the motive is a thorough understanding of all offender **activity** with the victim (or, in the case of arson, the targeted **property**). With a sexual assault, this exchange between the victim **and** offender would include verbal interaction as well as **physical** and sexual activity.

The tone of exchange between an offender and a **victim** of sexual assault is extremely helpful in directing the **investigator** to an appropriate classification. Excessively vulgar or abusive **language**, scripting, or apologetic language: each of these is common **to** a certain type of rapist.

Victimology is the *complete* ***history*** of **the** victim. (If the crime is an arson, that victimology **includes** targeted property.) A comprehensive victimology should include as much information **as** possible on the victim.

—adapted from *Crime Classification Manual: A Standard System for Investigating and Classifying Violent Crimes*, by John E. Douglas, Ann W. Burgess, Allen G. Burgess, and Robert K. Ressler

POST Practice Test 3

The following test is based on the POST exam given to police officer applicants in California. The test administered by the department you're applying to might include other sections that are not represented here. Regardless of the actual form of the test you'll take, you can only help your chances by developing your skills at standardized test taking.

Give yourself a total of two hours for the following test. An answer key and explanations follow the test.

Answer Sheet for Practice Test 3

Use the answer sheet to mark your choices for the multiple-choice questions. An answer key and explanations follow the test.

Clarity	Spelling	Context	Multiple-Choice Reading Comprehension
1. Ⓐ Ⓑ	1. Ⓐ Ⓑ Ⓒ Ⓓ	1. Ⓐ Ⓑ Ⓒ Ⓓ	1. Ⓐ Ⓑ Ⓒ Ⓓ
2. Ⓐ Ⓑ	2. Ⓐ Ⓑ Ⓒ Ⓓ	2. Ⓐ Ⓑ Ⓒ Ⓓ	2. Ⓐ Ⓑ Ⓒ Ⓓ
3. Ⓐ Ⓑ	3. Ⓐ Ⓑ Ⓒ Ⓓ	3. Ⓐ Ⓑ Ⓒ Ⓓ	3. Ⓐ Ⓑ Ⓒ Ⓓ
4. Ⓐ Ⓑ	4. Ⓐ Ⓑ Ⓒ Ⓓ	4. Ⓐ Ⓑ Ⓒ Ⓓ	4. Ⓐ Ⓑ Ⓒ Ⓓ
5. Ⓐ Ⓑ	5. Ⓐ Ⓑ Ⓒ Ⓓ	5. Ⓐ Ⓑ Ⓒ Ⓓ	5. Ⓐ Ⓑ Ⓒ Ⓓ
6. Ⓐ Ⓑ	6. Ⓐ Ⓑ Ⓒ Ⓓ	6. Ⓐ Ⓑ Ⓒ Ⓓ	6. Ⓐ Ⓑ Ⓒ Ⓓ
7. Ⓐ Ⓑ	7. Ⓐ Ⓑ Ⓒ Ⓓ	7. Ⓐ Ⓑ Ⓒ Ⓓ	7. Ⓐ Ⓑ Ⓒ Ⓓ
8. Ⓐ Ⓑ	8. Ⓐ Ⓑ Ⓒ Ⓓ	8. Ⓐ Ⓑ Ⓒ Ⓓ	8. Ⓐ Ⓑ Ⓒ Ⓓ
9. Ⓐ Ⓑ	9. Ⓐ Ⓑ Ⓒ Ⓓ	9. Ⓐ Ⓑ Ⓒ Ⓓ	9. Ⓐ Ⓑ Ⓒ Ⓓ
10. Ⓐ Ⓑ	10. Ⓐ Ⓑ Ⓒ Ⓓ	10. Ⓐ Ⓑ Ⓒ Ⓓ	10. Ⓐ Ⓑ Ⓒ Ⓓ
11. Ⓐ Ⓑ	11. Ⓐ Ⓑ Ⓒ Ⓓ	11. Ⓐ Ⓑ Ⓒ Ⓓ	11. Ⓐ Ⓑ Ⓒ Ⓓ
12. Ⓐ Ⓑ	12. Ⓐ Ⓑ Ⓒ Ⓓ	12. Ⓐ Ⓑ Ⓒ Ⓓ	12. Ⓐ Ⓑ Ⓒ Ⓓ
13. Ⓐ Ⓑ	13. Ⓐ Ⓑ Ⓒ Ⓓ	13. Ⓐ Ⓑ Ⓒ Ⓓ	13. Ⓐ Ⓑ Ⓒ Ⓓ
14. Ⓐ Ⓑ	14. Ⓐ Ⓑ Ⓒ Ⓓ	14. Ⓐ Ⓑ Ⓒ Ⓓ	14. Ⓐ Ⓑ Ⓒ Ⓓ
15. Ⓐ Ⓑ	15. Ⓐ Ⓑ Ⓒ Ⓓ	15. Ⓐ Ⓑ Ⓒ Ⓓ	15. Ⓐ Ⓑ Ⓒ Ⓓ
			16. Ⓐ Ⓑ Ⓒ Ⓓ
			17. Ⓐ Ⓑ Ⓒ Ⓓ
			18. Ⓐ Ⓑ Ⓒ Ⓓ
			19. Ⓐ Ⓑ Ⓒ Ⓓ
			20. Ⓐ Ⓑ Ⓒ Ⓓ

Book 1

Clarity

For each question, choose the sentence that is most clearly and correctly worded.

1. A. It is wrong to assumption things about people.
   B. It is wrong to assume things about people.

2. A. We promised to be together always.
   B. We promised to be to gether always.

3. A. The court's ruling is final.
   B. The courts ruling is final.

4. A. We bought four pounds a bananas.
   B. We bought four pounds of bananas.

5. A. The final lap, was the most strenuous.
   B. The final lap was the most strenuous.

6. A. They're going to the beach this summer.
   B. Their going to the beach this summer.

7. A. We couldn't resist the smell of the rich stew and, ate two bowls apiece.
   B. We couldn't resist the smell of the rich stew, and ate two bowls apiece.

8. A. The view from here are marvelous.
   B. The view from here is marvelous.

9. A. He wondered what went wrong.
   B. He wandered what went wrong.

10. A. There was too much pepper in the gumbo.

    B. There was to much pepper in the gumbo.

11. A. If, I die, please feed my cats for me.

    B. If I die, please feed my cats for me.

12. A. Far from home. There is a canyon.

    B. Far from home, there is a canyon.

13. A. He intended to return the book that he had borrowed from Mary and me.

    B. He intended to return the book that he had borrowed from Mary and I.

14. A. He's the tallest boy in the sixth grade.

    B. He'd the tallest boy in the sixth grade.

15. A. Her's is the brown suitcase.

    B. Hers is the brown suitcase.

Spelling

For each question, choose the correct spelling from among the four answers.

1. During the fight, he badly bruised his _____ .

    A. nuckle

    B. knuckle

    C. knukle

    D. nuckel

2. Soda fountains _____ mixtures of carbonation and flavored syrup.

    A. dispens

    B. despense

    C. dispense

    D. dispents

3. She got the promotion because she was honest, experienced, and _____ .

    A. savy

    B. savie

    C. savey

    D. savvy

4. After school, they went to the _____ to study.

    A. libary

    B. library

    C. librery

    D. librarie

5. The trash floated _____ .

    A. donstream

    B. downstreem

    C. dowstream

    D. downstream

6. Some of the older chairs on the porch were too _____ to be used anymore.

   A. rickety

   B. rickaty

   C. ricty

   D. rictey

7. To celebrate their anniversary, they went on a _____ .

   A. picknick

   B. picnic

   C. picnick

   D. picknic

8. When they went camping, they took a small portable _____ .

   A. ginerator

   B. generater

   C. gennerator

   D. generator

9. Caution should always be taken when handling _____ materials.

   A. corrosive

   B. corosive

   C. corossive

   D. carrosive

10. The pilgrims were asked to _____ before the shrine.

    A. neel

    B. kneal

    C. kneel

    D. neal

11. His _____ suit looks nice with his green shirt and aqua tie.

    A. bayge

    B. beige

    C. baige

    D. beyge

12. Flossing is an important part of maintaining good _____ health.

    A. orel

    B. orral

    C. oral

    D. orall

13. _____ products, like piano keys and figurines, are made from elephant tusks.

    A. Ivory

    B. Ivery

    C. Ivvary

    D. Ivary

14. The king is that country's _____ ruler.

    A. soveren

    B. sovereign

    C. sovren

    D. soverin

15. The city's population _____ many times over the years.

    A. mulltiplied

    B. multiplied

    C. multeiplied

    D. multiplide

Context

1. He does not believe in curfews or strict rules, and gives his son a lot of <u>latitude</u>.

   A. attitude

   B. freedom

   C. ignorance

   D. rebellion

2. The widow's cries of <u>lamentation</u> echoed throughout the church.

   A. sorrow

   B. indignation

   C. satisfaction

   D. discomfort

3. An <u>assemblage</u> of mismatched furniture filled the living room.

   A. set

   B. handful

   C. collection

   D. assessment

4. The driver used a <u>circuitous</u> route, trying to make sure no one followed them.

   A. spherical

   B. roundabout

   C. double-jointed

   D. well-marked

5. Her behavior was so <u>flagrant</u>, it almost seemed that she wanted to be caught.

   A. rapid

   B. graceful

   C. obvious

   D. sneaky

6. Worn out by the strike, the owner <u>acquiesced</u> to the union's demands.

    A. replied

    B. agreed

    C. referred

    D. denied

7. The <u>scurrilous</u> rumors involving his innocent children offended the candidate more than anything else.

    A. flattering

    B. faint

    C. contradictory

    D. offensive

8. She <u>defied</u> the teacher's order to return to her desk and was promptly sent to the principal's office.

    A. understood

    B. disobeyed

    C. noticed

    D. internalized

9. He is an <u>avid</u> reader of mystery novels; as soon as he finishes one, he starts another.

    A. reluctant

    B. indifferent

    C. enthusiastic

    D. weird

10. The right half of the sculpture looked like a reflection of the left half; it was a perfect example of <u>symmetry</u>.

    A. good taste

    B. interpretation

    C. balance

    D. confusion

11. Even after she explained her reasoning, he could not <u>fathom</u> her decision.

    A. understand

    B. oppose

    C. fund

    D. record

12. She was so slender and <u>lithe</u> that it was easy to believe she was a classical ballerina.

    A. small

    B. graceful

    C. nervous

    D. flashy

13. Always <u>circumspect</u>, she took her time making any decision.

    A. asleep

    B. alone

    C. cautious

    D. surrounded

14. He suffered a <u>grievous</u> loss when his wife died after a long illness.

    A. painful

    B. exhausting

    C. hopeful

    D. mysterious

15. His plan was so <u>asinine</u>, it was hard not to laugh in his face.

    A. reasonable

    B. ridiculous

    C. unearthly

    D. incomplete

Multiple-Choice Reading Comprehension

Read each paragraph or passage and choose the statement that best answers the question. Choose your answer solely on the basis of the material in the passage.

1. It has long been recognized that people eat for many reasons other than merely to satisfy hunger. A group of scientists investigating nonphysiological motivations for eating found a considerable difference between the eating patterns of obese individuals and those of normal-weight individuals. In one study, overweight subjects who listened to a detailed description of a food subsequently ate far more of that food than they usually did. Normal-weight individuals, meanwhile, displayed no change in their consumption levels after hearing the same description. Normal-weight subjects also ate as many nuts from a dimly lit dish as from a brightly lit dish. Obese subjects, on the other hand, ate twice as many nuts from the dish on which bright lights had been focused.

   Which one of the following is the most reliable conclusion to be drawn from the differences observed between obese and normal-weight individuals?

   A. Obese subjects' eating habits are more easily influenced by external cues than are those of normal-weight subjects.

   B. Normal-weight individuals eat less than do those who are obese.

   C. Obese individuals depend on food to satisfy emotional and psychological, rather than physiological, needs.

   D. Obese individuals have more acute senses than do normal-weight individuals.

2. Ptolemy was the first person to describe planetary orientation in terms of epicyclical motion, providing a foundation for the science of astronomy. At first this might seem to undermine the status of Copernicus, whose cosmological observations in the Renaissance earned him the epithet "father of modern astronomy." On closer consideration, however, the validity of Copernicus's celebrity is borne out: Ptolemy's model of planetary motion described a geocentric universe, in which the earth was the stationary element around which epicyclical motion took place. However, Copernicus's vision of a heliocentric universe, in which rotational movement takes place around the sun, was an important advance that allowed modern astronomy to proceed rapidly to its current advanced state.

   The author makes which one of the following arguments?

   A. If Ptolemy had not created the concept of epicyclical planetary motion, observations would not have been possible.

   B. Ptolemy's model of the universe, though important, is too unlike our present model to be considered truly modern.

   C. Ptolemy, the first proponent of epicyclical motion as the basis of universal order, is more deserving than Copernicus of the title "founder of modern astronomy."

   D. Copernicus's revision and reorientation of Ptolemy's model of the universe made possible the development of modern astronomy.

3. Very often one hears a person who has become famous or successful in their field of endeavor say that they "knew it all along." Although there may be a bit of rosy hindsight in such a claim, the fact remains that self-confidence is an indispensable component of success.

   The author of the passage above would most likely agree with which one of the following?

   A. It is not possible to become successful in one's field of endeavor unless one has a certain amount of self-confidence.

   B. Self-confidence is an innate trait, and cannot be influenced by such factors as environment and circumstance.

   C. What famous and successful people claim, and what is actually the case, are very often two different things.

   D. Although there may be successful people who are self-confident, there are many more self-confident people who are not successful.

4. The reputation of psychoanalysis continues to grow more tarnished, not because analysis is not a useful tool in certain circumstances, but rather because its application to certain people and situations is so often irrelevant—as irrelevant as an economic solution to a problem, such as a neurotic fear of success, that would be better addressed through psychoanalysis.

   The author probably believes that the reputation of psychoanalysis will worsen

   A. if it continues to fail to apply economic solutions to economic problems

   B. unless it is applied only to situations to which it is appropriate

   C. unless psychoanalysts come to understand the interrelationships among various academic disciplines

   D. unless it restricts itself to neuroses such as the fear of success

5. I believe the prime point of attack is in the educational media. Textbooks are visual disasters, as are educational films, buildings, and exhibits. Throughout their educational experience, our children are given an appreciation for literature, but never for art. One course in kindergarten, one field trip to a museum in high school, and one art appreciation course in college can hardly do the job, much less make up for the damage along the way. Imagine confining literature just to libraries visited only on field trips, or allowing the better literary works of man only one college semester in which to meet each new generation.

It can be inferred that the principal target of the author's attack is the

A. teaching of great works of literature in a single semester

B. lack of emphasis on art appreciation throughout the entire educational system

C. making of literature available only in libraries

D. usual approach to teaching art in kindergarten

6. Correlations between extended north-south strips of low magnetism on the ocean floor and heavily traveled whale navigation routes offer strong evidence that whales rely on magnetic fluctuations for directional guidance. Indeed, the majority of whale strandings analyzed in a recent study occurred near offshore magnetic anomalies.

If the statements in the passage above are true, which one of the following draws the most reliable conclusion from the passage?

A. Atypical magnetic patterns can mislead whales into entering too-shallow coastal waters.

B. Most whale strandings occur when whales leave the safety of the well-traveled north-south routes in search of higher magnetism.

C. Undersea routes that are heavily traveled by whales typically display high fluctuations in magnetic field.

D. Stretches of low magnetism on the ocean floor attract whales because they usually signal good feeding areas.

7. Despite the wide variety of so-called cold remedies on the market today, no genuine cure for the common cold exists; pills and liquids can offer only suppression of the overt symptoms of a cold, which must run its sometimes protracted course. Recent research involving chemically impregnated tissues has yielded interesting results, however. When cold sufferers sneeze into tissues treated with virus-killing liquids, the particles that would otherwise spread the cold to susceptible bystanders are to a large extent neutralized.

The passage above suggests that if the chemically impregnated tissues are used so as to capture droplets emitted when cold sufferers sneeze, they would be more effective than over-the-counter cold remedies in

   A. relieving the sore throat and swollen membranes common to many cold sufferers

   B. preventing the skin irritations sometimes caused by virus killers

   C. curing colds without harmful side effects

   D. reducing the spread of colds within a community

8. Those who sweepingly deplore conformity should take a closer look at how much the actual working of society, in the millions of fleeting interactions that occur each day, depends on unthinking and uncoerced adherence to rules of behavior. Waiting in line, sharing the sidewalk with other pedestrians, ordering coffee in a restaurant, even the self-proclaimed nonconformist shapes his behavior according to societal norms—and expects others to do so as well. That different rules govern comparable interactions in other societies is of no comfort to one whose own deeply embedded rules are challenged.

The passage above argues that

   A. nonconformists should reject even the societal norms that govern waiting in line

   B. conformity to social norms must be consciously sought

   C. conformity, on a certain level, is an essential aspect of living in a society

   D. society should develop stricter rules for behavior in public places

9. The earth's resources are currently endangered because of the method used for approaching environmental problems. Most pollution issues are viewed as the responsibility of a particular region or country. What government officials too often forget is that the earth is not physically divided along political boundaries. Air pollution may originate in the United States, but fall as acid rain somewhere in Canada. Governments, if they are at all attentive to pollution problems, spend much of their time quibbling about who should be held accountable for the problems, rather than working cooperatively to solve them.

The author of this passage argues that

   A. the only governments that have been successful in combating pollution problems are those that have devoted attention and resources to solutions

   B. the majority of acid rain reduction plans have failed because they were not specific in defining the problem and its possible solutions

   C. irrelevant issues of accountability have made countries less likely to accept proposals from others on combating pollution problems

   D. environmental issues are global and therefore require detailed, comprehensive solutions involving many countries

10. The common objection offered to the claim that "extrasensory perception" is within the realm of human potential points out that very few of us can show evidence of having ESP. This is true, but nonetheless trivial. Many persons who are ambidextrous do not discover their ability until an injury to their "strong" hand forces them to use their "weak" hand.

Which one of the following best describes the reason for the author's belief that the objection offered to ESP is trivial?

   A. We may all have untapped potentials of which we are unaware.

   B. Ambidexterity is a manifestation of psychic power.

   C. Psychic powers can only be discovered under circumstances of hardship.

   D. Everyone is ambidextrous, yet few people know this about themselves.

11. Municipal imposition of rent controls, designed to hold rents down during periods of housing shortages, can protect tenants from paying inordinate amounts of rent for decent housing. But in an era of rapid inflation like our own, high costs for fuel and maintenance can pose severe financial strain on landlords with fixed rent rolls. During such periods of economic hardship most landlords choose to defer all but the most vital building repairs before eliminating their own profit margin.

Which one of the following offers the most appropriate conclusion to the author's argument?

A. Decent housing is thus a relative concept, determined only by individuals choosing among options circumscribed by economic and technological factors in a society.

B. Landlords, who are categorically opposed to rent control because it inhibits their free reign over profits, should therefore defer maintenance in order to draw attention to what they deem to be unfair municipal regulations.

C. Thus, the construction of new housing would be a far more effective solution to shortages in available housing than the imposition of rent controls.

D. Rent control, which is intended to sustain fair market rents when decent housing is hard to find, can thus have the effect of actually lowering the quality of city housing.

Questions 12–13

One can only be thankful that Allen Ginsberg's great work, *Howl*, is beginning to gain long overdue critical recognition as one of the most innovative poems of the 20th century. Although many readers had been put off by the poem's energy and inventiveness, contemporary critics see in *Howl* that admixture of passion and disillusionment so unique to the modern American psyche. Even a poem as important as Eliot's *Waste Land* seems merely an echo of its literary antecedents when compared with *Howl*.

12. Which one of the following, if true, would most weaken the author's claim?

A. Some well-known critics have not changed their previously low assessment of *Howl*.

B. Although they agree that *Howl* is the first poem of its kind, many critics find *The Waste Land* more important.

C. In most recent critical opinion, *Howl* is strikingly similar in style, content, and use of language to the work of the 19th-century American poet, Walt Whitman.

D. Many scholars believe that the reason for the notoriety of Ginsberg's poem resides in its hedonistic content rather than in its actual value as a work of art.

13. The author of the passage would most likely agree with which one of the following opinions?

    A. All poems of merit eventually receive the appropriate acclaim.

    B. Initial critical reaction is usually a poor indication of a poem's worth.

    C. Passion and disillusionment are unique to 20th century poems.

    D. The initial reception of Ginsberg's poem *Howl* did not fully recognize its merit.

14. Our government guarantees us the right to worship in any way we want and yet this right is denied daily. School teachers are forbidden to lead all their students in collective prayer, even if the great majority of students in the class are religious in one way or another. The government is contradicting its promise of freedom of worship for all.

    The author of the above argument is logically committed to the view that

    A. atheism cannot be considered a religion and so is not protected under any guarantee of worship

    B. public worship does not amount to a repudiation of the doctrine of the separation of church and state

    C. if we allow religious freedom to wane, our other basic freedoms will soon be in jeopardy

    D. compelling someone to be present during the prayer does not violate that person's right of freedom of worship

15. Researchers have discovered a high correlation between skin cancer and the use of oil-based suntan lotion. On the basis of this finding, the lab recommended that all oil-based lotions be removed from the market. Despite the lab's implication that using these lotions causes skin cancer, however, the connection between using lotion and developing cancer becomes problematic when one considers that both may be effects produced by the same cause. It is known that excessive exposure to sunlight can lead to skin cancer. It should therefore come as no surprise that _____ .

    Which one of the following would most logically conclude the paragraph above?

    A. people who spend comparatively large amounts of time in the sun without the protection of suntan lotions are more likely than others to develop skin cancer

    B. the Central Laboratory has misinterpreted its data and come to a conclusion that is detrimental to the suntan lotion industry

    C. as a group, users of suntan lotion, most of whom spend inordinate amounts of time in the sun, have a high incidence of skin cancer

    D. the Central Laboratory emphasizes the dangers of using suntan lotion while ignoring the dangers of spending too much time in the sun

16. When parents allow their children to spend a large amount of time watching television, those children see many more images of violence than do children who watch very little television. The more violent images a child sees, the more violent that child will become. The more violent a child is, the more likely the child is to commit crimes as an adult. Thus, if parents permit their children to watch a lot of television, it is more likely that those children will grow up to be criminals.

    If the statements in the passage above are true, which of the following must also be true?

    A. If a child sees more images of violence on television, the likelihood of that child committing crimes as an adult increases.

    B. If parents did not allow their children to watch television, juvenile delinquency would be unlikely.

    C. No children will develop an aversion to violence if they are permitted to watch television.

    D. The more the parents in a particular family discourage their children from watching television, the more likely the children in that family are to become criminals.

Questions 17–18

We may define simple, cognitive apprehension as a mental state comprising nothing more than the conception of something, and lacking the holding of a belief about the thing, the passing of a judgment on the thing, or anything else extraneous to conceiving the thing in question. If we meant this to be a strict definition, one might reasonably respond that conception and apprehension are merely synonyms, and that we might just as easily define mental conception by cognitive apprehension. Yet, it must be remembered that a verbal definition of the mind's simplest operations cannot be derived with real exactitude. To perceive these operations with true clarity we must examine them as they occur in our own minds.

17. The main point of the passage above is that

    A. an exact understanding of simple mental operations can only be gained from examining one's own mind

    B. language obscures many distinctions that are vital to philosophic and psychological inquiry

    C. the highest orders of cognition cannot be expressed in human language

    D. one can define mental conception by mental apprehension as easily as one can define mental apprehension as mental conception

18. Which of the following can be most properly inferred from the passage above?

    A. Introspection is sufficient to derive the definition of any mental state or act.

    B. Beliefs and judgments about a thing inevitably obscure one's conception of that thing.

    C. Simple, cognitive apprehension does not require a belief in the existence of the apprehended object.

    D. Mental operations can be defined according to virtually any criteria.

19. Over-the-counter pain killers that contain two or more active ingredients may be harmful to users, according to a recent study. Drug products containing a single analgesic, such as aspirin or acetaminophen, appear to produce little or no risk; however, those that contain a combination of these ingredients may produce a form of kidney disease when taken over an extended period of time. Some experts estimate that as many as 400 out of every 20,000 cases of kidney failure reported annually may be caused by overuse of analgesic compounds.

    Which one of the following conclusions is most supported by the passage?

    A. It is safe to take a pain killer containing a single analgesic over a long period of time.

    B. People who take compound analgesics for extended periods of time will eventually suffer from kidney disease.

    C. Pain killers should only be taken for short-term illnesses.

    D. Restricting the availability of certain over-the-counter pain killers could reduce the rate of kidney disease.

20. Parents are generally responsible for imparting to their children basic survival techniques—how to cross the street, what to eat, what to wear when it's cold outside. More importantly, however, they should help children to develop the ability to reason and care for themselves. If parents are to prepare their children for the life ahead of them, they must treat these children not as playthings who will always be around, but rather as thinking, unique individuals in their own right.

    Which of the following is most clearly implied by the passage?

    A. Good parenting includes cultivating independent reasoning skills.

    B. Developing the capacity to think independently is dependent on having responsible parents.

    C. Parents should use disciplinary measures that teach their children how to be responsible for themselves.

    D. Parents should not tell their children how to behave.

Book 2

Reading Comprehension and Context

In the following two passages, certain words have been deleted. Write the missing word in the appropriate blank. The number in parentheses indicates the number of letters in the missing word. Note: A word may be used in your answers more than once.

Passage 1

The term "dangerous classes" has been used throughout history to _____ (8) individuals who are deemed a threat to law and _____ (5). Initially, the term described the environment in which one _____ (5), not the type of crime committed. An example of _____ (4) occurred in England in the mid-15th century, at the _____ (3) of the Hundred Years' War with France. Thousands of defeated English _____ (8) were demobilized, with none of the traditional spoils of _____ (3); at the same time, farmers were being pushed _____ (3) of their lands by changing economic conditions and property _____ (4). The homeless population skyrocketed. Because of their rootlessness and _____ (7), these people were considered the "dangerous class," and punishment for _____ (3) crime was severe. In the early 16th century, during the _____ (5) of Henry VIII, 72,000 major and _____ (5) thieves were hanged. Under Henry's daughter Queen Elizabeth I, vagabonds _____ (4) strung up in rows, as many as 300 or 400 _____ (2) a time. In this society, there was no _____ (7) at rehabilitation; the concept didn't exist.

This approach to _____ (11) and dealing with offenders began to change in 1838. _____ (4) year, the winning entry at the French Academy of Science and Politics _____ (3) titled, "The Dangerous Classes of the Population in Great Cities, and the Means of _____ (6) Them Better." "Dangerous class" was then used to describe individuals who were _____ (9) or who had the potential to become criminals, based on _____ (5) behavior; the term was no longer applied to all _____ (7) of certain social classes.

Later in the 19th century, the new field of statistics permitted a _____ (10) of crimes with factors such as race, age, sex, education _____ (3) geography. Cesare Lombrosos, a famed Italian physican, generally is _____ (8) with launching the scientific era of criminology. In 1872 he identified _____ (4) types of criminals: the born criminal, the insane criminal, the criminal by passion, the habitual criminal, and the occasional criminal.

> —adapted from *Crime Classification Manual: A Standard System for Investigating and Classifying Violent Crimes*, by John E. Douglas, Ann W. Burgess, Allen G. Burgess, and Robert K. Ressler

Passage 2

The crime scene of an organized offender suggests that _____ (4) sort of order was maintained before, during, and after _____ (3) offense. This sense of methodical organization suggests a carefully _____ (7) crime which includes the goal of deterring detection.

Although _____ (3) crime may be planned, the victim is often a _____ (8), someone targeted because he or she is in a _____ (10) location staked out by the offender. The victim _____ (7) a victim of opportunity; there is no personal connection _____ (7) the victim and the offender. Victims of serial murderers _____ (3) share common characteristics. The offender often has a preference _____ (3) a specific type of victim and thus may spend _____ (12) time searching for the "right" victim. As one offender _____ (4), "I'm a night person. Plenty of times that I _____ (4) out looking, but never came across anything, and just _____ (4) back home. I'd sit waiting and as I was _____ (7), I was reliving all the others." Common characteristics of _____ (7) selected by a specific murderer may include age, appearance, _____ (10), hairstyle, and lifestyle. Targeted victims of convicted serial murderers _____ (8) adolescent male youths, hitchhiking female college students, nurses, women _____ (11) bars, women sitting in automobiles with a male _____ (9), and solitary women driving two-door cars.

—adapted from *Sexual Homicide: Patterns and Motives,* by
Robert K. Ressler, Ann W. Burgess, John E. Douglas

POST Practice Test 3 Answers and Explanations

ANSWER KEY

Clarity	Spelling	Context	Multiple-Choice Reading Comprehension
1. B	1. B–knuckle	1. B	1. A
2. A	2. C–dispense	2. A	2. D
3. A	3. D–savvy	3. C	3. A
4. B	4. B–library	4. B	4. B
5. B	5. D–downstream	5. C	5. B
6. A	6. A–rickety	6. B	6. A
7. B	7. B–picnic	7. D	7. D
8. B	8. D–generator	8. B	8. C
9. A	9. A–corrosive	9. C	9. D
10. A	10. C–kneel	10. C	10. A
11. B	11. B–beige	11. A	11. D
12. B	12. C–oral	12. B	12. C
13. A	13. A–Ivory	13. C	13. D
14. A	14. B–sovereign	14. A	14. D
15. B	15. B–multiplied	15. B	15. C
			16. A
			17. A
			18. C
			19. D
			20. A

EXPLANATIONS

Book 1

Clarity

1. The correct answer is **B**. The correct word is the verb "assume." The word "assumption," in A, is the noun form of "assume."

2. **A** is the correct answer. "Together" is one word, and it's never divided, as it is in **B**, into "to" and "gether."

3. **A** is the correct answer. "Court's" is the proper possessive form of the word "court." "Courts" is the plural form, and is used incorrectly in place of the possessive in **B**.

4. The correct answer is **B**. The correct word is the preposition "of." In spoken English, "pounds of" can sound like "pounds a," but that doesn't make it correct when you're writing.

5. The correct answer is **B**. In **A**, the comma between "lap" and "was" is unnecessary.

6. **A** is the correct answer. The contraction of the words "they" and "are" is "they're." This is the correct word choice for the subject of the sentence. "Their" is a possessive pronoun, and is used incorrectly in **B**.

7. The correct answer is **B**. In **A**, the comma is misplaced. It should occur, as in **B** between "stew" and "and."

8. The correct answer is **B**. Since the subject, "the view," is singular, the correct verb form is "is."

9. **A** is the correct answer. The correct verb is "wondered." "Wandered" means to have traveled or moved around aimlessly

10. **A** is the correct answer. In **B**, the preposition "to" is used incorrectly. The correct word is the adverb "too."

11. The correct answer is **B**. In **A**, the comma between "if" and "I" is unnecessary and incorrect

12. The correct answer is **B**. There is a sentence fragment in **A**.

13. **A** is the correct answer. Since the objective case is indicated by the preposition "from," the correct pronoun is "me." A good way to figure out which pronoun to use is to just drop the words between the pronoun and the preposition. So in this case, you'd choose between "from me" and "from I." It's easier to see which one is correct this way.

14. **A** is the correct answer. "He's" is the correct contraction, as it combines the words "He" and "is." In **B**, the contraction of "He" and either "had" or "would" is used incorrectly.

15. The correct answer is **B**. "Hers" is the correct form of the possessive pronoun. "Her's" is not a word.

Context

1. **B** is correct.

2. **A** fits best in the context.

3. **C** is the correct answer.

4. **B** is the correct answer. This is a case where you can get closer to the meaning by linking the unfamiliar word to familiar ones. "Circle" and "circuit" are similar words, and both describe something enclosed, looping back on itself in some way. That helps you eliminate the incorrect answers. (Note that the route *couldn't* be spherical, unless the driver were orbiting the planet.)

5. **C** is the only answer that makes sense in the context.

6. **B** is the best answer. If the owner is worn out, you'd expect him to do something to end the strike—like give in.

7. **D** makes sense in context.

8. **B** is the correct answer.

9. **C** is the best answer.

10. **C** makes the most sense. We can't really judge taste here; interpretations can vary; the description doesn't make the sculpture sound confusing.

11. **A** is the best answer. "Even after" tells us to expect a contrast or contradiction. The only answer that *might* work is **C**, "fund," but that's a stretch. The more logical answer is "understand."

12. **B** is the correct answer. This is the only answer that definitely describes a ballerina's movements or appearance.

13. **C** is the only logical answer.

14. **A** is the best answer. You might have had to use process of elimination here. "Hopeful" is definitely out, and the death wasn't a mystery. A loss like this can be exhausting, but it's *always* painful.

15. **B** is the correct answer. Only a ridiculous plan would tempt you to laugh.

Multiple-Choice Reading Comprehension

1. **A**

   The experiments showed that obese people ate differing amounts with and without
   certain influences (spotlights, luscious descriptions, etcetera); normal-weight people,
   on the other hand, ate the same amounts with and without the influences. **A** sticks as
   close to the observed results as possible. It makes no claims as to why these observed
   differences exist between obese and normal-weight people; it just states the facts. **C** and
   D, which present guesses on the "why" of the observed results ("emotional needs,"
   "more acute senses," etcetera), are not as reliable as is **A**. And we have no grounds to
   conclude **B**. We have no comparison between actual amounts eaten by the two groups,
   just a comparison between what each group ate with and without external influences.

2. **D**

   Don't let the scientific details obscure the fact that the author believes Copernicus to be
   deserving of the title "father of modern astronomy." The author holds that "the validity
   of Copernicus's celebrity is borne out," however, because his reorientation of the
   Ptolemaic model (from geocentric to heliocentric) was "an advance that allowed
   modern astronomy to proceed." So **D** is the best description of the author's argument.
   A is too extreme—the author does believe that Copernicus owes much to Ptolemy, but
   not that Copernicus couldn't have developed his own theories without Ptolemy's
   precedent. The author may well believe what **B** says, but the actual argument is about
   why Copernicus is the father of modern astronomy, not about how far we've come
   from Ptolemy's model of the universe. **C** is contradicted by the author's stated belief
   that Copernicus deserves the title he has been given.

3. **A**

   The author of the argument says that although there is a bit of after-the-fact confidence
   in statements like "I knew it all along," eventual success *requires* self-confidence. The
   author, then, would agree with **A**, which says exactly this: Success requires self-
   confidence. We have no idea of what the author would think of **B** because it explains
   the origins of self-confidence, something the author never touched upon. **C** plays off
   the author's small concession to rosy hindsight. **C** exaggerates, however, by suggesting
   that the successful very often lie outright. **D** suggests the author's views on whether or
   not most self-confident people are successful. For all we know the author may believe
   that very *few* self-confident people are unsuccessful.

4. **B**

The author argues that psychoanalysis suffers because it is applied to situations where it is not applicable or relevant. She compares this irrelevant invoking of psychoanalysis to the absurdity of treating a neurosis via an economic approach. The reputation of psychoanalysis will continue to worsen, then, unless its application is confined to those situations to which it is truly appropriate, choice **B**. **A** and **C** confuse the author's method of argument with the content of her argument. The subject of this argument is psychoanalysis, not economics. Any choice that suggests that there is any other relationship between these two disciplines must be incorrect. **D**, the fear of success, is just one example of a problem that psychoanalysis might be appropriately applied to. There is nothing in the author's argument to suggest that only neuroses such as fear of success are appropriate to psychoanalysis.

5. **B**

The author argues that more attention should be paid to teaching people about the visual arts in school. He makes this point by comparing the teaching of literature with the teaching of visual arts. Since an appreciation for literature is taught *throughout* school, an appreciation of visual art should also be taught throughout school. Thus, **B** is correct. Choices **A** and **C** confuse the author's main subject with his supporting evidence. He is not arguing that literature should be taught less, but rather that art should be taught more. **D** is too specific to be the correct answer.

6. **A**

The author clearly feels that a strong case can be made that normal patterns of magnetism in the ocean are used by whales as directional signals. Changes in these patterns (or what he terms "magnetic anomalies") would, like a disturbance in any man-made guidance system, cause confusion. We can conclude that, for whales, the danger of being stranded would occur if magnetic anomalies near the shore fooled them into thinking that they are on course, when they're sliding into too-shallow coastal waters. This conclusion is found in **A**. **B** is out. In the first place, there's no support for the idea that whales seek out the magnetic anomalies; for another thing, there's no reason to conlude that such anomalies would always be characterized by magnetism higher than the "low magnetism" of the navigation routes. As for **C**, the author has told us only that low magnetism is typical of the north-south routes and that whales navigate by sensing magnetic fluctuations. Do the strips of low magnetism fluctuate themselves, or does the whale measure the fluctuation between the strip and an adjacent part of the ocean? We're told. Anyway, we are given no reason to believe that the fluctuation must be high. Choice **D** is wrong because it introduces a concept that isn't brought up or suggested in the passage.

7. **D**

The author claims that the common cold is susceptible to no known cure; such over-the-counter remedies as pills and liquids merely suppress the overt symptoms of the disease. She does note, however, that particles that can spread the cold to others are largely neutralized if the cold sufferer sneezes into tissues impregnated with virus-killing chemicals. In other words, as phrased in **D**, the use of such tissues might very well reduce the spread of colds within a community; they would certainly be "more effective than over-the-counter remedies" in this aim, since we are told that such products have the sole effect of relieving symptoms. As for **A**, the tissues have no effect upon the sufferer's symptoms, while over-the-counter remedies relieve common symptoms. In **B**, an idea is introduced that has not been mentioned or suggested by the author. Choice **C** goes too far. The tissues have caused "interesting results," but there is still no cure for the common cold. The additional idea that the supposed cure has no "harmful side effects" is meaningless.

8. **C**

As expressed in choice **C**, the passage is an argument for the social necessity of a certain level of conformity. **A** is the opposite of what the author thinks; he clearly believes that everyone should see the virtue of accepting and following such societal norms as waiting in line. The author does not mention the idea expressed in choice **B**. Instead, he suggests that conformity comes naturally to any member of society. As for **D**, the author neither praises nor questions the particular rules of any particular society.

9. **D**

The danger to resources is posed by the world's approach to pollution issues; nations quibble over who is responsible rather than working together to protect an environment. Since the author's emphasis throughout is on this theme of sharing, the best answer will likely advocate multinational cooperation in order to solve a multinational problem; and that is **D**. Since the author never explicitly mentions any country that has succeeded in solving its pollution problems his main point can't be **A**. **B** focuses on the "acid rain" details, which are offered as an example of how pollution problems are indeed global; the author's point is broader than that one example. **C**'s out because the point is not that the countries in question get stubborn and defensive and refuse to share solutions; the point is that the countries must share the responsibilities for the solutions, which is what correct choice **D** states.

10. **A**

The argument concludes that an objection offered to ESP, that too few people seem to have it, is true but trivial. The evidence supporting the objection is that few people manifest psychic powers. Thus, the objection runs, ESP can not truly be considered "within the realm of human potential." The assumption made by the objection is that since few people manifest psychic powers, few people actually possess psychic powers. This the author points out and denies with her analogy about ambidextrous people: Many were ambidextrous but didn't know it, or manifest it. So the author's reason for considering the claim that few people manifest ESP to be trivial is **A**. We may all have potentials, such as ambidexterity or psychic powers, yet simply be unaware of these potentials. **B** and **D** are wrong in linking what is said about psychic powers and ambidexterity.

11. **D**

Logically, the author has to take all the data about landlords and tie it back to the rent control issue. If landlords are hurt by high fuel and maintenance costs, a rent increase would cover those costs—but rent control won't permit an increase. Therefore, the landlord must delay most repairs and let the property decline. In this way **D** touches on all the points brought up in the paragraph and shows how they interrelate in a paradox. **A** makes it seem as if the topic of the paragraph were "decent housing," when in fact the topic is "the impact of rent control on landlord behavior." **B** takes the side of the landlords, supporting their withholding of repairs as an effort to gain publicity, but the author's tone is strictly neutral throughout, acknowledging difficulties faced by *both* tenants and landlords. The paragraph does suggest that the current rent-control system is somewhat faulty, but **C**'s recommendation of building new housing comes out of nowhere; by the end of the paragraph we're prepared for a summary of rent control's drawbacks but not for an alternative strategy.

12. **C**

The author's claim is that *Howl* is beginning to gain long overdue critical recognition as an innovative poem. The evidence behind this claim is that contemporary critics are starting to see it as expressing something unique to the modern American psyche, something that makes Eliot's famous work appear to be little more than an echo of his predecessors' works. **C** would weaken the argument by showing that poems basically similar to *Howl* were composed in the 19th century. This would damage the claim in the evidence that Ginsberg's poem expresses something unique and innovative. **A** is not a good weakener because what "some" critics still feel is irrelevant as long as some others are starting to appreciate the work. The reason the poem is notorious has nothing to do with the argument, so **D** is incorrect. As for **B**, the fact that many critics find another work to be more important need not detract from the author's claim that *Howl* is more innovative.

13. **D**

The author would certainly believe that *Howl* deserved more acclaim than it first received. Otherwise he could not call the work's newfound recognition "long overdue." **A** and **B** are too general to be inferred. The author may well believe that some good poems never get their appropriate acclaim, or that sometimes the initial critical reaction to a poem is perfectly correct. **C** is also too broad. The author recognized a particular "admixture" of these two themes, not the two themes themselves, as unique to the modern American psyche. The argument dealt only with *Howl*, so choice **D** is the best.

14. **D**

When you are "logically committed" to a view, it amounts to saying that that view is an assumption you must be making in the course of your argument. This author believes the notion that "freedom of worship for all" is violated when the government forbids a teacher to lead the whole class in prayer, given that most students are "religious in one way or another." But what will happen to the nonreligious students who would be forced to stay in the room during such a group prayer? The author must be assuming that those students' rights will not be violated, so **D** is a view to which the author is "logically committed." Students' possible atheism, **A**, is not an issue; the author believes that the rights of nonreligious students will not be violated. As for the issue of "separation of church and state," **B**, we don't know the author's view on that matter. Nor are we given evidence pointing to any fears on the part of the author about future jeopardization of other freedoms, **C**.

15. **C**

The author tells you that the researchers think the lotion causes skin cancer, but she has a different idea. She says that using the lotion and contracting skin cancer both may be symptoms produced by a completely separate cause. The passage tells you that excessive exposure to sunlight causes skin cancer. Thus, excessive exposure to sunlight must be that common cause, the thing that accounts for both the use of suntan lotion and skin cancer. **C** makes it clear that overexposure to the sun is what causes the apparent link between the use of suntan oil and skin cancer. **A** misses the point of the passage by suggesting a negative relationship between the use of suntan lotion and skin cancer. **B** is out because there's nothing here to imply that it's to be expected that the researchers would misinterpret data. **D** suggests that there *are* dangers associated with using suntan lotion, but the point of the passage is that there aren't necessarily any dangers associated with lotion use.

16. **A**

The point of the passage's argument is that the more TV a child sees, the greater are the chances of the child becoming violent and criminal. But the argument leaves open the possibility that other factors can cause an increase in violence. For this reason we can toss out **B**. **B** infers that delinquency is unlikely if children's TV viewing is restrained. Not necessarily; other factors may make delinquency just as likely. **C** is too strong a conclusion. The argument just claims that more TV violence leads to more violent children. **C** infers that no child who is permitted to watch TV will develop an aversion to violence. **D** directly contradicts the argument. The argument says that allowing children to view TV will make them more likely to become criminals. Choice **A** works. If, the passage says, children see more violent images, they become more violent, more likely to commit crimes as adults. Choice **A** just moves from the violent images to the increased likelihood of criminality.

17. **A**

The passage defines cognitive apprehension as grasping the bare idea of a thing, without any judgments or beliefs about the thing. The passage points out that this cannot be considered a strict definition, because a strict, verbal definition about such a simple, mental operation is impossible. The main point, then, is choice **A**. Simple, mental operations can be exactly understood only if one examines one's own mind. Choice **B** is too broad a claim. We aren't told of any other distinctions save that between cognitive apprehension and other mental operations. Nor are we given reason to believe that language is responsible for obscuring anything. Simply because a verbal definition is not exact does not mean that it obscures anything. Choice **C** speaks of the highest orders of cognition, which hasn't come up in the passage. Cognitive apprehension is called a simple, mental operation. **D** just points out the author's admission of the inadequacy of his proposed definition. This is not his main point. The main point is the reason for this definition's inadequacy.

18. **C**

Since we've been told that simple, cognitive apprehension doesn't comprise beliefs, we can infer that it doesn't comprise or require a belief in the existence of the thing being apprehended. So **C** is correct. **A** infers that introspection alone can give us the definition of any mental state or act. But we've only been told of *some* cases where examining one's own mind is necessary; we can't infer that in *all* cases, this is sufficient. As for **B**, the passage only says that beliefs and judgments are not part of the definition of simple, cognitive apprehension, not that they *obscure* simple, cognitive apprehension. **D** goes too far. The author says that the mind's simplest operations can't be described exactly, not that they can be defined by virtually any criteria.

19. **D**

Here we're presented with some evidence and are asked to choose the conclusion that the evidence best supports. **D** sticks closest to the evidence, so it's the best answer. The evidence claims that long-term use of multiple-ingredient pain killers causes a certain number of cases of kidney disease. It is not much of a jump from this evidence to a conclusion that restricting the availability of such pain killers (preventing them from being used over a long period) could reduce the rate of kidney disease, since those cases that were caused by the long-term use of multiple-ingredient pain killers would be fewer in number. **A** is not supported; merely by saying that single-ingredient pain killers do not appear to cause kidney ailments, we do not prove that such pain killers are safe. Perhaps they cause other, non-kidney-related ailments. **B** is too extreme to be supported by the evidence; we know that long-term use of compound analgesics *can* cause kidney disease, not that long-term use invariably *must* cause it. **C** is too categorical, since it talks about all pain killers; **C** would be better if it just said that multiple-ingredient pain killers should only be taken for short-term illnesses.

20. **A**

The author grants that parents must teach children "basic survival techniques," but believes that parents must do more than that if they want their child to be adequately prepared for life. They must help their children "develop the ability to reason and care for themselves"; they must treat their children like "thinking, unique individuals." All of this points to **A** as the clearest implication. **B** fails because of the word "dependent." The author does believe that parents should teach independent thinking, but that does not mean that having responsible parents is the only way kids can learn independent thinking. Eliminate **C**, since the author never even mentions anything about discipline. And **D** is contradicted by the author's saying that parents should tell their kids "what to eat, etcetera."

Book 2

Reading Comprehension and Context

Passage 1

The term "dangerous classes" has been used throughout history to **describe** individuals who are deemed a threat to law and **order**. Initially, the term described the environment in which one **lived**, not the type of crime committed. An example of **this** occurred in England in the mid-15th century, at the **end** of the Hundred Years' War with France. Thousands of defeated English **soldiers** were demobilized, with none of the traditional spoils of **war**; at the same time, farmers were being pushed **out** of their lands by changing economic conditions and property **laws**. The homeless population skyrocketed. Because of their rootlessness and **poverty**, these people were considered the "dangerous class," and punishment for **any** crime was severe. In the early 16th century, during the **reign** of Henry VIII, 72,000 major and **minor** thieves were hanged. Under Henry's daughter Queen Elizabeth I, vagabonds **were** strung up in rows, as many as 300 or 400 **at** a time. In this society, there was no **attempt** at rehabilitation; the concept didn't exist.

This approach to **classifying** and dealing with offenders began to change in 1838. **That** year, the winning entry at the French Academy of Science and Politics was titled, "The Dangerous Classes of the Population in Great Cities, and the Means of **Making** Them Better." "Dangerous class" was then used to describe individuals who were **criminals** or who had the potential to become criminals, based on **their** behavior; the term was no longer applied to all **members** of certain social classes.

Later in the 19th century, the new field of statistics permitted a **comparison** of crimes with factors such as race, age, sex, education **and** geography. Cesare Lombrosos, a famed Italian physician, generally is **credited** with launching the scientific era of criminology. In 1872 he identified **five** types of criminals: the born criminal, the insane criminal, the criminal by passion, the habitual criminal, and the occasional criminal.

—adapted from *Crime Classification Manual: A Standard System for Investigating and Classifying Violent Crimes*, by John E. Douglas, Ann W. Burgess, Allen G. Burgess, and Robert K. Ressler

Passage 2

The crime scene of an organized offender suggests that **some** sort of order was maintained before, during, and after **the** offense. This sense of methodical organization suggests a carefully **planned** crime which includes the goal of deterring detection.

Although **the** crime may be planned, the victim is often a **stranger**, someone targeted because he or she is in a **particular** location staked out by the offender. The victim **becomes** a victim of opportunity; there is no personal connection **between** the victim and the offender. Victims of serial murderers **may** share common characteristics. The offender often has a preference **for** a specific type of victim and thus may spend **considerable** time searching for the "right" victim. As one offender **said**, "I'm a night person. Plenty of times that I **went** out looking, but never came across anything, and just **went** back home. I'd sit waiting and as I was **waiting**, I was reliving all the others." Common characteristics of **victims** selected by a specific murderer may include age, appearance, **occupation**, hairstyle, and lifestyle. Targeted victims of convicted serial murderers **included** adolescent male youths, hitchhiking female college students, nurses, women **frequenting** bars, women sitting in automobiles with a male **companion**, and solitary women driving two-door cars.

—adapted from *Sexual Homicide: Patterns and Motives*, by
Robert K. Ressler, Ann W. Burgess, John E. Douglas

POST Practice Test 4

The following test is based on the POST exam given to police officer applicants in California. The test administered by the department you're applying to might include other sections that are not represented here. Regardless of the actual form of the test you'll take, you can only help your chances by developing your skills at standardized test taking.

Give yourself a total of two hours for the following test. An answer key and explanations follow the test.

Answer Sheet for Practice Test 4

For each question, select the best answer choice. Use the answer sheet to mark your choices. An answer key and explanations follow the test.

Clarity	Spelling	Context	Multiple-Choice Reading Comprehension
1. (A) (B)	1. (A) (B) (C) (D)	1. (A) (B) (C) (D)	1. (A) (B) (C) (D)
2. (A) (B)	2. (A) (B) (C) (D)	2. (A) (B) (C) (D)	2. (A) (B) (C) (D)
3. (A) (B)	3. (A) (B) (C) (D)	3. (A) (B) (C) (D)	3. (A) (B) (C) (D)
4. (A) (B)	4. (A) (B) (C) (D)	4. (A) (B) (C) (D)	4. (A) (B) (C) (D)
5. (A) (B)	5. (A) (B) (C) (D)	5. (A) (B) (C) (D)	5. (A) (B) (C) (D)
6. (A) (B)	6. (A) (B) (C) (D)	6. (A) (B) (C) (D)	6. (A) (B) (C) (D)
7. (A) (B)	7. (A) (B) (C) (D)	7. (A) (B) (C) (D)	7. (A) (B) (C) (D)
8. (A) (B)	8. (A) (B) (C) (D)	8. (A) (B) (C) (D)	8. (A) (B) (C) (D)
9. (A) (B)	9. (A) (B) (C) (D)	9. (A) (B) (C) (D)	9. (A) (B) (C) (D)
10. (A) (B)	10. (A) (B) (C) (D)	10. (A) (B) (C) (D)	10. (A) (B) (C) (D)
11. (A) (B)	11. (A) (B) (C) (D)	11. (A) (B) (C) (D)	11. (A) (B) (C) (D)
12. (A) (B)	12. (A) (B) (C) (D)	12. (A) (B) (C) (D)	12. (A) (B) (C) (D)
13. (A) (B)	13. (A) (B) (C) (D)	13. (A) (B) (C) (D)	13. (A) (B) (C) (D)
14. (A) (B)	14. (A) (B) (C) (D)	14. (A) (B) (C) (D)	14. (A) (B) (C) (D)
15. (A) (B)	15. (A) (B) (C) (D)	15. (A) (B) (C) (D)	15. (A) (B) (C) (D)
			16. (A) (B) (C) (D)
			17. (A) (B) (C) (D)
			18. (A) (B) (C) (D)
			19. (A) (B) (C) (D)
			20. (A) (B) (C) (D)

Book 1

Clarity

1. A. He ran all the way home after the bully pushed him down.

   B. He run all the way home after the bully pushed him down.

2. A. They, chose the prettiest china, and ordered four place settings.

   B. They chose the prettiest china, and ordered four place settings.

3. A. He swore he could of eaten four entire pies.

   B. He swore he could've eaten four entire pies.

4. A. Her boss never offer her a raise.

   B. Her boss never offered her a raise.

5. A. He bought a pony instead of a horse.

   B. He bought a pony instead from a horse.

6. A. His flowers were large red and lovely.

   B. His flowers were large, red, and lovely.

7. A. High in the sky. There is a thin, gray cloud.

   B. High in the sky, there is a thin, gray cloud.

8. A. They forgotted where they had parked their car.

   B. They forgot where they had parked their car.

9. A. She ate her food and left in a hurry.

   B. She eat her food and left in a hurry.

10. A. Fried chicken is not the healthiest of all foods.

    B. Fried chicken is not the healthier of all foods.

11. A. Wishful thinking will get you nowhere.

    B. Wishful thinking will, get you nowhere.

12. A. She growed quickly.

    B. She grew quickly.

13. A. The bright lights were colorful and pretty.

    B. The bright lights was colorful and pretty.

14. A. Its a shame that we missed the concert.

    B. It's a shame that we missed the concert.

15. A. He and his girlfriend have a great idea for a fireworks display.

    B. He and his girlfriend has a great idea for a fireworks display.

Spelling

1. It is impolite to _____ on other people's conversations.

    A. eevesdrop

    B. evesdrop

    C. eavesdrop

    D. eavsdrop

2. His shirt got caught on a nail and one of his _____ popped off.

    A. buttens

    B. butons

    C. buttenns

    D. buttons

3. The new roommates soon developed a comfortable _____ .

   A. rootine

   B. routtine

   C. routine

   D. rutine

4. After years of use, tables often lose their _____ .

   A. varnnish

   B. vernish

   C. varnishe

   D. varnish

5. He defended himself against several serious _____ .

   A. alegations

   B. allegations

   C. aleggations

   D. alleggations

6. The children were taught not to _____ against those who mistreated them.

   A. retalliate

   B. retaliat

   C. retaliate

   D. rettaliate

7. The story's themes were _____ .

   A. universsal

   B. universal

   C. universeal

   D. unniversal

8. He intends to keep a _____ for the next year.

   A. jernal

   B. jearnal

   C. journel

   D. journal

9. Many problems face _____ as we look to the future.

   A. humanity

   B. humannity

   C. humanety

   D. humanitie

10. The chef loves his new _____ oven.

    A. convecksion

    B. connvection

    C. convection

    D. cunvection

11. The runners will have to _____ for the race before they can compete.

    A. qualify

    B. quallify

    C. qualifie

    D. qualefy

12. The influence of the ancient _____ is still felt today.

    A. impire

    B. empire

    C. impyre

    D. impeire

13. After being undercharged for his groceries, the man's _____ bothered him.

    A. contience

    B. consience

    C. conscience

    D. consceince

14. The freedom to purchase and own _____ is a hotly debated topic these days.

    A. firarms

    B. feirarms

    C. fireams

    D. firearms

15. My friend thinks that the matter is _____ .

    A. triviel

    B. trivial

    C. triviale

    D. trevial

Context

1. The surviving passenger answered the investigator's questions, but her account was rather <u>sketchy</u> and not very helpful.

    A. incomplete

    B. detailed

    C. long-winded

    D. critical

2. No one was aware of the group's <u>clandestine</u> plotting, until they put their plans into action.

    A. complicated

    B. contradictory

    C. heavy-handed

    D. hidden

3. The innkeeper said the path along the shore could be unsafe, and he <u>admonished</u> us to avoid the high cliffs on our walks.

    A. begged

    B. warned

    C. expected

    D. commanded

4. She's the most <u>placid</u> person I know; I've never seen her rushed or angry.

    A. unintelligent

    B. nervous

    C. calm

    D. forgetful

5. He is a great hockey player because he is both <u>nimble</u> and observant.

    A. long-limbed

    B. smart

    C. quick

    D. small

6. She offered a(n) <u>justification</u> for her actions, but no one felt it was adequate.

    A. addition

    B. explanation

    C. schedule

    D. denial

7. She seemed reluctant, and he <u>implored</u> her to accept his proposal.

    A. expected

    B. encouraged

    C. begged

    D. dissuaded

8. The salary they <u>proffered</u> was not enough to lure her away from her old job.

    A. perceived

    B. found

    C. regretted

    D. offered

9. She had a(n) <u>visceral</u> response to the sounds, and dove behind her desk before she even realized they were gunshots.

    A. instinctive

    B. unexpected

    C. combative

    D. wicked

10. The mossy wood <u>smoldered</u>, but it was too damp to burn.

    A. stank

    B. smoked

    C. collapsed

    D. glittered

11. The sirens wailed louder, and his actions grew more <u>frenetic</u> as he tried to dispose of the counterfeit bills before the police arrived.

    A. clumsy

    B. disconnected

    C. relaxed

    D. hurried

12. Weighed down by his clothes and shoes, the man <u>floundered</u> in the water.

    A. struggled

    B. splashed

    C. dove

    D. snagged

13. Standing at the edge of the room, watching the lively party, the awkward teenager felt <u>excluded</u>.

    A. nervous

    B. left out

    C. social

    D. warm

14. Some scientists believe that certain vitamins <u>fortify</u> a person's immune system, increasing overall health.

    A. stress

    B. attack

    C. lengthen

    D. strengthen

15. They plan to <u>remain</u> at the beach for two weeks, instead of spending one week at the beach and one week in the mountains.

    A. play

    B. swim

    C. stay

    D. rest

Multiple-Choice Reading Comprehension

Read each paragraph or passage and choose the statement that best answers the question. Choose your answer solely on the basis of the material in the passage.

1. Clearly, a tactical intent of members of the Dada art movement was to shock bourgeois members of society. By unsettling the respectable and taste-setting opinion makers of a relatively conservative European community, the artists were able to free themselves from the strictest standards of artistic achievement. Reeling from the shock, bourgeois critics were not immediately able to distinguish fraud from genius, profligacy from skill, the obscene from the adventurous. Dadaism thus protected its practitioners from incisive criticism by its aggressive shock tactics.

   The main point of the passage is that

   A. Dadaists used shock tactics to obscure the fact that their art did not meet high standards of achievement

   B. members of the Dadaist movement felt that there was little difference between genius and fraud

   C. Dadaists realized that shock tactics would disarm potential critics by making traditional standards seem inapplicable

   D. Dadaist artists set out to show that art was only important if it had the capacity to shock

2. The scientific process places the burden of proof upon the person advancing a new hypothesis. A new hypothesis cannot be regarded as true until ample evidence has been amassed to support it. This is not to say that an unproven hypothesis must be regarded as false. If it were, then _____ .

   Which one of the following best completes the passage?

   A. the hypothesis would be accepted without being put to the test

   B. the hypothesis would actually be true

   C. anyone advancing a new hypothesis would be all the more eager to defend it

   D. a new hypothesis would never receive a hearing

3. The elderly increasingly look to government rather than to family members for support and comfort in their declining years. Many factors—the high cost of medical care, the struggle of finding adequate living space, and the differing values of subsequent generations—make it difficult for most middle-aged working couples to take care of their parents in the home. Instead, government and society have worked to create many programs tending to the needs of the aged. Inevitably, a family pays the price in terms of diminished closeness.

    The passage above provides the most support for which one of the following conclusions?

    A. Neither society nor the family provides adequate resources to care for the elderly.

    B. The more government cares for the needs of the elderly, the more tenuous family ties become.

    C. Middle-aged working couples are under stress because of the high cost of medical care for their aging parents.

    D. Despite its good intentions, government should not interfere in family relationships.

4. The success of recent legislative efforts to reduce crime may be overstated. Most crimes are committed by men under 30, so the crime rate tends to increase or decrease along with the number of such men in the population. As the number of young men in the population has declined over the last few years, so has the crime rate. Thus, it may be that there is little relationship between the present crime rate and _____ .

    Which one of the following would best complete the passage above?

    A. stiffer criminal penalties recently enacted in some states

    B. the rising average age of the population

    C. the decreasing child mortality rates and increasing life expectancy of recent years

    D. the strong anticrime rhetoric of public officials around the country

5. An ability to create believable, living characters is one of the essential gifts for a novelist, since strong characterization induces the reader's emotional commitment to the story and reinforces the general aura of verisimilitude. If fiction is to remain a significant art form, its practitioners must concentrate on creating credible characters in their work.

    The author of the argument above would most probably agree with which one of the following statements?

    A. If a novel has strong characters, it must necessarily be a significant work of art.

    B. A novel without credible characters will never become a bestseller.

    C. If a novel does not have credible characters, it will probably not be very significant.

    D. The novel is the only art form that should aspire to verisimilitude.

6. A small independent country may well be invaded if its defenses are not adequately prepared against a potential aggressor. But the individual in a stable society, having cast his lot with others in a social contract, need not arm himself or barricade his home against intruders, for the state will protect him and his property.

    Of the following, which one best sums up the passage above?

    A. The individual in a state is less well protected than is the average small independent country.

    B. When an individual does not abide by the implied terms of the social contract, the state has no obligation to offer him protection from harm.

    C. When the state does not adequately protect the life and property of a citizen, he or she has the right to bear arms for self defense.

    D. Although a small independent state must fend for itself, the individual in a stable society has the protection of the state.

7. "Litigiousness" is the habit of unnecessarily taking to court matters that could probably be settled fairly by other means. According to judicial experts, the United States is rapidly becoming the most litigious country in the world. Disputes that could easily have been settled out of court in any number of ways, including binding arbitration, now clog the average court calendar in all parts of the nation.

   Which one of the following statements, if true, best supports the argument?

   A. An increasing number of court cases involve employee-employer disputes, which can be handled by government administrative boards.

   B. The greater the number of unnecessary court cases in a society, the larger the number of trial lawyers who are gainfully employed.

   C. Litigiousness is not necessarily a socially negative trait, since it may encourage shy individuals to defend their own rights.

   D. Studies of litigiousness may not have taken into account the average American's lack of sophistication about courtroom procedure.

8. Lest charity become confused with self-interest, it is well to remember that we can hope to rehabilitate a convicted felon without demanding that he or she be remade in our own image. To insist that the former pusher be willing to become a social worker, or the former burglar a bank clerk, is to deny the very individuality of expression that true rehabilitative programs should develop.

   Which one of the following sentences best completes the statement of the position put forth in the passage above?

   A. For proper rehabilitation, however, the convicted felon must follow the advice of professionals in choosing a career.

   B. Moreover, forcing an unsuitable career upon the subject for rehabilitation might pressure him or her to return to the criminal life out of frustration.

   C. In particular, it is unlikely that any individual will find self-expression in work that involves reporting daily to an institution.

   D. Furthermore, many a social worker has less knowledge of the motivations behind criminal acts than a felon who has actually committed a crime.

9. Thus, a man's desire for his own good may be a beneficial desire or a malevolent desire. For, if this desire is too strong (as when one is motivated by an excessive love of life), then it is undoubtedly vicious; and if it is vicious, then he who is moved by it is vicious, and cannot be otherwise when moved by it. Therefore, if, through an earnest and passionate love of life, a man is accidentally induced to do good, he is no more a good man because of this good he does than a man is an honest or good man who pleads for a just cause, or fights for a good cause, merely for the sake of his fee or stipend.

Based solely on the passage above, which one of the following is a criterion that the author considers important in identifying the good man?

A. motivation

B. wisdom

C. consequences

D. honesty

10. It is barbarous in the extreme to equate murder with simple acquiescence in the choice of a pain-wracked, dying friend to find self-deliverance from an onerous life. To assist a friend in suicide is to give solace, to respect the individual's free choice; to murder, of course, is to perform the ultimate act of disrespect for individual civil rights. Both our legislators and our justices must be urged to use reason rather than to respond as they have with traditional prejudice.

It can be inferred from the passage that

A. the concept of murder in any given society is related to that society's interpretation of the idea of individual rights

B. terminally ill patients frequently contemplate suicide

C. our legislators and our justices do not agree with the author of the passage that assisting a suicide is not an act of murder

D. suicide should always be considered an act of self-deliverance, just as murder should be considered an act of disrespect for individual civil rights

11. Without the profound structural changes in the Irish agricultural economy that began with the first grudging acceptance of the potato into the human diet, the great Potato Famine of the 1840s would never have been the disaster it was. Although other staples continued to be cultivated, primarily for export to England, the total dependence of much of the Irish population on potatoes turned the blight-induced failure of several potato crops in the latter part of the decade into a sweeping sentence of death or emigration.

    Which one of the following conclusions can most reliably be drawn from the statements in the passage?

    A. The adoption of the potato as the staple of the Irish diet represented a nationalistic rejection of English social patterns.

    B. Other staples are less susceptible to crop failure than is the potato.

    C. Reliance on a single crop made Ireland a fertile ground for revolutionary activity when that crop failed.

    D. Absence of alternative sources of food left much of the Irish population with nothing to eat when the potato crop failed.

12. In our society, personality is considered an expression of individuality. We like to see ourselves as self-created, distinct from the influences of the past, bent upon our own development as self. Effects upon us are viewed as intrusions. But in the tribal society of the Bambara peoples, personality is the sum of many parts—less an individual phenomenon than a reflection of the family, less a single unit than an integer of a larger, sustaining tribal identity. Personality is richer because it is not self-centered, maturer because it benefits from diversity, and stronger because it draws its strength from the clan.

    The argument has been designed to emphasize the supposed interrelationship between

    A. richness of personality and integration in a society

    B. individuality of expression and development of the self

    C. diversity of personality and self-centeredness

    D. a sustaining tribal identity and the strength of the clan

13. Recent studies have indicated that a certain type of freshwater cod has more tumors than other species of fish in the Hudson. Long before this phenomenon was recognized, significant strides had been made in clearing the river of chemical and other kinds of industrial pollution thought to promote tumorous growth.

Which one of the following conclusions can most reliably be drawn from the statements above?

   A. The mentioned studies provide no evidence that the number of tumors in the freshwater cod is related to the level of industrial pollution in the river.

   B. A sudden change in the river environment has had a drastic effect on the freshwater cod.

   C. Efforts to clear the Hudson of chemical and other kinds of industrial pollution have not been vigorous enough.

   D. No other fish but the freshwater cod is susceptible to the effects of chemical and other kinds of industrial pollution.

14. Early in this century, the doctor was a comforter, expected to predict the progress of a disease or to help the patient cope with a struggle or an imminent defeat, but not to work miracles. This situation changed with the coming of such drugs as penicillin, insulin, and the antibiotics. Add the rapid technological developments of contemporary medicine, and we find the medical professional under pressure to defeat every disease, correct every physical defect, and maximize the patient's quality of life. Society no longer is satisfied with the dedicated efforts of human beings; it now demands perfect performance of technicians as foolproof as the most sophisticated machines.

Which one of the following can be most reasonably inferred from the passage?

   A. Today's physician does not view comforting the patient as part of his or her job.

   B. The patient today expects results rather than sympathy from his or her physician.

   C. As medical technology has advanced, health-care workers have become less sensitive to the feelings of their patients.

   D. Because doctors cannot meet the often unrealistic expectations of their patients, they are subjected to an ever-increasing number of malpractice suits.

15. The unexpected plummet of the stock market in September badly shook the economy. For this past holiday season, retail sales comprised a lower percentage of total annual sales than it has in any of the previous twenty years. Retailers and legislators are worried. New rules that govern trading on the stock exchange may be put into effect.

The main point of the passage is that

A. the stock exchange wishes to enlist the aid of the government

B. legislators typically do not become concerned until a real market effect is felt

C. new rules governing the trading of stocks will increase the volume of retail sales

D. the decline in the percentage of retail sales was due to the September stock market fall

16. In this age of mechanization, when nearly everyone wears a watch and many even wear stopwatches, time is an omnipresent specter. People in agrarian societies of the past measured their days by the position of the sun—in winter they simply had less time in which to accomplish their chores and accordingly did less. Now we count every second spent unwisely, or unaccounted for, as time lost. A missed traffic light or a delayed train can affect an entire day. Yet electricity allows us to create daylight whenever we wish, theoretically extending the day indefinitely.

The main point of this passage is most probably that

A. the attitudes of agrarian societies toward the passage of time are different from those of industrial societies

B. members of the agrarian societies of the past were more attuned than we to changes in their natural surroundings

C. people who may be said to have more time nevertheless feel that they must watch it more closely

D. modern industrialization has produced more mechanisms by which time can be calculated

17. Economists can directly compare how effectively different economic systems perform specific tasks—for example, the number of automobiles or tons of steel produced at what cost in labor—simply by referring to the relevant statistics. Assuming the statistics are accurate, one system then can be fairly judged better or worse than others in terms of its operational effectiveness. In comparing systems as a whole, however, the difficulty of comparing their unquantifiable aspects—such as what constitutes an acceptable level of unemployment or a fair distribution of income—may produce widely diverging opinions among economists who otherwise concur in their analyses of the systems' relative operational merits.

    If all of the statements in the passage are true, which one of the following must also be true on the basis of them?

    A. An economic system's effectiveness in performing specific tasks cannot be accurately determined by statistical analysis alone.

    B. The statistics on unemployment and income distribution within a given economic system are frequently considered unreliable by economic analysts.

    C. In comparing economic systems as a whole, economists must inevitably make value judgments about certain aspects of the systems' performances.

    D. Most economists would agree that the relative merits of different economic systems should not be assessed on the basis of their productive capabilities.

Questions 18–19

    Are we an active or a reactive society? Do we attempt to shape the world to our desires or do we merely respond by reflex to the harms that the world deals us? Most people would claim that we define ourselves as the former kind of society. Why, then, do many of these same people advocate capital punishment, a totally reactive response to crime? To execute violent criminals is to admit defeat, to assert that people cannot be changed or rehabilitated. Is it not better to be constructive rather than destructive, to regard criminals as flawed elements in our society that can be corrected, rather than irrevocable failures who must be written off?

18. Which one of the following best describes the point made by the author above?

    A. The execution of criminals is not consistent with the idea of an active, constructive society.

    B. We should outlaw capital punishment because it violates the spirit of our laws.

    C. We should reconsider our conception of ourselves as an active society.

    D. Our professed image of ourselves as a society is often at odds with our actions as a society.

19. The author of the above argument would most likely agree with which one of the following principles?

    A. Capital punishment makes a society as culpable as the criminals it executes.

    B. Our society's treatment of criminals should be more rehabilitative and less punitive.

    C. A society that admits defeat in the matter of violent crime will not survive.

    D. Destroying human life is inappropriate for a society in any situation.

20. Although we tend to measure the phenomenon of aging in a casual way by referring to the passing of chronological time, this really provides an incomplete description of an animal's or a human being's real physiological age. Physiological, or "true," age relates the physiological changes brought about in the animal by the passing of chronological time to the whole aging process of its species. A fifteen-year-old cat could aptly be described as "very old," which would not be true of a horse younger than twenty years, while a fifty-year-old human being nowadays could be considered still relatively young.

    It can be most properly inferred from the above that

    A. people are better able to make an accurate determination of another person's age than of an animal's age

    B. the idiosyncrasies of animal physiology preclude any meaningful use of words such as old or young in descriptions of age

    C. evaluating an animal's physiological condition is not the most accurate way of determining its true age

    D. knowing the chronological age of any animal is meaningful as a measure of true age only when its species' life span is also known

Book 2

Reading Comprehension and Context

In the following two passages, certain words have been deleted. Write the missing word in the appropriate blank. The number in parentheses indicates the number of letters in the missing word. Note: A word may be used in your answers more than once.

Passage 1

Child and family researchers often suggest that the structure _____ (3) quality of family interaction is an important factor in a _____ (6) development. The child's early life attachments (sometimes called bonding) _____ (4) a pattern for relationships that lasts long beyond _____ (9). The adult's interactions with society are shaped by the child's _____ (10) within the family. Because of the importance of these _____ (5) life attachments, we were especially interested in identifying specific _____ (7) within family relationships that most clearly indicated the offenders' levels of _____ (10) to other people.

When interviewing these offenders, we discovered _____ (4) nearly all reported multiple problems in their families. These _____ (8) included alcoholism, drug abuse, frequent unemployment, violence, sexual abuse, _____ (3) serious psychiatric problems. Given the severity of these problems, which _____ (9) when they are combined, it is reasonable to _____ (7) that relationships among family members were inconsistent and unreliable, _____ (2) well as emotionally inadequate. Thus, the possibility that most of _____ (5) offenders experienced significant positive interactions with family members seems _____ (8).

When examining the patterns described by the murderers regarding _____ (5) own families, we discovered an extremely high degree of _____ (11) in home structure. Only one-third of the men reported _____ (7) up in one location throughout childhood. Over half said _____ (4) experienced occasional instability, and a third reported chronic instability or _____ (8) moving, sometimes as often as four or five _____ (5) a year. In addition, nearly half of the offenders _____ (8) that they had left the family home before age 18.

—adapted from *Sexual Homicide: Patterns and Motives*, by
Robert K. Ressler, Ann W. Burgess, John E. Douglas

Passage 2

It is widely believed that infertile couples who adopt a _____ (5) are afterwards more likely to conceive than similar _____ (7) who do not. The usual explanation for this remarkable _____ (10) involves the reduction of stress. Couples who adopt, it is said, _____ (6) less obsessed with their reproductive failure and their newfound _____ (5) of mind boosts their chances for success.

On closer _____ (10), however, it becomes clear that the remarkable occurrence we _____ (4) to explain is not why adoption increases fertility; clinical research _____ (3) shown that it does not. What needs explanation is _____ (3) so many people hold this belief when it is _____ (3) true.

People who must decide who is to be admitted to a prestigious _____ (6) or a competitive executive training program all think they can _____ (4) more effective admissions decisions if each candidate is seen in a _____ (5), personal interview. They cannot. Research indicates that decisions _____ (5) on objective criteria alone (such as grades and test _____ (6)) are at least as effective as those influenced by subjective _____ (11) formed in an interview. But why then do people _____ (7) the interview to be informative?

Nurses who work on _____ (9) wards believe that more babies are born when the _____ (4) is full. They are mistaken. Again, why do _____ (4) believe it if it "just ain't so"?

—adapted from *How We Know What Isn't So: The Fallibility of Human Reason in Everyday Life,* by Thomas Gilovich

POST Practice Test 4 Answers and Explanations

ANSWER KEY

Clarity	Spelling	Context	Multiple-Choice Reading Comprehension
1. A	1. C–eavesdrop	1. A	1. C
2. B	2. D–buttons	2. D	2. D
3. B	3. C–routine	3. B	3. B
4. B	4. D–varnish	4. C	4. A
5. A	5. B–allegations	5. C	5. C
6. B	6. C–retaliate	6. B	6. D
7. B	7. B–universal	7. C	7. A
8. B	8. D–journal	8. D	8. B
9. A	9. A–humanity	9. A	9. A
10. A	10. C–convection	10. B	10. C
11. A	11. A–qualify	11. D	11. D
12. B	12. B–empire	12. A	12. A
13. A	13. C–conscience	13. B	13. A
14. B	14. D–firearms	14. D	14. B
15. A	15. B–trivial	15. C	15. D
			16. C
			17. C
			18. A
			19. B
			20. D

EXPLANATIONS

Book 1

Clarity

1. The correct answer is **A**. Since the sentence is in the past tense, the correct verb form is "ran."

2, The correct answer is **B**. In **A**, there shouldn't be a comma between "they" and "chose."

3. The correct answer is **B**. This is another example of the difference between written and spoken English. What you say and hear is "could of eaten." But it's actually a contraction ("could've eaten") for the correct phrase: "could have eaten." Always use the correct grammar in your writing.

4. The correct answer is **B**. "Offer" is the first or second person verb:"I offer," "we offer," "you offer." Since the subject ("He") is third person, the verb has to match: "He offered."

5. The correct answer is **A**. The correct phrase is "instead of." The second sentence doesn't make much sense, and seems to be saying a horse was selling a pony.

6. The correct answer is **B**. There should be commas separating the adjectives in **A**. The commas in **B** are placed correctly.

7. The correct answer is **B**. There is a sentence fragment in **A**. "High in the sky"—what?

8. The correct answer is **B**. The correct form of the verb is "forgot." "Forgotted" isn't a word.

9. The correct answer is **A**. Again, you have to make sure the subject and verb match.

10. The correct answer is **A**. The correct form of the adjective is the superlative "healthiest." That's because you're comparing fried chicken to all the other foods in the world. If you were comparing only two items, you'd use "healthier," as in: Fried chicken is healthier than a tub of pure lard.

11. The correct answer is **A**. In **B**, the comma breaks up the verb.

12. The correct answer is **B**. The past tense form of "grow" is "grew." I've heard "growed" a million times, and I'll bet you have too, but that doesn't make it a word.

13. The correct answer is **A**. The subject, "the bright lights," is plural, so you need to use the plural form of the verb. Of your two choices, only "were" is plural.

14. The correct answer is **B**. The correct pronoun is "it's," which is a contraction of the words "it" and "is." Remember, "its" is the possessive form of "it."

15. The correct answer is **A**. Since the subject, "he and his girlfriend," is plural, the correct verb form is "have."

Context

1. **A** is the best answer. You're looking for something that will make the passenger's answers unhelpful. "Incomplete" is the only logical answer.

2. **D** is most logical.

3. **B** is the correct answer. You wouldn't expect an innkeeper to either beg or command his guests. He might expect them to take a hint and avoid the cliffs, but it makes more sense to think he'd go ahead and warn them.

4. **C** makes the most sense.

5. **C** is the best answer. "Small" and "long-limbed" don't work; "smart" might seem okay, but think about it. "Smart" and "observant" describe very similar qualities. Considering the use of the word "both," it makes more sense that the writer would combine two different attributes in this phrase.

6. **B** is the correct answer. "Denial" is the only other possibility, but we don't really think of denials as being adequate or inadequate.

7. **C** is the best answer. This one's a little tricky. You can eliminate "expected" because that sentence makes no sense. "Encouraged" seems pretty weak. If you're trying to overcome someone's reluctance, it's going to take more than encouragement. "Dissuaded," or argued against, is exactly the opposite meaning. What if you weren't sure what "dissuaded" meant? Remember the prefixes and suffixes: "dis" is wrong, against, negative in some way. If you think about words similar to "dissuaded," you'll come up with "persuaded." Even if you couldn't come up with an exact definition, you could probably figure out that "dissuaded" is a negative kind of persuasion.

8. **D** makes sense in the context.

9. **A** is the best answer. "Unexpected" might work, but "instinctive" makes more sense.

10. **B** is the correct answer. The "but" signals a contrast; of these four, the best contrast to fire ("to burn") is smoke.

11. **D** is the best answer. He might have grown more clumsy, but he'd definitely have been in a big hurry.

12. **A** is the best answer. If you're burdened with clothes, you're going to be doing a lot more struggling than splashing, and diving is pretty much out.

13. **B** is the best answer. The choice is between "nervous" and "left out." Either would work in the sentence, but "left out" a better match for "excluded." Again, remember the prefixes. "Ex-" indicates something outside, as in "external."

14. **D** makes sense in context.

15. **C** is the best answer. They'll probably play, swim, and rest at the beach, but the phrase "instead of" lets you know there's a contrast or opposition. The only verb that gives you that is "stay."

Multiple-Choice Reading Comprehension

1. **C**

The author tells us that the Dadaists wanted to shock "to free themselves from the strictest standards of artistic achievement" by unsettling the critics. **C** is the best description of the main point. **A** is wrong since the intent of the shock tactics was to free the Dadaists from traditional standards, not to obscure the fact that their work was inferior. Eliminate **B** because the author says nothing to give us the impression that Dadaists saw no distinction between genius and fraud. The author says only that bourgeois critics could not distinguish Dada genius from Dada fraud. As for **D**, the Dadaists used shocking art to achieve an end; that does not mean that they believed that the only important art was shocking art.

2. **D**

The blank must be filled with a consequence of considering all unproven hypotheses false. Well, if we were to consider all new hypotheses false, then there would be no need to amass proof on behalf of them. They would be dismissed without a hearing. That's choice **D**, which best completes the passage. **A** is incorrect because considering new hypotheses false would certainly not lead to their being accepted. **B** is out because accepting or rejecting hypotheses has nothing to do with causing them to be true or false. **C** says that considering new hypotheses false would lead to staunch defenses of them. Maybe, but then again maybe not.

3. **B**

This passage makes the point that responsibility for care of the elderly has shifted increasingly from the family to the government. The author argues that these "innovations" threaten the family as a unit. Correct choice **B** is practically a paraphrase of the final sentence of the passage. Choices **A** and **C** come close, but one goes too far while the other one doesn't go far enough. The author says it's tough on the children of the elderly and that government is trying to pick up the slack, but **A** implies that both are trying and failing. And **C** applies only to those couples who are bearing the financial burden of their parents' medical care, while the main thrust of the passage concerns those families where the middle-aged couples are not housing and taking care of their parents. As for **D**, the author is not warning us flat out to stop the government from interfering in our family lives; he's simply saying that this trend in caring for the elderly has created the problem of diminished closeness.

4. **A**

The subject of this passage is the questionable success of recent anticrime legislation. The blank must be some kind of anticrime legislation, since that's what the author's argument is targeting. The only choice that mentions some kind of legislation is **A**, so that's our answer. **B** contradicts the passage: The author is suggesting that the rising average age of the population *does* have something to do with the shrinking crime rate, because there are fewer young men around to commit violent crimes. **C** brings in two irrelevant ideas: the child mortality rate and the increased life expectancy in our country. **D** sounds like it's on the right track, but **A** is better because it refers to anticrime legislation, which is mentioned in context, rather than anticrime rhetoric, which is not.

5. **C**

The author would probably agree with statement **C**: A novel won't be significant if it doesn't have credible characters. **A** is incorrect because the author never claims that believable characters alone will suffice to make a novel significant. Choice **B** is out because no mention is made in the passage of a possible relationship between credible characters and a novel's popularity. The author never concerns himself with other art forms, so it should have been pretty easy for you to dismiss choice **D**.

6. **D**

The logic of the passage runs as follows: A small country may be invaded if it isn't adequately prepared to defend itself, but a person in a stable society need not prepare to defend himself because the state will defend him. The choice that best sums up this argument is **D**. **A** skews the point of the argument, which contrasts what individuals and small countries must do to protect themselves; the argument does not discuss how well each is protected. **B** distorts the argument; the author never warns that dire things will happen to the person who fails to abide by the terms of the social contract. **C** goes against the author's argument, which is that unlike a small nation, a person doesn't have to bear arms to defend himself. The individual's right to self-defense is not discussed in the passage.

7. **A**

The author's conclusion is that our nation's courts are currently clogged with disputes that could be solved by other means. The passage contains no real evidence for this, citing only the opinion of judicial experts, but no real facts. So the answer choice which best supports the passage will be the one that does provide examples or other evidence to support the author's claim. Only choice **A** gives us the needed examples. Choice **B** fails to support the conclusion; it merely indicates an effect of litigiousness: low unemployment among lawyers. Choice **C** tries to justify litigiousness on the grounds that it has redeeming social value. But the issue is whether our legal system suffers from an excess of litigiousness. **D** casts doubt on the validity of studies of litigiousness, but the passage never mentions any such studies.

8. **B**

We can thus expect a concluding statement which completes this theme, that convicts must be permitted free choice in determining their new careers. Only choice **B** takes this approach. If we try to rehabilitate convicts in careers of our choosing, we may frustrate them to the point that they return to a life of crime. Choice **A** contradicts the author's message by arguing that someone else should have the power to determine a convict's new career. **C** is a broad generalization that comes from left field. Finally, the motivation behind the criminal act, choice **D**, is irrelevant to the issue of whether a convict should be allowed to choose his or her new career.

9. **A**

The author has concluded that the desire for one's own good can be good or bad, depending on degree. Examples of acts that would be good but for their selfish motivation are given: fighting for a good cause as a mercenary and pleading for a good cause solely to earn a buck. So **A**, motivation, is correct. From what we can tell, the author considers a man's motivation to be the *most* important criterion for judging his character. Since the author does not consider a man who fights the good cause only to make a profit to be good, he can't consider the consequences of an act to be an important criterion in judging a man, so **C** is incorrect. **B** comes from left field, as nowhere in the passage is wisdom ever mentioned. As for **D**, the author does not consider a man to be honest simply because his acts are honest, so **D** is out.

10. **C**

This author argues that an individual ought to be allowed to help a "pain-wracked, dying friend" to commit suicide. The correct inference can be drawn from the final sentence of the passage, where the author concludes that lawmakers and judges must treat such cases reasonably. We can infer, then, that lawmakers and judges disagree with the author. Choice **C** is the correct answer: Lawmakers and judges, according to the author, feel that assistance of suicide is murder, and the author wishes to change their minds. **A** is sensible but can't be inferred from the passage. The author never discusses his idea in the context of other societies, so we can't infer a universal application for it. **B** is wrong because the passage tells us nothing about the thoughts and feelings of the terminally ill; perhaps very few contemplate suicide. Choice **D** goes too far. The author very carefully describes exactly the type of assistance of suicide he thinks is justified, and never implies that the act of suicide is *always* an act of self-deliverance.

11. **D**

The author argues that, since much of the Irish population had become totally dependent on the potato for the bulk of its diet, successive failures of the yearly potato crop resulted in a national famine. **D** is the best conclusion, because if much of the population was totally dependent on the potato for its diet, then it follows that much of the population was left without alternative food sources when the potato crops continued to fail. There's no reason to conclude that the adoption of the potato as a staple of the Irish diet represented a rejection of English social patterns, choice **A**. Choice **B** is out because all the author tells us about other crops is that they continued to be cultivated, but "primarily for export to England." Choice **C** is also out; the author never implies that the great Potato Famine caused any revolutionary activity.

12. **A**

This passage sets up a distinction between two apparently different concepts of "personality," as the author views them: our current idea of self-created individuality, and the traditional Bambara notion of the individual as part of a larger whole. He argues that the latter is preferable; the personality that is "the sum of many parts" will be the richer type. In other words, as stated in choice **A**, the author believes that richness of personality has a relationship with the degree to which one is integrated with a society. Choice **B** describes two related aspects of our society's idea of personality. These are similar ideas, however, not ideas presented as a relationship that is central to making the main argument of the passage. Choice **C** is out: Far from arguing that diversity of personality and self-centeredness are in any way related, the author states that the reverse is true. The relationship in choice **D** is not discussed by the author; furthermore, it can't be reasonably inferred from the passage that he would agree that such a relationship exists. In any event, he does not present his argument in terms of such a relationship.

13. **A**

First, we are told that one Hudson River fish, a cod, suffers more from tumors than do other fish in the river. Second, we learn that pollution thought to cause such growths was being cleaned out of the river long before the cod tumors were discovered. What relationship does the second fact have to the first? The correct choice is **A**; that is to say, there is no evident relationship at all between the two facts, at least as far as we can tell from the study. Choice **B** plays fast and loose with the facts. There was no "sudden change" in the river; rather, the passage suggests a gradual change in the amount of pollution. And sudden or not, the change can't be linked to the appearance of the tumors, simply on the basis of the information in the passage. There is no indication that choice **C** is a reasonable conclusion; on the contrary, the author cites the "significant strides" made. It is always possible that the efforts could be more vigorously pursued, but we have no reason to suspect that to be the case. **D** makes two unwarranted assumptions: that the Hudson River pollution causes the cod tumors, and it would only affect the freshwater cod.

14. **B**

We are told that the great strides in combating disease have led patients nowadays to expect that medical professionals, once less able to heal than to give comfort, should always deliver technically proficient service rather than, as **B** says, "sympathy." **B** is a condensed version of the idea expressed in the last sentence of the paragraph. As for **A**, we are not told how the physician views his or her job; the emphasis is on the expectations patients may have of medical professionals. **C** goes too far. There is no suggestion here that health-care workers have become less sensitive; again, the emphasis is on the *patients' expectations*. And **D** is beyond the scope, as malpractice suits are never mentioned at all in the passage.

15. **D**

We're told that the September stock market fall shook the economy. Then we're told that retail sales during the holiday season were lower, when compared to the total annual sales, than in any of the previous twenty years. This is followed with the statement that retailers and lawmakers are worried, and that they may institute new rules concerning stock trading. Well, what inference leaps out at us? The inference that the stock market plummet is responsible for the fall in retail sales. This piece of information is necessary to make sense of the argument. As a result, **D** is the point being made. Choice **A** is outside the scope of the passage. Although the legislature is considering rules, we have no indication that the market *desires* such rules, or any other "aid." Similarly, the typical habits of legislators, in choice **B**, are also outside the argument's scope. As for **C**, all that can be inferred from this piece of journalism is that the new rules might protect the market and retail sales, not that they *will increase* the volume of retail sales.

16. **C**

The author is creating a contrast between the perception of time in the past and in the present "age of mechanization." There is a sense of paradox in the contrast, signaled by the keyword "yet" at the beginning of the last sentence. Present societies, though they theoretically have "more" time, are nonetheless more concerned about time's passing. So choice **C** best describes the author's point. **A** misstates the exact contrast the author is making, which is between the past and the present, not between agrarian and industrial societies. **B** is wrong because the passage is clearly about perceptions of time and its passing, not about perceptions of changes in natural surroundings. While **D** is a true statement that the author would agree with, it is definitely not the main idea here, which is about *perceptions* of time.

17. **C**

The passage refers to the use of statistics to judge economic systems in two ways: with respect to operational effectiveness, and "as a whole." When judging operational effectiveness, the passage suggests that the statistics speak for themselves. However, when looking at the big picture, economists need to determine the significance, or "value," of unquantifiable aspects. Choice **C** stays consistent with the passage's theme. **A** is out because contradictory to the first sentence of the passage, this is the area in which statistical analysis can be used with reliability. As for **B**, the issues here comprise the "unquantifiable aspects" of systems as a whole, so statistics aren't relevant. **D** is out because the passage strongly implies that productivity is a good way of comparing economic systems, and the author doesn't address what "most economists would agree" upon.

18. **A**

The author wants to point out an apparent hypocrisy, and to call on society to reconcile this hypocrisy in accordance with the author's beliefs. We say we're an "active" society, but going by the author's definitions, advocating capital punishment is more a part of a "reactive" society. **B** is out because the author doesn't deal with the idea of punishment violating the spirit of our laws. Instead, he argues against capital punishment by saying that we should work to reform criminals rather than execute them. As for **C**, the author would rather we retain the concept of being "active," and change our view of capital punishment to fit that mold. **D** is too broad to be the author's main point, which, of course, is the issue of capital punishment.

19. **B**

The last sentence and choice **B** say essentially the same thing: An active society, for which the author argues, would work to "correct the flawed elements in society" or, in other words, rehabilitate criminals rather than simply react and punish them. **A** is too extreme. The author simply argues that there are better, more productive routes to take than capital punishment. **C** is too extreme. The author does believe that the use of capital punishment is an admission of defeat, but that doesn't mean he'd agree that a society with this mindset won't survive. **D** is too vague. War, for example, involves the destruction of human lives, which the author may feel is okay in some situations.

20. **D**

The difference between chronological age and physiological age is that the latter is a more complete description, because it places the chronological age of a species into the context of the life span of that species. **D** sticks very closely to this theme and is reinforced by the illustration in the last sentence. **A** is off the mark. The passage deals with the issue of how to assign meaning to a particular age; figuring out that age isn't discussed. In **B**, the words *old* and *young* have meaning, but those meanings merely vary from one animal to another. **C** is beyond the scope. At no point is anything said about an animal's physiological condition.

Book 2

Reading Comprehension and Context

Child and family researchers often suggest that the structure **and** quality of family interaction is an important factor in a **child's** development. The child's early life attachments (sometimes called bonding) **form** a pattern for relationships that lasts long beyond **childhood**. The adult's interactions with society are shaped by the child's **experience** within the family. Because of the importance of these **early** life attachments, we were especially interested in identifying specific **factors** within family relationships that most clearly indicated the offenders' levels of **attachment** to other people.

When interviewing these offenders, we discovered **that** nearly all reported multiple problems in their families. These **problems** included alcoholism, drug abuse, frequent unemployment, violence, sexual abuse, **and** serious psychiatric problems. Given the severity of these problems, which **increases** when they are combined, it is reasonable to **suggest** that relationships among family members were inconsistent and unreliable, **as** well as emotionally inadequate. Thus, the possibility that most of **these** offenders experienced significant positive interactions with family members seems **unlikely**.

When examining the patterns described by the murderers regarding **their** own families, we discovered an extremely high degree of **instability** in home structure. Only one-third of the men reported **growing** up in one location throughout childhood. Over half said **they** experienced occasional instability, and a third reported chronic instability or **frequent** moving, sometimes as often as four or five **times** a year. In addition, nearly half of the offenders **reported** that they had left the family home before age 18.

—adapted from *Sexual Homicide: Patterns and Motives*,
by Robert K. Ressler, Ann W. Burgess, John E. Douglas

It is widely believed that infertile couples who adopt a **child** are afterwards more likely to conceive than similar **couples** who do not. The usual explanation for this remarkable **occurrence** involves the reduction of stress. Couples who adopt, it is said, **become** less obsessed with their reproductive failure and their newfound **peace** of mind boosts their chances for success.

On closer **inspection**, however, it becomes clear that the remarkable occurrence we **need** to explain is not why adoption increases fertility; clinical research **has** shown that it does not. What needs explanation is why so many people hold this belief when it is **not** true.

People who must decide who is to be admitted to a prestigious **school** or a competitive executive training program all think they can **make** more effective admissions decisions if each candidate is seen in a **brief**, personal interview. They cannot. Research indicates that decisions **based** on objective criteria alone (such as grades and test scores) are at least as effective as those influenced by subjective **impressions** formed in an interview. But why then do people **believe** the interview to be informative?

Nurses who work on **maternity** wards believe that more babies are born when the **moon** is full. They are mistaken. Again, why do **they** believe it if it "just ain't so"?

—adapted from *How We Know What Isn't So: The Fallibility of Human Reason in Everyday Life*, by Thomas Gilovich.

APPENDIX 1
California Law Enforcement Agencies

This section lists over 500 departments throughout the state, organized by county. The number you see to the right of the department name tells you the number of sworn officers in that department.

Alameda County

County

Alameda County Sheriff's Department   939
1401 Lakeside Drive, 12th Floor
Oakland, CA 94612
(510) 272-6878

Municipal

Alameda Police Department   111
1555 Oak Street
Alameda, CA 94501
(510) 748-4508

Albany Police Department   27
1000 San Pablo Avenue
Albany, CA 94706-2295

Bay Area Rapid Transit (BART) Police
Department   177
800 Madison Street
Oakland, CA 94608
(510) 464-7061

Berkeley Police Department   201
2171 McKinley Avenue
Berkeley, CA 94703

(510) 644-6698
East Bay Regional Parks
District Police Department   49
17930 Lake Chabot Road
Castro Valley, CA 94546-1950

Emeryville Police Department   37
2449 Powell Street
Emeryville, CA 94608

Fremont Police Department   205
2000 Stevenson Boulevard
Fremont, CA 94538
(510) 790-6800

Hayward Police Department   180
300 W. Winton Avenue
Hayward, CA 94544-1137
(510) 293-7078

Livermore Police Department   82
1110 S. Livermore Avenue
Livermore, CA 94550-9534
(925) 371-4900

Moraga Police Department 12
350 Rheem Boulevard
Moraga, CA 94567

Newark Police Department 56
37101 Newark Boulevard
Newark, CA 94560-9986
(510) 790-7267

Oakland Police Department 672
Police Administration Building
455 Seventh Street
Oakland, CA 94607
(510) 777-3333

Piedmont Police Department 20
403 Highland Avenue
Piedmont, CA 94611

Pleasanton Police Department 80
P.O. Box 909
4833 Bernal Avenue
Pleasanton, CA 94566

San Leandro Police
Department 95
901 E. 14th Street
San Leandro, CA 94577

Union City Police Department 74
34009 Alvarado-Niles Road
Union City, CA 94587

Alpine
County
Alpine County Sheriff's Department 10
P.O. Box 278
Markleeville, CA 96120

Amador
County
Amador County District Attorney's Office
708 Court Street
Jackson, CA 95642
(209) 223-6444

Amador County Sheriff's Department 41
700 Court Street
Jackson, CA 95642-2130

Municipal
Ione Police Department 5
P.O. Box 398
1 E. Main Street
Ione, CA 95640-0398

Jackson Police Department
33D Broadway
Jackson, CA 95642 10

Butte
County
Butte County District Attorney's Office
25 County Center Drive
Oroville, CA 95965-3385
(530) 538-7411

Butte County Sheriff's Department 99
33 County Center Drive
Oroville, CA 95965

Municipal
Chico Police Department 74
1460 Humboldt Road
Chico, CA 95928
(530) 895-4981

Gridley Police Department   12
685 Kentucky Street
Gridley, CA 95948

Oroville Police Department   24
2055 Lincoln Street
Oroville, CA 95966-5385

Paradise Police Department   23
5595 Black Olive Drive
Paradise, CA 95969

Calaveras
County
Calaveras County District Attorney's Office
891 Mountain Ranch Road
San Andreas, CA 95249
(209) 754-6330

Calaveras County Sheriff's Department   48
891 Mountain Ranch Road
San Andreas, CA 95249
(209) 754-6500

Colusa
County
Colusa County Sheriff's Department   34
929 Bridge Street
Colusa, CA 95932

Municipal
Colusa Police Department   9
260 Sixth Street
Colusa, CA 95932

Williams Police Department   7
P.O. Box 310
688 Seventh Street
Williams, CA 95987

Contra Costa
County
Contra Costa County District
Attorney's Office
P.O. Box 670
Courthouse, 725 Court Street at Main
Martinez, CA 94553
(925) 646-4500

Contra Costa County Sheriff's
Department   654
P.O. Box 391
651 Pine Street
Martinez, CA 94553
(925) 335-1500

Municipal
Antioch Police Department   98
300 "L" Street
Antioch, CA 94509-1100

Brentwood Police Department   25
500 Chestnut Street
Brentwood, CA 94513

Clayton Police Department   10
6000 Heritage Trail
Clayton, CA 94517-1249

Concord Police Department   150
1350 Galindo Street
Concord, CA 94520-2809
(925) 671-3333

El Cerrito Police Department   34
10900 San Pablo Avenue
El Cerrito, CA 94530-2391
(510) 215-4400

Hercules Police Department   21
111 Civic Drive
Hercules, CA 94547-1771

Kensington Police Department   10
217 Arlington Avenue
Kensington, CA 94707

Martinez Police Department   37
525 Henrietta Street
Martinez, CA 94553

Pinole Police Department   22
880 Tennent Avenue
Pinole, CA 94564-1724

Pittsburg Police Department   73
65 Civic Avenue
Pittsburg, CA 94565

Pleasant Hill Police Department   43
330 Civic Drive
Pleasant Hill, CA 94523

Richmond Police Department   186
401 27th Street
Richmond, CA 94803

San Pablo Police Department   42
13880 San Pablo Avenue
San Pablo, CA 94806

Walnut Creek Police Department   80
1666 N. Main Street
Walnut Creek, CA 94596

Del Norte
County
Del Norte County District Attorney's Office
450 "H" Street, #171
Crescent City, CA 95531

Del Norte County Sheriff's Department   38
650 Fifth Street
Crescent City, CA 95531
(707) 464-4191

Municipal
Crescent City Police Department   12
686 "G" Street
Crescent City, CA 95531

El Dorado
County
El Dorado County Sheriff's Department   149
300 Fair Lane
Placerville, CA 95667
(530) 621-5703

Municipal
Placerville Police Department   18
730 Main Street
Placerville, CA 95667

South Lake Tahoe Police Department   50
1352 Johnson Boulevard
South Lake Tahoe, CA 96150

Fresno
County
Fresno County District Attorney's Office
Golden State Plaza
2220 Tulare Street, Ste. 1000
Fresno, CA 93721
(559) 488-3141

Fresno County Sheriff's Department 430
P.O. Box 1788
2200 Fresno Street
Fresno, CA 93717
(559) 488-3931

Municipal
Clovis Police Department 81
1033 Fifth Street
Clovis, CA 93612

Coalinga Police Department 21
270 N. Sixth Street
Coalinga, CA 93210

Firebaugh Police Department 12
1575 11th Street
Firebaugh, CA 93622

Fowler Police Department 7
128 S. Fifth Street
Fowler, CA 93625-2401

Fresno Police Department 693
P.O. Box 1271
Fresno, CA 93715-1271

2326 Fresno Street
Fresno, CA 93721
(559) 498-1450

Huron Police Department 11
P.O. Box 339
36389 Lassen Avenue
Huron, CA 93234

Kerman Police Department 16
850 S. Madera Avenue
Kerman, CA 93630

Kingsburg Police Department 15
P.O. Box 575
1440 Marion Street
Kingsburg, CA 93631

Parlier Police Department 8
8770 S. Mendocino Avenue, Suite A
Parlier, CA 93648

Reedley Police Department 23
843 "G" Street
Reedley, CA 93654

Sanger Police Department 27
1700 Seventh Street
Sanger, CA 93657

Selma Police Department 28
1935 E. Front Street
Selma, CA 93662

Glenn
County
Glenn County District Attorney's Office
P.O. Box 430
540 W. Sycamore Street
Willows, CA 95988
Glenn County Sheriff's Department 33
543 W. Oak Street
Willows, CA 95988
(530) 934-645

Municipal
Orland Police Department 10
817 Fourth Street
Orland, CA 95963

Willows Police Department 9
201 N. Lassen Street
Willows, CA 95988

Humboldt
<u>County</u>
Humboldt County District Attorney's Office
Courthouse
825 Fifth Street
Eureka, CA 95501

Humboldt County Sheriff's Department 78
825 Fifth Street
Eureka, CA 95501

<u>Municipal</u>
Arcata Police Department 27
736 "F" Street
Arcata, CA 95521

Blue Lake Police Department 4
P.O. Box 458
City Hall, 111 Greenwood
Blue Lake, CA 95525

Eureka Police Department 52
604 "C" Street
Eureka, CA 95501-0341

Ferndale Police Department 3
P.O. Box 1096
834 Main Street
Ferndale, CA 95536-1096

Fortuna Police Department 15
P.O. Box 545
621 11th Street
Fortuna, CA 95540

Rio Dell Police Department 6
675 Wildwood Avenue
Rio Dell, CA 95562

Trinidad Police Department 10
P.O. Box 390
409 Trinity Street
Trinidad, CA 95570

Imperial
<u>County</u>
Imperial County District Attorney's Office
Courthouse
939 Main Street
El Centro, CA 92243

Imperial County Sheriff's Department 78
P.O. Box 1040
El Centro, CA 92244
328 Applestill Road
El Centro, CA 92243

<u>Municipal</u>
Brawley Police Department 27
351 Main Street
Brawley, CA 92227

Calexico Police Department 43
420 E. Fifth Street
Calexico, CA 92231

Calipatria Police Department 2
P.O. Box 668
101 N. Lake Avenue
Calipatria, CA 92233

El Centro Police Department 50
150 N. 11th Street
El Centro, CA 92243
(760) 337-4648

Imperal Police Department 11
424 S. Imperial Avenue
Imperial, CA 92251

Westmorland Police Department 4
355 S. Center
Westmorland, CA 92281

Inyo
County
Inyo County District Attorney's Office
PO Drawer "D"
Courthouse, 168 Edwards Street
Independence, CA 93526

Inyo County Sheriff's Department 36
P.O. Box "S"
550 S. Clay Street
Independence, CA 93526

Municipal
Bishop Police Department 13
207 W. Line Street
Bishop, CA 93514

Kern
County
Kern County District Attorney's Office
1215 Truxton Avenue, 4th Floor
Bakersfield, CA 93301

Kern County Sheriff's Department 456
P.O. Box 2208
Bakersfield, CA 93301

1350 Norris Road
Bakersfield, CA 93308
(661) 391-7500

Municipal
Arvin Police Department 12
P.O. Box 548
200 Campus Drive
Arvin, CA 93203-0548

Bakersfield Police Department 300
P.O. Box 59
Bakersfield, CA 93302
1601 Truxtun Avenue
Bakersfield, CA 93301
(661) 327-7111

Bear Valley Police Department 6
25101 Bear Valley Road
Tehachapi, CA 93561

California City Police Department 12
21130 Hacienda Boulevard
California City, CA 93505

Delano Police Department 35
P.O. Box 218
1022 12th Street
Delano, CA 93216-0218

Maricopa Police Department 6
P.O. Box 548
400 California Street
Maricopa, CA 93252-0548

Ridgecrest Police Department 31
100 W. California Avenue
Ridgecrest, CA 93555-4054

Shafter Police Department 12
201 Central Valley Highway
Shafter, CA 93263

Stallion Springs Police Department 4
28500 Stallion Springs Drive
Tehachapi, CA 93561

Taft Police Department 12
320 Commerce Way
Taft, CA 93268

Kings
County
Kings County District Attorney's Office
Government Center
1400 W. Lacey Boulevard
Hanford, CA 93230

Kings County Sheriff's Department 73
P.O. Box 986
Hanford, CA 93232-0986
1444 W. Lacey Boulevard
Hanford, CA 93230

Municipal
Corcoran Police Department 17
1031 Chittenden Avenue
Corcoran, CA 93212

Hanford Police Department 44
425 N. Irwin Street
Hanford, CA 93230

Lemoore Police Department 23
210 Fox Street
Lemoore, CA 93245

Lake
County
Lake County District Attorney's Office
Courthouse
255 N. Forbes Street
Lakeport, CA 95453

Lake County Sheriff's Department 69
P.O. Box 489
Lakeport, CA 95453
(707) 263-2212

Municipal
Clearlake Police Department 24
P.O. Box 2440
14050 Olympic Drive
Clearlake, CA 95422

Lakeport Police Department 12
445 N. Main Street
Lakeport, CA 95453

Lassen
County
Lassen County Sheriff's Department 30
Courthouse Annex
220 S. Lassen Street
Susanville, CA 96130

Municipal
Susanville Police Department 18
1801 Main Street
Susanville, CA 96130

Los Angeles

State

Dept. of Corporations—Enforcement
    Division
3700 Wilshire Boulevard, Suite 600
Los Angeles, CA 90010-3001

County

Los Angeles County District Attorney's Office
Criminal Courts Building
210 W. Temple Street, Rm. 18-709
Los Angeles, CA 90012
(213) 974-3610

Los Angeles County Sheriff's   8,417
    Department
4700 Ramona Boulevard, 4th Floor
Monterey Park, CA 91754-2169
(323) 526-5541

Municipal

Alhambra Police Department   91
211 S. First Street
Alhambra, CA 91801-3706
(626) 570-5095

Arcadia Police Department   73
P.O. Box 60021
250 W. Huntington Drive
Arcadia, CA 91066-6021
(626) 574-5405

Azusa Police Department   58
725 N. Alameda Avenue
Azusa, CA 91702

Baldwin Park Police Department   76
14403 East Pacific Avenue
Baldwin Park, CA 91706

Bell Gardens Police Department   57
7100 Garfield Avenue
Bell Gardens, CA 90201-3293

Bell Police Department   29
6326 Pine Avenue
Bell, CA 90201-1290

Beverly Hills Police Department   134
464 North Rexford Drive
Beverly Hills, CA 90210-4817

Burbank Police Department   162
P.O. Box 6459
Burbank, CA 91510-6459
200 N. Third Street
Burbank, CA 91502

Claremont Police Department   39
570 W. Bonita Avenue
Claremont, CA 91711-4624

Compton Police Department   132
301 S. Willowbrook
Compton, CA 90220
(310) 605-5500

Covina Police Department   58
444 N. Citrus Avenue
Covina, CA 91723-2065
(626) 331-0111

Culver City Police Department   122
4040 Duquesne Avenue
Culver City, CA 90232
(310) 837-1221

Downey Police Department 115
P.O. Box 7016
10911 Brookshire Avenue
Downey, CA 90241-7016
(562) 904-2319

El Monte Police Department 150
P.O. Box 6008
El Monte, CA 91732
11333 Valley Boulevard
El Monte, CA 91731-3292
(626) 580-2100

El Segundo Police Department 69
348 Main Street
El Segundo, CA 90245-3885

Gardena Police Department 73
1718 W. 162nd Street
Gardena, CA 90247-3732
(310) 217-9116

Glendale Police Department 229
140 N. Isabel Street
Glendale, CA 91206-4382
(818) 548-3117

Glendora Police Department 55
150 S. Glendora Avenue
Glendora, CA 91741

Hawthorne Police Department 86
4440 W. 126th Street
Hawthorne, CA 93230

Hermosa Beach Police Department 36
Civic Center
1315 Valley Drive
Hermosa Beach, CA 90254-3885

Huntington Park Police Department 70
6542 Miles Avenue
Huntington Park, CA 90255-4386

Inglewood Police Department 176
P.O. Box 6500
One Manchester Boulevard
Inglewood, CA 90301
(310) 412-5210

Irwindale Police Department 20
5050 N. Irwindale Avenue
Irwindale, CA 91706

La Verne Police Department 41
2061 Third Street
La Verne, CA 91750

Long Beach Police Department 842
400 W. Broadway
Long Beach, CA 90802
(562) 570-7260

Los Angeles Police Department 9,475
P.O. Box 30158
Los Angeles, CA 90030
150 N. Los Angeles Street
Los Angeles, CA 90012
(213) 485-4051

Manhattan Beach Police Department 63
420 15th Street
Manhattan Beach, CA 90266

Maywood Police Department 25
4317 E. Slauson Avenue
Maywood, CA 90270-2897

Monrovia Police Department   61
140 E. Lime Avenue
Monrovia, CA 91016

Montebello Police Department   92
1600 W. Beverly Boulevard
Montebello, CA 90640
(213) 887-1275

Monterey Park Police Department   82
320 W. Newmark Avenue
Monterey Park, CA 91754-2896

Palos Verdes Estates Police Department   23
340 Palos Verdes Drive W.
Palos Verdes Estates, CA 90274

Pasadena Police Department   235
207 N. Garfield Avenue
Pasadena, CA 91101-1791
(626) 744-4366

Redondo Beach Police Department   105
P.O. Box 639
401 Diamond Street
Redondo Beach, CA 90277-0639
(310) 318-0659

San Fernando Police Department   37
910 First Street
San Fernando, CA 91340

San Gabriel Police Department   55
P.O. Box 130
San Gabriel, CA 91778-0130
625 S. Del Mar
San Gabriel, CA 91776

San Marino Police Department   28
2200 Huntington Drive
San Marino, CA 91108-2639

Santa Monica Police Department   209
P.O. Box 2200
Santa Monica, CA 90407-2200

1685 Main Street
Santa Monica, CA 90401
(310) 395-9931

Sierra Madre Police Department   11
242 W. Sierra Madre
Sierra Madre, CA 91024

Signal Hill Police Department   30
1800 E. Hill Street
Signal Hill, CA 90806

South Gate Police Department   92
8620 California Avenue
South Gate, CA 90280

South Pasadena Police Department   33
1422 Mission Street
South Pasadena, CA 91030

Torrance Police Department   249
3300 Civic Center Drive
Torrance, CA 90503-5056
(310) 328-3456

Vernon Police Department   59
4305 Santa Fe Avenue
Vernon, CA 90058

West Covina Police Department 114
P.O. Box 2166
West Covina, CA 91793

1444 W. Garvey Avenue
West Covina, CA 91791
(626) 814-8501

Whittier Police Department 150
7315 Painter Avenue
Whittier, CA 90602
(562) 945-8250

Madera
<u>County</u>
Madera County District Attorney's Office
Government Center
209 W. Yosemite Avenue
Madera, CA 93637
Madera County Sheriff's Department 71
14143 Road 28
Madera, CA 93638

<u>Municipal</u>
Chowchilla Police Department 14
122 Trinity Avenue
Chowchilla, CA 91708-0667

Madera Police Department 47
203 W. Fourth Street
Madera, CA 93637
(209) 661-5400

Marin
<u>County</u>
Marin County District Attorney's Office
3501 Civic Center Drive, Room 183
San Rafael, CA 94903

Marin County Sheriff's Department 208
3501 Civic Center Drive, Room 145
San Rafael, CA 94903
(415) 499-7250

<u>Municipal</u>
Belvedere Police Department 7
450 San Rafael Avenue
Belvedere, CA 94920

Fairfax Police Department 13
144 Bolinas Road
Fairfax, CA 94930

Mill Valley Police Department 23
P.O. Box 1029
1 Hamilton Drive
Mill Valley, CA 94942-1029

Novato Police Department 58
909 Machin Avenue
Novato, CA 94947

Ross Police Department 8
P.O. Box 320
33 Sir Frances Drake Boulevard
Ross, CA 94957

San Anselmo Police Department 17
525 San Anselmo Avenue
San Anselmo, CA 94960

San Rafael Police Department 72
P.O. Box 151560
1400 Fifth Avenue
San Rafael, CA 94915-1560

Sausalito Police Department 21
P.O. Box 35
Sausalito, CA 94966

300 Locust Street
Sausalito, CA 94965

Tiburon Police Department 14
1155 Tiburon Boulevard
Tiburon, CA 94920

Twin Cities Police Department 31
250 Doherty Drive
Larkspur, CA 94939

Mariposa
County
Mariposa County District Attorney's Office
P.O. Box 748
5088 Bullion Street
Mariposa, CA 95338

Mariposa County Sheriff's Department 33
P.O. Box 276
4963 Tenth Street
Mariposa, CA 95338

Mendocino
County
Mendocino County District Attorney's
Office
P.O. Box 1000
State & Perkins Streets
Ukiah, CA 95482

Mendocino County Sheriff's 66
Department
951 Low Gap Road
Ukiah, CA 95482
(707) 463-4411

Municipal
Fort Bragg Police Department 18
250 Cypress Street
Fort Bragg, CA 95437-3693

Ukiah Police Department 29
300 Seminary Avenue
Ukiah, CA 95482

Willits Police Department 13
125 E. Commercial Street, Suite 150
Willits, CA 95490

Merced
County
Merced County District Attorney's Office
Mail: 2222 "M" Street
County Courts Building
Merced, CA 95340

627 W. 21st Street
Merced, CA 95340

Merced County Sheriff's Department 72
2222 "M" Street
Merced, CA 95340

Municipal
Atwater Police Department 24
750 Bellevue Road
Arwater, CA 95301-2898

Dos Palos Police Department 9
1546 Golden Gate Avenue
Dos Palos, CA 93620

Gustine Police Department 9
P.O. Box 16
682 Third Avenue
Gustine, CA 95322

Livingston Police Department 18
P.O. Box 308
1446 "C" Street
Livingston, CA 95334-9534

Los Banos Department of Public Safety 28
P.O. Box 31
945 Fifth Street
Los Banos, CA 93635

Merced Police Department 81
611 W. 22nd Street
Merced, CA 95340

Modoc

County
Modoc County District Attorney's Office
P.O. Box 1171
Alturas, CA 96101

Modoc County Sheriff's Department 12
PO Drawer 460
102 S. Court Street
Alturas, CA 96101

Municipal
Alturas Police Department 8
220 W. North Street
Alturas, CA 96101

Mono

County
Mono County District Attorney's Office
P.O. Box 617
Courthouse
Bridgeport, CA 93517

Mono County Sheriff's Department 27
P.O. Box 616
100 Bryant Street
Bridgeport, CA 93517

Municipal
Mammoth Lakes Police Department 15
P.O. Box 2799
City Hall—437 Old Mammoth Road
Mammoth Lakes, CA 93546

Monterey

County
Monterey County District Attorney's Office
P.O. Box 1369
240 Church Street, Room 101
Salinas, CA 93902

Monterey County Sheriff's Department 346
1414 Natividad Road
Salinas, CA 93906
(831) 755-3744

Municipal
Carmel Police Department 15
P.O. Box 600
Carmel, CA 93921
Fourth and Junipero
Carmel, CA 93923

Gonzales Police Department 11
P.O. Box 647
109 Fourth Street
Gonzales, CA 93926

Greenfield Police Department 13
P.O. Box 306
215 El Camino Real
Greenfield, CA 93927

King City Police Department 16
415 Bassett Street
King City, CA 93930

Marina Department of Public Safety 30
211 Hillcrest Avenue
Marina, CA 93933

Monterey Police Department 61
351 Madison Street
Monterey, CA 93940
(408) 646-3822

Pacific Grove Police Department 30
580 Pine Avenue
Pacific Grove, CA 93950

Salinas Police Department 160
222 Lincoln Avenue
Salinas, CA 93901
(831) 758-7292

Sand City Police Department 6
1 Sylvan Park
Sand City, CA 93955

Seaside Police Department 40
P.O. Box 810
440 Harcourt Avenue
Seaside, CA 93955-0810

Soledad Police Department 15
P.O. Box 606
237 Soledad Street
Soledad, CA 93960

Napa
County
Napa County District Attorney's Office
P.O. Box 720
Napa, CA 94559-0720

931 Parkway Mall
Napa, CA 94559

Napa County Sheriff's Department 74
1125 Third Street
Napa, CA 94559

Municipal
Calistoga Police Department 11
1235 Washington Street
Calistoga, CA 94515

Napa Police Department 75
1539 First Street
Napa, CA 94559

Saint Helena Police Department 12
1480 Main Street
Saint Helena, CA 94574

Nevada

County

Nevada County Sheriff's Department 96
950 Maidu Avenue
Nevada City, CA 95959-8617

Municipal

Grass Valley Police Department 20
City Hall—129 S. Auburn Street
Grass Valley, CA 95945

Nevada City Police Department 9
317 Broad Street
Nevada City, CA 95959

Orange

County

Orange County District Attorney's Office
P.O. Box 808
700 Civic Center Drive W.
Santa Ana, CA 92702

Orange County Sheriff's Department 1,483
P.O. Box 449
Santa Ana, CA 92702-0449
550 N. Flower Street
Santa Ana, CA 92702
(714) 647-1881

Municipal

Anaheim Police Department 400
P.O. Box 3369
425 S. Harbor Blvd
Anaheim, CA 92805
(714) 765-1900

Brea Police Department 108
No. 1 Civic Center Circle
Brea, CA 92821-5732
(714) 990-7715

Buena Park Police Department 90
P.O. Box 5009
Buena Park, CA 90622-5009
6650 Beach Blvd.
Buena Park, CA 90620

Costa Mesa Police Department 156
P.O. Box 1200
99 Fair Drive
Costa Mesa, CA 92626-1200
(714) 754-5280

Cypress Police Department 56
P.O. Box 609
5275 Orange Avenue
Cypress, CA 90630
(714) 229-6630

Fountain Valley Police Department 63
10200 Slater Avenue
Fountain Valley, CA 92702-8030

Fullerton Police Department 150
237 W. Commonwealth Avenue
Fullerton, CA 92832
(714) 738-6800

Garden Grove Police Department 159
P.O. Box 3070
11301 Acacia Parkway
Garden Grove, CA 92842
(714) 741-5704

Huntington Beach Police Department 232
P.O. Box 70
Huntington Beach, CA 92648
2000 Main Street
Huntington Beach, CA 92648
(714) 960-8811

Irvine Police Department 145
P.O. Box 19575
Irvine, CA 92623-9575
1 Civic Center Plaza
Irvine, CA 92606
(949) 724-6201

La Habra Police Department 69
150 N. Euclid Street
La Habra, CA 90631

La Palma Police Department 23
7792 Walker Street
La Palma, CA 90623

Laguna Beach Police Department 47
505 Forest Avenue
Laguna Beach, CA 92651
(714) 497-0375

Los Alamitos Police Department 24
3201 Katella Avenue
Los Alamitos, CA 90720

Newport Beach Police Department 134
P.O. Box 7000
Newport Beach, CA 92658-7000

870 Santa Barbara Drive
Newport Beach, CA 92660
(949) 644-3667

Orange Police Department 155
1107 N. Batavia Street
Orange, CA 92867
(714) 744-7255

Placentia Police Department 51
401 E. Chapman Avenue
Placentia, CA 92670

Santa Ana Police Department 366
P.O. Box 1981
Santa Ana, CA 92702
60 Civic Center Plaza
Santa Ana, CA 92702
(714) 245-8665

Santa Ana Unified School District Police
Department
1601 E. Chestnut Avenue
Santa Ana, CA 92701

Seal Beach Police Department 33
911 Seal Beach Boulevard
Seal Beach, CA 90740

Tustin Police Department 89
300 Centennial Way
Tustin, CA 92680

Westminster Police Department 102
8200 Westminster Boulevard
Westminster, CA 92683
(714) 898-3315

Placer
County
Placer County District Attorney's Office
11562 "B" Avenue, DeWitt Center
Auburn, CA 95603

Placer County Sheriff's Department 214
P.O. Box 6990
Auburn, CA 95604-6990

11500 "A" Avenue
Auburn, CA 95603
(530) 889-7800

Municipal

Auburn Police Department	21
1215 Lincoln Way	
Auburn, CA 95603-5004	

Lincoln Police Department	12
472 "E" Street	
Lincoln, CA 95648	

Rocklin Police Department	29
P.O. Box 1380	
4060 Rocklin Road	
Rocklin, CA 95677	

Roseville Police Department	79
401 Oak Street, #400	
Roseville, CA 95678	

Plumas

County

Plumas County Sheriff's Department	35
P.O. Box 1106	
1400 E. Main Street	
Quincy, CA 95971	

Riverside

County

Riverside County District Attorney's Office
4075 Main Street
Riverside, CA 92501

Riverside County Sheriff's	1,209
Department	
P.O. Box 592	
4095 Lemon Street	
Riverside, CA 92502	
(909) 955-2460	

Municipal

Banning Police Department	32
P.O. Box 1177	
125 East Ramsey	
Banning, CA 92220	

Beaumont Police Department	16
660 Orange Avenue	
Beaumont, CA 92223	

Blythe Police Department	24
240 N. Spring Street	
Blythe, CA 92225	

Cathedral City Police Department	46
68-625 Perez Road	
Cathedral City, CA 92234	

Coachella Police Department	26
1515 Sixth Street	
Coachella, CA 92236	

Corona Police Department	131
849 W. Sixth Street	
Corona, CA 92882	
(909) 736-2332	

Hemet Police Department	61
210 N. Juanita Street	
Hemet, CA 92543	

Indio Police Department	52
46-800 Jackson Street	
Indio, CA 92201	

Murrieta Police Department	29
40080 California Oaks Road	
Murrieta, CA 92562	

Palm Springs Police Department   80
P.O. Box 1830
Palm Springs, CA 92263-1830

200 S. Civic Drive
Palm Springs, CA 92262

Riverside Police Department   336
4102 Orange Street
Riverside, CA 92501
(909) 782-5808

San Jacinto Police Department   22
160 W. Sixth Street
San Jacinto, CA 92583

Sacramento
State
California Exposition & State Fair Police
1600 Exposition Boulevard
Sacramento, CA 95815

California Highway Patrol
P.O. Box 942898
Sacramento, CA 94298-0001

2555 First Avenue
Sacramento, CA 95818
(916) 322-5380

California Horse Racing Board
1010 Hurley Way, Suite 190
Sacramento, CA 95825

California State Lottery
650 N. Tenth Street
Sacramento, CA 95814

Dept. of Alcoholic Beverage Control
3810 Rosin Court, Suite 150
Sacramento, CA 95834
(562) 402-0659

Dept. of Consumer Affairs
Board of Dental Examiners
1432 Howe Avenue, Suite 85
Sacramento, CA 95825-3241

Dept. of Consumer Affairs
Division of Investigation
444 N. 3rd Street, Suite 110
Sacramento, CA 95814-0215

Dept. of Consumer Affairs—
Medical Board of CA
Enforcement Division/Field Ops
1434 Howe Avenue, Suite 84
Sacramento, CA 95825-3236

Dept. of Developmental Services
Office of Special Investigations
1600 Ninth Street, Room 240
Sacramento, CA 95814

Dept. of Fish and Game
Wildlife Protection Branch
1416 Ninth Street, Room 1326
Sacramento, CA 95814

Dept. of Forestry and Fire Protection
P.O. Box 944246
Sacramento, CA 94244-2460

Dept. of Health Services
Investigations Branch
P.O. Box 942732
Sacramento, CA 94234-7320

Dept. of Insurance
Fraud Division
9342 Tech Center Drive, Suite 500
Sacramento, CA 95825

Dept. of Justice
Division of Law Enforcement
P.O. Box 903281
Sacramento, CA 94203-2810

Dept. of Justice
AG's Medical Fraud Unit
1300 "I" Street, Suite 1540
Sacramento, CA 95814

Dept. of Mental Health
Special Investigators Unit
1600 Ninth Street
Sacramento, CA 95814

Dept. of Motor Vehicles
Division of Investigations
P.O. Box 932389, MSN-223
Sacramento, CA 94232-3890

2415 Burnett Way
Sacramento, CA 95818

Dept. of Parks and Recreation
Public Safety Section
P.O. Box 942896
Sacramento, CA 94296-0001

Dept. of Toxic Substances Control
Criminal Investigations Branch
P.O. Box 806
Sacramento, CA 95812-0806

400 "P" Street, 4th Floor
Sacramento, CA 95812-0806

Employment Development Department
Investigation Division
800 Capitol Mall, MIC 43
Sacramento, CA 95814

State Controllers Office
P.O. Box 942850
Sacramento, CA 94250

Office of Emergency Services (OES)
2800 Meadowview Road
Sacramento, CA 95832-1499

Secretary of State—Office of Investigations
1500 11th Street
Sacramento, CA 95814

County
Sacramento County District Attorney's
Office
P.O. Box 749
Sacramento, CA 95804

901 "G" Street
Sacramento, CA 95814

Sacramento County Sheriff's
Department   1,355
P.O. Box 988
Sacramento, CA 95812-0988

711 "G" Street
Sacramento, CA 95814
(916) 874-5092

Municipal
Folsom Police Department   42
46 Natoma Street
Folsom, CA 95630

Galt Police Department 20
380 Civic Drive
Galt, CA 95632

Isleton Police Department 3
P.O. Box 716
210 Jackson Boulevard
Isleton, CA 95641

Sacramento Police Department 627
900 Eighth Street
Sacramento, CA 95814-2506
(916) 264-5263

San Benito
County
San Benito County District Attorney's Office
375 Sixth Street
Hollister, CA 95023

San Benito County Sheriff's Department 20
P.O. Box 700
Hollister, CA 95024-0700
451 Fourth Street
Hollister, CA 95023

Municipal
Hollister Police Department 25
395 Apollo Way
Hollister, CA 95023-2508

San Bernardino
County
San Bernardino County District Attorney's
Office
316 N. Mountain View Ave.
San Bernardino, CA 92415-0004

San Bernardino County Sheriff's
Department 1,418
P.O. Box 569
San Bernardino, CA 92402

655 E. Third Street
San Bernardino, CA 92415-0061
(909) 387-3750

Municipal
Adelanto Police Department 29
P.O. Box 10
11613 Bartlett Avenue
Adelanto, CA 92301

Barstow Police Department 44
220 E. Mt. View Street
Barstow, CA 92311-2889
(619) 256-3531

Chino Police Department 83
P.O. Box 667
Chino, CA 91708-0667

13250 Central Avenue
Chino, CA 91710

Colton Police Department 63
650 N. LaCadena Drive
Colton, CA 92324

Montclair Police Department 52
P.O. Box 2308
5111 Benito Street
Montclair, CA 91763

Ontario Police Department 225
200 N. Cherry Avenue
Ontario, CA 91764-4197
(909) 988-6481

Redlands Police Department   76
P.O. Box 1025
212 Brookside Avenue
Redlands, CA 92373

Rialto Police Department   105
128 N. Willow Avenue
Rialto, CA 92376-5894
(909) 820-2540

San Bernardino Police Department   300
P.O. Box 1559
San Bernardino, CA 92402-1559

710 N. "D" Street
San Bernardino, CA 92401
(909) 384-5742

Upland Police Department   89
1499 W. 13th Street
Upland, CA 91786

San Diego

<u>County</u>
San Diego County District Attorney's Office
P.O. Box X-1011
Hall of Justice
330 N. Broadway, Suite 1300
San Diego, CA 92101

San Diego County Sheriff's   2,084
   Department
P.O. Box 429000
San Diego, CA 92142-9000

9621 Ridgehaven Court
San Diego, CA 92142-9000
(858) 974-2001

<u>Municipal</u>
Carlsbad Police Department   90
2560 Orion Way
Carlsbad, CA 92008-7280

Chula Vista Police Department   178
P.O. Box 1087
Chula Vista, CA 91912

276 Fourth Avenue
Chula Vista, CA 91910
(619) 691-5137

Coronado Police Department   42
700 Orange Avenue
Coronado, CA 92118

El Cajon Police Department   135
100 Fletcher Parkway
El Cajon, CA 92020
(619) 579-3311

Escondido Police Department   153
700 W. Grand Avenue
Escondido, CA 92025
(760) 839-4706

La Mesa Police Department   63
8181 Allison Avenue
La Mesa, CA 91941-5099

National City Police Department   79
1200 National City Boulevard
National City, CA 91950

Oceanside Police Department   167
3855 Mission Avenue
Oceanside, CA 92054
(760) 435-4900

Port of San Diego Harbor Police
P.O. Box 488
3380 N. Harbor Drive
San Diego, CA 92101

San Diego Police Department   2,000
P.O. Box 1431
San Diego, CA 92112

1401 Broadway, MS706
San Diego, CA 92101
(619) 531-2126

San Francisco
County
San Francisco County District Attorney's Office
Hall of Justice
850 Bryant Street, 3rd Floor
San Francisco, CA 94103

San Francisco County Sheriff's   695
    Department
Room 456 City Hall
One Dr. Carlton B. Goodlett Place
San Francisco, CA 94102
(415) 554-7225

Municipal
San Francisco Police Department   2,092
850 Bryant Street
San Francisco, CA 94103
(415) 553-0123

San Joaquin
County
San Joaquin County District Attorney's Office
P.O. Box 990
Stockton, CA 95201

222 E. Weber Avenue, Room 202
Stockton, CA 95202

San Joaquin County Sheriff's   350
    Department
7000 N. Michael Canlis Boulevard
French Camp, CA 95231-9781
(209) 468-4400

Municipal
Escalon Police Department   8
P.O. Box 248
1855 Coley Avenue
Escalon, CA 95320-1930

Lodi Police Department   78
230 W. Elm Street
Lodi, CA 95240
(209) 333-6723

Manteca Police Department   53
1001 W. Center Street
Manteca, CA 95336

Ripon Police Department   15
259 N. Wilma Avenue
Ripon, CA 95366-9640

Stockton Police Department   395
22 E. Market Street
Stockton, CA 95202
(209) 937-8377

Tracy Police Department   47
1000 Civic Center Drive
Tracy, CA 95376

San Luis Obispo
County
San Luis Obispo County District
    Attorney's Office
Room 450, County Government Center
San Luis Obispo, CA 93408

San Luis Obispo County Sheriff's 144
Department
P.O. Box 32
San Luis Obispo, CA 93406

1585 Kansas Avenue
San Luis Obispo, CA 93401
(805) 781-4540

<u>Municipal</u>
Arroyo Grande Police Department 25
200 N. Halcyon Road
Arroyo Grande, CA 93420

Atascadero Police Department 28
P.O. Box 911
5505 El Camino Real
Atascadero, CA 93423

Grover Beach Police Department 19
P.O. Box 365
Grover Beach, CA 93483
711 Rockaway
Grover Beach, CA 93433

Morro Bay Police Department 20
850 Morro Bay Boulevard
Morro Bay, CA 93442

Paso Robles Police Department 36
840 Tenth Street
Paso Robles, CA 93446

Pismo Beach Police Department 20
1000 Bello Street
Pismo Beach, CA 93449

San Luis Obispo Police Department 55
P.O. Box 1328
San Luis Obispo, CA 93406

1042 Walnut
San Luis Obispo, CA 93401

San Mateo
<u>State</u>
Department of Social Service
Community Care Licensing
Coastal Regional Office
801 Traeger Avenue, Suite 105
San Bruno, CA 94066-3045

<u>County</u>
San Mateo County District Attorney's Office
Hall of Justice & Records
400 County Center
Redwood City, CA 94063
(650) 599-1664

San Mateo County Sheriff's 331
Department
400 County Center
Redwood City, CA 94063
(650) 599-1664

<u>Municipal</u>
Belmont Police Department 35
1215 Ralston Avenue
Belmont, CA 94002

Brisbane Police Department 15
50 Park Lane
Brisbane, CA 94005

Broadmoor Police Department 9
388 88th Street
Broadmoor, CA 94015-1717

Burlingame Police Department 45
P.O. Box 551
Burlingame, CA 94011

1111 Trousdale Drive
Burlingame, CA 94010

Colma Police Department 11
1198 El Camino Real
Colma, CA 94014

Daly City Police Department 115
333 90th Street
Daly City, CA 94015-1895
(650) 991-8119

East Palo Alto Police Department 47
2415 University Avenue
East Palo Alto, CA 94303

Foster City Police Department 43
1030 E. Hillsdale Boulevard
Foster City, CA 94404-1604

Half Moon Bay Police Department 17
537 Kelly Avenue
Half Moon Bay, CA 94019

Hillsborough Police Department 27
1600 Floribunda Avenue
Hillsborough, CA 94010

Menlo Park Police Department 50
Civic Center
801 Laurel Street
Menlo Park, CA 94025-3482

Millbrae Police Department 20
P.O. Box 850
621 Magnolia Avenue
Millbrae, CA 94030

Pacifica Police Department 36
1850 Francisco Boulevard
Pacifica, CA 94044-2506

Redwood City Police Department 90
P.O. Box 189
Redwood City, CA 94064-0189

1301 Maple Street
Redwood City, CA 94063

San Bruno Police Department 50
567 El Camino Real
San Bruno, CA 94066

San Carlos Police Department 36
600 Elm Street
San Carlos, CA 94070

San Mateo Police Department 110
2000 S. Delaware Street
San Mateo, CA 94403
(650) 522-7710

South San Francisco Police Department 75
33 Arroyo Drive
South San Francisco, CA 94080

Santa Barbara
<u>County</u>
Santa Barbara County District Attorney's
Office
1105 Santa Barbara Street
Santa Barbara, CA 93101

Santa Barbara County Sheriff's
Department 282
P.O. Box 6427
Santa Barbara, CA 93160-6427

4434 Calle Real
Santa Barbara, CA 93110
(805) 681-4100

Municipal

Guadalupe Police Department   8
4490 Tenth Street, Room 5
Guadalupe, CA 93434-1420

Lompoc Police Department   44
107 Civic Center Plaza
Lompoc, CA 93436
(805) 736-2341

Santa Barbara Police Department   145
P.O. Box 539
Santa Barbara, CA 93102

215 E. Figueroa Street
Santa Barbara, CA 93101
(805) 897-2300

Santa Maria Police Department   86
222 E. Cook Street
Santa Maria, CA 93454

Santa Clara

County

Santa Clara County District Attorney's
     Office
70 W. Hedding Street
5th Floor, West Wing
San Jose, CA 95110

Santa Clara County Sheriff's
Department   455
55 W. Younger Avenue
San Jose, CA 95110-1721
(408) 299-3127

Municipal

Campbell Police Department   45
70 N. First Street
Campbell, CA 95008

Gilroy Police Department   39
7370 Rosanna Street
Gilroy, CA 95020
(408) 848-0400

Los Altos Police Department   30
1 N. San Antonio Road
Los Altos, CA 94022

Los Gatos Police Department   42
P.O. Box 973
Los Gatos, CA 95031

110 E. Main Street
Los Gatos, CA 95030

Milpitas Police Department   85
1275 N. Milpitas Boulevard
Milpitas, CA 95035
(408) 942-2448

Morgan Hill Police Department   29
17605 Monterey Road
Morgan Hill, CA 95037

Mountain View Police Department   96
1000 Villa Street
Mountain View, CA 94041

Palo Alto Police Department   96
275 Forest Avenue
Palo Alto, CA 94301

San Jose Police Department   1,308
201 W. Mission Street
San Jose, CA 95110
(408) 277-8900

Santa Clara Police Department 145
1541 Civic Center Drive
Santa Clara, CA 95050
(408) 261-5300

Sunnyvale Police Department 215
P.O. Box 3707
700 All American Way
Sunnyvale, CA 94088-3707
(408) 730-7100

Santa Cruz
County
Santa Cruz County District Attorney's Office
P.O. Box 1159
701 Ocean Street, Room 250
Santa Cruz, CA 95061

Santa Cruz County Sheriff's 146
Department
701 Ocean Street, Room 340
Santa Cruz, CA 95060
(831) 454-2414

Municipal
Capitola Police Department 23
422 Capitola Avenue
Capitola, CA 95010

Santa Cruz Police Department 93
212 Locust Street
Santa Cruz, CA 95060

Scotts Valley Police Department 21
One Civic Center Drive
Scotts Valley, CA 95066

Watsonville Police Department 60
P.O. Box 1930
Watsonville, CA 95077

215 Union Street
Watsonville, CA 95076

Shasta
County
Shasta County District Attorney's Office
1525 Court Street
Redding, CA 96001-1632

Shasta County Sheriff's Department 149
1525 Court Street
Redding, CA 96001
(530) 245-6000

Municipal
Anderson Police Department 15
P.O. Box 1804
2220 North Street
Anderson, CA 96007

Redding Police Department 104
1313 California Street
Redding, CA 96001-0698
(530) 225-4565

Sierra
County
Sierra County Sheriff's Department 10
P.O. Box 66
Courthouse Square
Downieville, CA 95936

Siskiyou
County
Siskiyou County Sheriff's Department 54
311 Lane Street
Yreka, CA 96097

<u>Municipal</u>
Lake Shastina District Police Department 4
16309 Everhart Drive
Weed, CA 96094

Mount Shasta Police Department 0
303 N. Mount Shasta Boulevard
Mount Shasta, CA 96067

Tulelake Police Department 4
P.O. Box 400
470 "C" Street
Tulelake, CA 96134

Weed Police Department 9
P.O. Box 470
550 Main Street
Weed, CA 96094

Yreka Police Department 14
412 W. Miner Street
Yreka, CA 96097

Solano
<u>County</u>
Solano County District Attorney's Office
Hall of Justice
600 Union Avenue
Fairfield, CA 94533

Solano County Sheriff's Department 89
530 Union Avenue, #100
Fairfield, CA 94533-6306

<u>Municipal</u>
Benicia Police Department 36
200 East "L" Street
Benicia, CA 94510
(707) 746-4265

Dixon Police Department 18
201 W. "A" Street
Dixon, CA 95620

Fairfield Police Department 101
1000 Webster Street
Fairfield, CA 94533-4883
(707) 428-7300

Rio Vista Police Department 11
P.O. Box 745
One Main Street
Rio Vista, CA 94571

Suisun City Police Department 28
701 Civic Center Boulevard
Suisun City, CA 94585-2693

Vacaville Police Department 96
630 Merchant Street
Vacaville, CA 95688

Vallejo Police Department 145
P.O. Box 1031
111 Amador Street
Vallejo, CA 94590-6301
(707) 648-4321

Sonoma
<u>County</u>
Sonoma County District Attorney's Office
600 Administration Drive, Room 212 J
Santa Rosa, CA 95403-2831

Sonoma County Sheriff's Department 228
600 Administration Drive, Room 103-J
Santa Rosa, CA 95403

Municipal
Cloverdale Police Department 11
112 Broad Street
Cloverdale, CA 95425

Cotati Police Department 12
201 W. Sierra Avenue
Cotati, CA 94928

Healdsburg Police Department 16
238 Center Street
Healdsburg, CA 95448

Petaluma Police Department 63
969 Petaluma Boulevard N.
Petaluma, CA 94952-6320

Santa Rosa Police Department 163
P.O. Box 1678
Santa Rosa, CA 95402-1678

965 Sonoma Avenue
Santa Rosa, CA 95404
(707) 543-3559

Sebastopol Police Department 16
P.O. Box 1776
Sebastopol, CA 95473-1776

370 Johnson Street
Sebastopol, CA 95472

Sonoma Police Department 16
175 First Street W.
Sonoma, CA 95476

Stanislaus
County
Stanislaus County District Attorney's Office
P.O. Box 442
1100 "I" Street
Modesto, CA 95353

Stanislaus County Sheriff's Department 191
P.O. Box 858
Modesto, CA 95353-0858

250 E. Hackett Road
Modesto, CA 95358
(209) 525-7114

Municipal
Ceres Police Department 38
2727 Third Street
Ceres, CA 95307

Hughson Police Department 8
P.O. Box 9
7018 Pine Street
Hughson, CA 95326

Modesto Police Department 258
P.O. Box 3313
601 11th Street
Modesto, CA 95353
(209) 572-9500

Newman Police Department 11
1200 "O" Street
Newman, CA 95360

Oakdale Police Department 23
245 N. Second Avenue
Oakdale, CA 95361

Patterson Police Department 14
344 W. Las Palmas
Patterson, CA 95363-0667

Turlock Police Department 57
250 Centennial Way
Tustin, CA 92680

Waterford Police Department   11
P.O. Box 199
320 "E" Street
Waterford, CA 95386

Sutter
<u>County</u>
Sutter County District Attorney's Office
Courthouse Annex
442 Second Street
Yuba City, CA 95991

Sutter County Sheriff's Department   56
P.O. Box 1555
Yuba City, CA 95991
1077 Civic Center Boulevard
Yuba City, CA 95993

<u>Municipal</u>
Yuba City Police Department   43
P.O. Box 3447
Yuba City, CA 95992

1545 Poole Boulevard
Yuba City, CA 95993

Tehama
<u>County</u>
Tehama County District Attorney's Office
P.O. Box 519
633 Washington Street
Red Bluff, CA 96080

Tehama County Sheriff's Department   78
P.O. Box 729
502 Oak Street
Red Bluff, CA 96080

<u>Municipal</u>
Corning Police Department   15
774 Third Street
Corning, CA 96021

Red Bluff Police Department   25
555 Washington Street
Red Bluff, CA 96080

Trinity
<u>County</u>
Trinity County District Attorney's Office
P.O. Box 310
Courthouse
101 Court Street
Weaverville, CA 96093

Trinity County Sheriff's Department   23
P.O. Box 1228
101 Memorial
Weaverville, CA 96093

Tulare
<u>County</u>
Tulare County District Attorney's Office
2350 Burrell Avenue
Visalia, CA 93291

Tulare County Sheriff's Department   385
County Civic Center
2404 Burrel Avenue
Visalia, CA 93291-4580
(559) 733-6220

<u>Municipal</u>
Dinuba Police Department   20
420 E. Tulare Street
Dinuba, CA 93618

Exeter Police Department 14
115 S. "B" Street
Exeter, CA 93221

Farmersville Police Department 11
147 E. Front Street
Farmersville, CA 93223

Lindsay Department of Public Safety 18
P.O. Box 369
185 N. Gale Hill Avenue
Lindsay, CA 93247

Porterville Police Department 45
350 N. "D" Street
Porterville, CA 93257

Tulare Police Department 50
260 S. "M" Street
Tulare, CA 93274

Visalia Police Department 95
303 S. Johnson Street
Visalia, CA 93291

Woodlake Police Department 12
350 N. Valencia Boulevard
Woodlake, CA 93286

Tuolumne
County
Tuolumne County District Attorney's Office
2 S. Green Street
Sonora, CA 95370

Tuolumne County Sheriff's Department 53
28 N. Lower Sunset Drive
Sonora, CA 95370

Municipal
Sonora Police Department 14
100 S. Green Street
Sonora, CA 95476

Ventura
County
Ventura County District Attorney's Office
800 S. Victoria Avenue, #L2730
Ventura, CA 93009

Ventura County Sheriff's Department 755
800 S. Victoria
Ventura, CA 93009
(805) 654-2311

Municipal
Oxnard Police Department 196
251 S. "C" Street
Oxnard, CA 93030
(805) 385-7740

Port Hueneme Police Department 21
250 N. Ventura Road
Port Hueneme, CA 93401

Santa Paula Police Department 29
214 S. Tenth Street
Santa Paula, CA 93060

Simi Valley Police Department 121
3901 Alamo Street
Simi Valley, CA 93063
(805) 583-6950

Ventura Police Department 122
1425 Dowell Drive
Ventura, CA 93003-7382
(805) 339-4400

Yolo

County

Yolo County Sheriff's Department   77
41793 Gibson Road
Woodland, CA 95776

Municipal

Davis Police Department   53
226 "F" Street
Davis, CA 95616

West Sacramento Police Department   55
P.O. Box 428
305 Third Street
West Sacramento, CA 95605

Winters Police Department   10
318-A First Street
Winters, CA 95694

Woodland Police Department   59
520 Court Street
Woodland, CA 95695

Yuba

County

Yuba County Sheriff's Department   64
P.O. Box 1389
215 Fifth Street
Marysville, CA 95901

Municipal

Marysville Police Department   27
P.O. Box 670
316 Sixth Street
Marysville, CA 95901

Wheatland Police Department   5
413 Second Street
Wheatland, CA 95692-9457

APPENDIX 2

Sample Personal History Statement

Personal History Statement

Personal

The following information is requested of you for verification and contact purposes:

1. Your Name *(Please print or type)*		
Last	First	Middle

Other names (including nicknames) you have used or been known by:

2. Please list address at which you can be contacted.				
Number	Street	City	State	Zip Code

3. Please list the local telephone number(s) at which you can be contacted.		
	( ) _____ Hrs. you can be contacted:	( ) _____ Hrs. you can be contacted:

4. Birthdate (Month) (Day) (Year)	5. You must be a citizen of the United States or a permanent resident alien who is eligible for and has applied for citizenship. Can you provide such documentation? ☐ Yes ☐ No

6. Social Security Number	(In accordance with the Federal Privacy Act of 1974, disclosure is voluntary. The SSN will be used for identification purposes to ensure that proper records are obtained.)

7. For the purposes of identification, please provide the following:			
Height	Weight	Hair Color	Eye Color

Scars, tatoos, or other distinguishing marks

Relatives and References

During the course of the background investigation, persons who know you will be asked to comment upon your suitability for the position of peace officer. Inquiries will be confined to job-relevant matters.

8. Please supply the appropriate information in the spaces provided below. If a category is not applicable, write in "N/A."

If living, name of your:	Address where person can be contacted (Include City, State and Zip Code)	Telephone at which person can be contacted
Father	☐ Home ☐ Work ☐ Other	☐ Home ☐ Work ☐ Other
Mother	☐ Home ☐ Work ☐ Other	☐ Home ☐ Work ☐ Other
Father-in-Law	☐ Home ☐ Work ☐ Other	☐ Home ☐ Work ☐ Other
Mother-in-Law	☐ Home ☐ Work ☐ Other	☐ Home ☐ Work ☐ Other
Spouse	☐ Home ☐ Work ☐ Other	☐ Home ☐ Work ☐ Other
Former Spouse(s)	☐ Home ☐ Work ☐ Other	☐ Home ☐ Work ☐ Other
	☐ Home ☐ Work ☐ Other	☐ Home ☐ Work ☐ Other

POST 2-251 (Rev. 5/94)   Page 3

Personal History Statement

Relatives and References Continued

If living, name of your:		Address where person can be contacted (Include City, State and Zip Code)	Telephone at which person can be contacted
Brother(s) and Sister(s)			
		☐ Home ☐ Work ☐ Other	☐ Home ☐ Work ☐ Other
		☐ Home ☐ Work ☐ Other	☐ Home ☐ Work ☐ Other
		☐ Home ☐ Work ☐ Other	☐ Home ☐ Work ☐ Other
Step-mother			
		☐ Home ☐ Work ☐ Other	☐ Home ☐ Work ☐ Other
Step-father			
		☐ Home ☐ Work ☐ Other	☐ Home ☐ Work ☐ Other
Step-brother(s) and Step-sister(s)			
		☐ Home ☐ Work ☐ Other	☐ Home ☐ Work ☐ Other
		☐ Home ☐ Work ☐ Other	☐ Home ☐ Work ☐ Other
		☐ Home ☐ Work ☐ Other	☐ Home ☐ Work ☐ Other
Other relatives with whom you have a close personal relationship (including children).			
	Relationship		
		☐ Home ☐ Work ☐ Other	☐ Home ☐ Work ☐ Other
		☐ Home ☐ Work ☐ Other	☐ Home ☐ Work ☐ Other
		☐ Home ☐ Work ☐ Other	☐ Home ☐ Work ☐ Other
		☐ Home ☐ Work ☐ Other	☐ Home ☐ Work ☐ Other

9. Below, please list those individuals with whom you have resided during the last 10 years (list no information prior to your 15th birthday). Exclude family members.

	Address	Telephone
	☐ Home ☐ Work ☐ Other	☐ Home ☐ Work ☐ Other
	☐ Home ☐ Work ☐ Other	☐ Home ☐ Work ☐ Other
	☐ Home ☐ Work ☐ Other	☐ Home ☐ Work ☐ Other
	☐ Home ☐ Work ☐ Other	☐ Home ☐ Work ☐ Other
	☐ Home ☐ Work ☐ Other	☐ Home ☐ Work ☐ Other
	☐ Home ☐ Work ☐ Other	☐ Home ☐ Work ☐ Other

POST 2-251 (Rev. 5/94) Page 4

SAMPLE ONLY: DO NOT USE

Personal History Statement

Relatives and References   Continued

10. In the space below, please list as references 3-5 individuals who have knowledge of you and your qualifications. Exclude relatives and former employers.

Name	Address where person can be contacted (Include City, State and Zip Code)	Telephone at which person can be contacted
	☐ Home ☐ Work ☐ Other	☐ Home ☐ Work ☐ Other
	☐ Home ☐ Work ☐ Other	☐ Home ☐ Work ☐ Other
	☐ Home ☐ Work ☐ Other	☐ Home ☐ Work ☐ Other
	☐ Home ☐ Work ☐ Other	☐ Home ☐ Work ☐ Other
	☐ Home ☐ Work ☐ Other	☐ Home ☐ Work ☐ Other

Education

11. The Commission on Peace Officer Standards and Training requires a peace officer to possess a U.S. high school diploma or its equivalent. Please indicate your current situation with regard to this requirement by checking one of the appropriate boxes.

☐ I possess a high school diploma from a U.S. institution.

☐ I passed the G.E.D. (General Educational Development) test.

☐ I passed the California High School Proficiency Examination.

☐ I possess a two-year college degree.

☐ I possess a four-year college or university degree.

☐ I do not currently have a high school diploma or its equivalent, but I plan to satisfy the requirement in the future as follows:

When: _____

How: _____

_____

12. Please indicate below all the schools you have attended beginning with high school. During the background investigation, persons who have known you in a learning environment will be contacted. A review of your school records may be made in conjunction with those contacts.

Name of School	Location of School (City & State)	Dates Attended From Month/Year	To Month/Year	School References (teachers, counselors, etc.)

POST 2-251 (Rev. 5/94)   Page 5

SAMPLE ONLY: DO NOT USE

Personal History Statement

Education Continued

13. Have you ever been suspended or expelled from any high school or post-secondary school? (Post-secondary schools include two- and four-year colleges, universities, and business and vocational schools -- any formal education beyond the high school level.)

☐ Yes ☐ No

If "yes," please explain (include school, date, and circumstances). _____

_____

_____

_____

_____

_____

Residence

Individuals who have become acquainted with you by reason of your residing in different locations, are often helpful in providing useful information for the background investigation.

14. Please list all of your residences during the last 10 years (list no information prior to your 15th birthday). Begin with your most current residence.

Address of Residence	City, State & Zip Code	Dates From Month/Year	To Month/Year	If rented, give name & address of the person responsible for the collection of rent

SAMPLE ONLY: DO NOT USE

Personal History Statement

Experience and Employment

15. Beginning with your most current employment, please list all jobs (including part-time, temporary, and voluntary positions) you have held in the past 10 years. (For the purposes of this personal history statement, volunteer work should be included as employment.) For identification and verification, please indicate the nature of the activity; i.e., full-time, part-time, or voluntary. If you have had intervening periods of military service or unemployment, please list those periods in sequence in the spaces provided.

SAMPLE ONLY: DO NOT USE

Dates of employment	Name and address of employer	Name of supervisor
From / To Mo. Yr.		
☐ Full-time	Telephone No.	Names(s) of co-worker(s)
☐ Part-time	Title or duties (for identification purposes)	
☐ Voluntary		
Reason for leaving		
☐ Military Service ☐ Not employed From Mo./Yr. To Mo./Yr.		

Dates of employment	Name and address of employer	Name of supervisor
From / To Mo. Yr.		
☐ Full-time	Telephone No.	Names(s) of co-worker(s)
☐ Part-time	Title or duties (for identification purposes)	
☐ Voluntary		
Reason for leaving		
☐ Military Service ☐ Not employed From Mo./Yr. To Mo./Yr.		

Dates of employment	Name and address of employer	Name of supervisor
From / To Mo. Yr.		
☐ Full-time	Telephone No.	Names(s) of co-worker(s)
☐ Part-time	Title or duties (for identification purposes)	
☐ Voluntary		
Reason for leaving		
☐ Military Service ☐ Not employed From Mo./Yr. To Mo./Yr.		

Dates of employment	Name and address of employer	Name of supervisor
From / To Mo. Yr.		
☐ Full-time	Telephone No.	Names(s) of co-worker(s)
☐ Part-time	Title or duties (for identification purposes)	
☐ Voluntary		
Reason for leaving		
☐ Military Service ☐ Not employed From Mo./Yr. To Mo./Yr.		

POST 2-251 (Rev. 5/94)   Page 7

329

Personal History Statement

Experience and Employment Continued

15. (Continued)

Dates of employment	Name and address of employer		Name of supervisor
From To Mo. Yr. Mo. Yr. ___/___ ___/___		Telephone No.	Names(s) of co-worker(s)
☐ Full-time ☐ Part-time ☐ Voluntary	Title or duties (for identification purposes)		
Reason for leaving			

☐ Military Service	☐ Not employed		From	Mo. / Yr.	To	Mo. / Yr.

Dates of employment	Name and address of employer		Name of supervisor
From To Mo. Yr. Mo. Yr. ___/___ ___/___		Telephone No.	Names(s) of co-worker(s)
☐ Full-time ☐ Part-time ☐ Voluntary	Title or duties (for identification purposes)		
Reason for leaving			

☐ Military Service	☐ Not employed		From	Mo. / Yr.	To	Mo. / Yr.

Dates of employment	Name and address of employer		Name of supervisor
From To Mo. Yr. Mo. Yr. ___/___ ___/___		Telephone No.	Names(s) of co-worker(s)
☐ Full-time ☐ Part-time ☐ Voluntary	Title or duties (for identification purposes)		
Reason for leaving			

☐ Military Service	☐ Not employed		From	Mo. / Yr.	To	Mo. / Yr.

Dates of employment	Name and address of employer		Name of supervisor
From To Mo. Yr. Mo. Yr. ___/___ ___/___		Telephone No.	Names(s) of co-worker(s)
☐ Full-time ☐ Part-time ☐ Voluntary	Title or duties (for identification purposes)		
Reason for leaving			

☐ Military Service	☐ Not employed		From	Mo. / Yr.	To	Mo. / Yr.

SAMPLE ONLY: DO NOT USE

SAMPLE ONLY: DO NOT USE

Personal History Statement

Experience and Employment Continued

16. Would any problem result if your present employer was contacted during the course of the background investigation? ☐ Yes ☐ No

    If "no," when should such contact be made? _____

17. If you have had no prior employment, please explain in the space below.

18. Have you had any extended work absences for reasons other than earned vacations? ☐ Yes ☐ No

    If "yes," please explain (include when, name of employer, why).

19. Have you ever been fired or asked to resign from any place of employment? ☐ Yes ☐ No

    If "yes," please give details (include when, where, circumstances).

20. Have you ever been a successful or unsuccessful candidate for another position requiring peace officer powers? ☐ Yes ☐ No

    If "yes," please give details (include when, name of agency, circumstances).

Military Service

21. If you are a male under age 26, please provide the following:

Selective Service Number	Approximate Date of Registration	Address at Time of Registration

22. Have you ever served in the armed forces, National Guard or military reserves? ☐ Yes ☐ No.

    If "yes," please supply the following information:

Branch of Service	Service Number	Dates of Service	Type of Discharge
		___ / ___ to ___ / ___	

23. Are you *currently* participating in any military reserve or National Guard program? ☐ Yes ☐ No

24. Have you ever been the subject of any judicial or non-judicial disciplinary action while in the military, National Guard or military reserves?

    ☐ Yes ☐ No

    If "yes," please give details (include branch of service, when, where, circumstances).

POST 2-251 (Rev. 5/94)   Page 9

Personal History Statement

Military Service Continued

25. Past commanding officers or military acquaintances are potential sources of relevant information pertaining to your background. Please list those individuals who know you well enough to provide accurate information about you.

Name	Contact Address	Contact Telephone	Years Known From	To
		( )		
		( )		
		( )		
		( )		

Financial

26. The management of personal finances is relevant to an individual's qualifications for the position of peace officer. Therefore, please fill in the financial statement below. Be complete and accurate. The amount of indebtedness in itself will not be used in evaluating your qualifications, but rather the behavior exhibited in meeting your financial obligations.

Current Monthly Income	$		Current Monthly Expenditures	$	
Monthly salary			Real Estate (mortgage) payment(s)		
Spouse's salary			Rent		
Other monthly income - describe:			Other monthly payments - describe:		
			Estimated monthly cost of living (include utilities, food, gasoline, home and car maintenance, entertainment, etc.) and any other obligations . . .		
TOTAL MONTHLY INCOME	$		TOTAL MONTHLY EXPENDITURES	$	

Current Assets	$		Current Liabilities	$	
Savings			Real Estate Indebtedness		
Checking			Long-term Loans		
Real Estate			Charge Accounts		
Stocks and Bonds			Other Liabilities - describe:		
Life Insurance (cash value of whole life policy)					
Autos					
Other Assets - describe:					
TOTAL ASSETS	$		TOTAL LIABILITIES	$	

POST 2-251 (Rev. 5/94)   Page 10

SAMPLE ONLY: DO NOT USE

Personal History Statement

Financial Continued

27. Please supply more detailed information about your charge accounts, contracts, or other financial liabilities.		
Name of Firm	Address	Account Number

28. Have you ever filed for or declared bankruptcy? ☐ Yes ☐ No
If "yes," please give details (include when, where, why).

29. Have any of your bills ever been turned over to a collection agency? ☐ Yes ☐ No
If "yes," please give details (include when, firms involved, circumstances).

30. Have you ever had purchased goods repossessed? ☐ Yes ☐ No
If "yes," please give details (include when, firms involved, circumstances).

POST 2-251 (Rev. 5/94)   Page 11

SAMPLE ONLY: DO NOT USE

Personal History Statement

Financial Continued

31. Have your wages ever been garnisheed? ☐ Yes ☐ No
    If "yes," please give details (include when, where, why).

32. Have you ever been delinquent on income or other tax payments? ☐ Yes ☐ No
    If "yes," please give details (include when, where, why).

Legal

33. If you have ever been arrested or convicted for any crime (excluding traffic citations), please give the following information: *(An arrest resulting in participation in a diversion program, or the fact that your record may have been affected by a sealing, an expungement, a release, or a pardon has specific legal implications as to how you should answer this question. Please see the cover page for details.)*

Approx. Date	Police Agency	Circumstances

34. Have you ever been placed on court probation as an adult? ☐ Yes ☐ No
    If "yes," please give details (include when, where, why).

35. Were you ever required to appear before a juvenile court for an act which would have been a crime if committed by an adult?
    ☐ Yes ☐ No
    If "yes," please give details (include when, where, why).

POST 2-251 (Rev. 5/94) Page 12

SAMPLE ONLY: DO NOT USE

Personal History Statement

Legal Continued

36. Have you ever been reported to a law enforcement agency as a missing person or a runaway? ☐ Yes ☐ No
   If "yes," please give details (include date, law enforcement agency, circumstances).

37. Are you now or have you ever been involved as a plaintiff or defendant in any civil court action? ☐ Yes ☐ No
   If "yes," please give details (include when, where, name and location of court, circumstances).

Motor Vehicle Operation

Operation of a motor vehicle is an integral part of the position of patrol officer. An investigation of your driving history will be made through a records check. To expedite this procedure, please supply the following information:

38. California driver's license number	Expiration date
Name under which license was granted	

39. Please list other states where you have been licensed to operate a motor vehicle.

State	State	State	State
Name under which license was granted	Name under which license was granted	Name under which license was granted	Name under which license was granted

40. Have you ever been refused a driver's license by any state? ☐ Yes ☐ No
   If "yes," please explain (include when, where, why).

41. California law requires that operators and owners of motor vehicles be covered by automobile liability insurance or bond or deposit of $35,000 with the Department of Motor Vehicles. Therefore, please list the current liability insurance you have with your motor vehicles.

Company	Address	Policy Number	Date of Expiration

If you are bonded or have deposited $35,000 to meet your motor vehicle financial responsibility, please indicate.
☐ Bond   ☐ $35,000

SAMPLE ONLY: DO NOT USE

Personal History Statement

Motor Vehicle Operation Continued

42. Please list all traffic citations (exclude parking citations) you have received within the last 5 years.			
Nature of violation	Location (city)	Approximate Date	Indicate whether fined or action taken on driver's license

43. Have you ever been involved as a driver in a motor vehicle accident within the last 5 years? ☐ Yes ☐ No
If "yes," please give details for each accident.

Date	Location		☐ Injury ☐ Non-injury
Police investigation? ☐ Yes ☐ No	Police Agency		
Date	Location		☐ Injury ☐ Non-injury
Police investigation? ☐ Yes ☐ No	Police Agency		
Date	Location		☐ Injury ☐ Non-injury
Police investigation? ☐ Yes ☐ No	Police Agency		
Date	Location		☐ Injury ☐ Non-injury
Police investigation? ☐ Yes ☐ No	Police Agency		
Date	Location		☐ Injury ☐ Non-injury
Police investigation? ☐ Yes ☐ No	Police Agency		

44. If there is anything you wish to discuss about your driving record, please use the space below.

45. Has your license ever been suspended, revoked, or placed on negligent operator's probation? ☐ Yes ☐ No
If "yes," please give details (include what, when, where, why).

POST 2-251 (Rev. 5/94)   Page 14

SAMPLE ONLY: DO NOT USE

Personal History Statement

General Information

46. Have you ever been refused insurance for any reason other than failure to pay a premium? ☐ Yes ☐ No
If "yes," please explain (include company name and address, date, and reason).

47. Have you ever applied for a permit to carry a concealed weapon? ☐ Yes ☐ No
If "yes," please provide the following information:

Permit granted? ☐ Yes ☐ No	Date	Name of law enforcement agency

Purpose

I hereby certify that all statements made in this personal history statement are true and complete, and I understand that any misstatements of material facts will subject me to disqualification or dismissal.

Signature in full	Date completed

SAMPLE ONLY: DO NOT USE

How Did We Do? Grade Us.

Thank you for choosing a Kaplan book. Your comments and suggestions are very useful to us. Please answer the following questions to assist us in our continued development of high-quality resources to meet your needs.

The Kaplan book I read was: _____

My name is: _____

My address is: _____

_____

My e-mail address is: _____

What overall grade would you give this book?   Ⓐ Ⓑ Ⓒ Ⓓ Ⓕ

How relevant was the information to your goals?   Ⓐ Ⓑ Ⓒ Ⓓ Ⓕ

How comprehensive was the information in this book?   Ⓐ Ⓑ Ⓒ Ⓓ Ⓕ

How accurate was the information in this book?   Ⓐ Ⓑ Ⓒ Ⓓ Ⓕ

How easy was the book to use?   Ⓐ Ⓑ Ⓒ Ⓓ Ⓕ

How appealing was the book's design?   Ⓐ Ⓑ Ⓒ Ⓓ Ⓕ

What were the book's strong points? _____

How could this book be improved? _____

Is there anything that we left out that you wanted to know more about?

Would you recommend this book to others?   ☐ YES   ☐ NO

Other comments: _____

_____

_____

Do we have permission to quote you?   ☐ YES   ☐ NO

Thank you for your help. Please tear out this page and mail it to:

Dave Chipps, Managing Editor
Kaplan Educational Centers
888 Seventh Avenue
New York, NY 10106

Or, you can answer these questions online at www.kaplan.com/talkback.

Thanks!

Just in case the rock star thing doesn't work out.

Kaplan gets you in.

For over 60 years, Kaplan has been helping students get into college. Whether you're facing the SAT, PSAT or ACT, take Kaplan and get the score you need to get into the schools you want.

1-800-KAP-TEST
kaptest.com AOL keyword: kaplan

*Test names are registered trademarks of their respective owners.

KAPLAN®
World Leader in Test Prep

About

Educational Centers

Kaplan Educational Centers is one of the nation's leading providers of premier education and career services. Kaplan is a wholly owned subsidiary of The Washington Post Company.

TEST PREPARATION & ADMISSIONS

Kaplan's nationally recognized test prep courses cover more than 20 standardized tests, including secondary school, college and graduate school entrance exams and foreign language and professional licensing exams. In addition, Kaplan offers private tutoring and comprehensive, one-to-one admissions and application advice for students applying to graduate programs. Kaplan also provides information and guidance on the financial aid process.

SCORE! EDUCATIONAL CENTERS

SCORE! after-school learning centers help K-8 students build confidence, academic and goal-setting skills in a motivating, sports-oriented environment. Its cutting-edge, interactive curriculum continually assesses and adapts to each child's academic needs and learning style. Enthusiastic Academic Coaches serve as positive role models, creating a high-energy atmosphere where learning is exciting and fun. SCORE! Prep provides in-home, one-on-one tutoring for high school academic subjects and standardized tests.

KAPLAN LEARNING SERVICES

Kaplan Learning Services provides customized assessment, education and professional development programs to K-12 schools and universities.

KAPLAN INTERNATIONAL PROGRAMS

Kaplan services international students and professionals in the U.S. through a series of intensive English language and test preparation programs. These programs are offered at Kaplan City Centers and four new campus-based centers in California, Washington and New York via Kaplan/LCP International Institute. Kaplan and Kaplan/LCP offer specialized services to sponsors including placement at top American universities, fellowship management, academic monitoring and reporting, and financial administration.

KAPLAN PUBLISHING

Kaplan Publishing produces books, software and online services. Kaplan Books, a joint imprint with Simon & Schuster, publishes titles in test preparation, admissions, education, career development and life skills; Kaplan and Newsweek jointly publish guides on getting into college, finding the right career, and helping your child succeed in school. Through an alliance with Knowledge Adventure, Kaplan publishes educational software for the K-12 retail and school markets.

KAPLAN PROFESSIONAL

Kaplan Professional provides recruitment and training services for corporate clients and individuals seeking to advance their careers. Member units include Kaplan Professional Career Services, the largest career fair provider in North America; Perfect Access/CRN, which delivers software education and consultation for law firms and businesses; HireSystems, which provides web-based hiring solutions; and Kaplan Professional Call Center Services, a total provider of services for the call center industry.

DISTANCE LEARNING DIVISION

Kaplan's distance learning programs include Concord School of Law, the nation's first online law school; and National Institute of Paralegal Arts and Sciences, a leading provider of degrees and certificates in paralegal studies and legal nurse consulting.

COMMUNITY OUTREACH

Kaplan provides educational resources to thousands of financially disadvantaged students annually, working closely with educational institutions, not-for-profit groups, government agencies and other grass roots organizations on a variety of national and local support programs. Kaplan enriches local communities by employing high school, college and graduate students, creating valuable work experiences for vast numbers of young people each year.

Want more information about our services, products, or the nearest Kaplan center?

Call our nationwide toll-free numbers:

1-800-KAP-TEST for information on our courses, private tutoring and admissions consulting

1-800-KAP-ITEM for information on our books and software

1-888-KAP-LOAN* for information on student loans

Connect with us in cyberspace:

On AOL, keyword:"Kaplan"

On the World Wide Web, go to:

1. www.kaplan.com
2. www.kaptest.com
3. www.eSCORE.com
4. www.dearborn.com
5. www.BrassRing.com
6. www.concord.kaplan.edu
7. www.kaplancollege.com

Via e-mail: info@kaplan.com

**Write to:**

 Kaplan Educational Centers
888 Seventh Avenue
New York, NY 10106